M B A
HANDBOOK
for
HEALTHCARE
PROFESSIONALS

M B A
HANDBOOK
for
HEALTHCARE
PROFESSIONALS

Edited by

JOSEPH S. SANFILIPPO, MD, MBA

Department of Obstetrics, Gynecology and Reproductive Sciences,
University of Pittsburgh School of Medicine, Magee-Womens Hospital, Pittsburgh, PA

THOMAS E. NOLAN, MD, MBA

Department of Obstetrics, Gynecology and Medicine, Louisiana State University,
Health Sciences Center, New Orleans, LA

BATES H. WHITESIDE, CPA, PFS

Gulf Coast Professional Planners, LLC, New Orleans, LA

The Parthenon Publishing Group
International Publishers in Medicine, Science & Technology

A CRC PRESS COMPANY
BOCA RATON   LONDON   NEW YORK   WASHINGTON, D.C.

Published in the USA by
The Parthenon Publishing Group Inc.
345 Park Avenue South
10th Floor
New York, NY 10010, USA

Published in the UK and Europe by
The Parthenon Publishing Group Ltd.
23–25 Blades Court, Deodar Road
London, SW15 2NU, UK

Library of Congress Cataloging-in-Publication Data
MBA handbook for healthcare professionals / edited by Joseph S. Sanfilippo,
Thomas E. Nolan, and Bates H. Whiteside
         p.   ;   cm
   Includes index.
   ISBN 1-84214-074-4 (alk. paper)
    1. Medicine—Practice—Finance—Handbooks, manuals, etc. 2. Medical
offices—Personnel management—Handbooks, manuals, etc. I. Sanfilippo, J. S.
(Joseph S.) II. Nolan, Thomas E. III. Whiteside, Bates H.
   [DNLM: 1. Practice Management—organization & administration. 2. Office
Management—organization & administration. W 80 M478 2001]
R728.M335 2001
610'.68—dc21   2001050001

British Library Cataloguing in Publication Data
MBA handbook for healthcare professionals
   1. Medicine – Practice   2. Medical offices – Management
   I. Sanfilippo, J. S. (Joseph S.) II. Nolan, Thomas E. III. Whiteside, Bates H.
   362.1'068

   ISBN 1-84214-074-4

Typeset by Martin Lister Publishing Services, Carnforth, UK
Printed and bound by Butler & Tanner Ltd., Frome and London, UK

Contents

List of Contributors

Joseph S. Sanfilippo, MD, MBA
Professor, Obstetrics, Gynecology &
  Reproductive Sciences
The University of Pittsburgh School of Medicine
Vice Chairman, Reproductive Sciences
Magee-Womens Hospital
Pittsburgh, PA 15213

Joseph Balestreire, MEd
Adjunct Associate Professor
Heinz School, Public Policy and Management
Carnegie Mellon University
Vice President and Manager
Quality and Performance Improvement
Treasury Management
PNC Financial Services Group
Pittsburgh, Pennsylvania

Robert Bartolacci, MS, CPA, CIA
Adjunct Assistant Professor of Finance
Carnegie Mellon University
Chief Financial Officer, Treasurer
Vanadium Enterprises Corporation
Pittsburgh, Pennsylvania

Neil Baum, MD
Associate Clinical Professor
Department of Urology
Tulane Medical School and Louisiana State
  Medical School
New Orleans, LA 70115

Arthur Boerner, MD
Associate Clinical Professor
University of Louisville
Louisville, KY 40292

Stephen M. Crow, PhD
Endowed Chair
Health Care Management
Department of Management
University of New Orleans
New Orleans, LA 70148

Joseph T. Donnelly, CPA
Principal
Advisors in Health Finance Ltd.
Pittsburgh, PA 15237

Rhona Ferguson, RN, BS, CPC
Operational Director, Department of Surgery
Allegheny General Hospital
Pittsburgh, PA 15212

Larry R. Glazerman, MD
Clinical Assistant Professor
Penn State University
Hershey Medical Center
Philadelphia, PA 17033

Professor Mahesh Gupta
University of Louisville
Department of Management
College of Business and Public Administration
Louisville, KY 40292

Stephen K. Klasko, MD, MBA
Vice Dean, Professor, Obstetrics and
  Gynecology
MCH Hahnemann University
Philadelphia, PA 19102

Thomas E. Nolan, MD, MBA
Professor of Obstetrics, Gynecology &
 Medicine
Department of Ob/Gyn and Medicine
Louisiana State University – Health Sciences
 Center
Hospital Center Director, Women's and
 Newborn Services
Medical Center of Louisiana
New Orleans, LA 70112

Professor Louis Raho
University of Louisville
Department of Management
College of Business and Public Administration
Louisville, KY 40292

Steven Smith, JD, MA
Dean
California Western School of Law
San Diego, CA 92101

David B. Toub, MD
Medical Director
Newton Interactive
Pennington, NJ 08534

Jeroen Walstra
Marketing and Economic Consultant
Partner, Cohen and Walstra
Adjunct Professor of Marketing
Chatham College and Point Park College
Pittsburgh, Pennsylvania

Bates H. Whiteside, CPA, PFS
Gulf Coast Professional Planners, LLC
938 Lafayette Street
New Orleans, LA 70113

Introduction

Practice management continues to be an area of growing importance, especially in light of the increasing visibility of managed care with respect to private practice. The business aspects of medicine have acquired even greater significance. Clinicians are called upon to be more efficient with regard to their organizational behavior within a practice setting. It is imperative that they have the ability to deal with the effect that managed care has had on practice management, and therefore, there is a need to provide a succinct method of equipping clinicians with the armamentarium prerequisite to a successful clinical practice with competitive advantage.

Establishing a mission statement for a practice allows one to convey who we are, what we want to be and how we get there. This may seem a simple, straightforward concept, but allowing a practice to be 'focused' is an investment that will pay big dividends. How does a clinician establish competitive advantage? This term is used in the business world with regard to the effort to be 'a step ahead'. Once a competitive advantage is achieved, how does one maintain a 'sustained competitive advantage'? The 'business of medicine', mission statement for a practice, the four 'Ps' of marketing, dealing with managed care and improving office efficiency are several of the objectives of our handbook. Provision of the most accurate information with respect to current procedural terminology (CPT) coding, leadership skills within an office practice, patients as 'raving fans', organizational behavior, attending to the fine print in a contract and financial planning in an office setting complement the educational component of the book; these basic tenets are conveyed in the *MBA Handbook for Healthcare Professionals*.

How does one proceed with marketing a practice in a cost-efficient manner? The four Ps of marketing, including product (or in most cases services), price, promotion and production (distribution), are applied to medical services. Methods of increasing efficiency within the office practice and decreasing overhead to compensate for the financial remuneration associated with many third-party payers is another objective of this book. Keeping a focus on patients as 'customers', with the basic marketing tenet of providing for their wants and needs, leads one to periodic surveys and reassessment within an office practice. To deal with conflict within the office, healthcare professionals must have appropriate leadership skills and be able to handle conflict, and, ideally, avoid it whenever possible. How to establish 'raving fans', specifically patients who market your practice for you, is another issue clinicians must address. The letters 'OB' have taken on a new meaning in medicine, and now signify 'organizational behavior'. What are the best ways to orchestrate office behavior and modify it appropriately? Getting employees to 'buy in' to the design and implementation of activities is most worthwhile.

If you are given a third-party payer contract, it is in your best interest to have the appropriate individual(s) 'explain the contract and its fine print'. One would be wise to document this discussion to serve as a future reference point.

Financial planning is paramount. Knowledge with regard to Keoghs, 401(k), defined contribution, SEP–IRA, SIMPLE plans, and other retirement options and methods of preparing for the future are especially important. It is also of interest to have a basic understanding and knowledge of the law as applied to medical practice. This is conveyed in a separate chapter entitled 'Applied law for the non-attorney'.

A sincere effort to address the practice management aspects of medicine succinctly for health professionals has been the primary objective of the *MBA Handbook for Healthcare Professionals.*

Negotiation

Joseph S. Sanfilippo

Healthcare professionals are very capable of being good negotiators. If one stops to think, we are 'negotiating' all the time. What is negotiating? It is an interactive communication process that, in essence, occurs when there is a need to obtain something from someone else or they want something from you. The most important point with respect to negotiation is 'proper preparation'. There are two basic assumptions with respect to negotiating: first, everyone negotiates for one and only one reason, that is, to achieve their own goals; second, no one ever does anything that is not in their best interests, at least as they perceive those interests. One's style of negotiating should reflect entering into the process by 'being yourself'. Attempts to adopt a negotiating technique that does not feel comfortable can lead to credibility problems or, at least, the perception of such. Key points include the tone of the conversation, making the request in a dignified manner, and creating a circumstance in which it is in the other party's best interests to say 'yes'. Bargaining tools, willingness to compromise and effectiveness in being accommodated by the request are paramount (Table 1).

Table 1 The four stages of negotiating

Preparation
Information exchange
Bargaining
Implementation

Preparation includes identifying your needs, their needs and any third-party needs. In addition, what are the interests, both shared and conflicting? How many issues are at stake? How many parties are involved? Will there be an ongoing relationship between parties? What are the 'leverage' factors? Preparation includes identifying specific goals, being alert and not being a victim of asking for something after you close, i.e. resetting the negotiation. Be effective! Be the first to take command of the situation/circumstance. Ideally, try to arrange it so that the other party makes the first offer. Keep a straight face – bargain a little, no matter what.

- High expectations are extremely important

- Reputation for integrity is important

- Effective listening tools as well as communication skills and self-confidence are paramount

- Determine what your bottom line is

- Determine what would be a fair resolution

- Determine your high expectations target

- Determine the other party's bottom line

- As part of the preparation, be sure you make a list beforehand.

The important strategic points are *goals* and *targets*.

The key foundations, with respect to negotiation, include goals (motivation), their needs (the power of self-interest), your leverage (potential loss versus potential gain), standards and norms (consistency and fairness) and personal relationships (reciprocity) (Table 2).

Table 2 Negotiation style

HIGH Expectations		LOW Expectations
Collaborator: Problem Solver		Accommodator
	Compromiser	
Competitor		Conflict Avoider

Be prepared to 'declare war', thus lining up your allies and your own defense, if necessary. Identify when you are being tested, i.e. know when to say 'no'. Be careful of the 'Mr Nice Guy' concept and that 'everything will be all right'.

The importance of a messenger must be emphasized. If you feel the negotiations would best proceed with a messenger intervening, then this merits consideration. A memo prior to the negotiation may also be helpful. Avoid bribes; focus on control and/or autonomy.

Use the following rules of negotiation:

(1)   Never use a sheet – have it all memorized;

(2)   There is no tomorrow, it must be done today;

(3)   Upon finishing, do not talk about the negotiation, but 'shake hands'.

You can learn from the success of others:

(1)   Leverage makes a significant difference.

(2)   The most important single success factor in negotiation is planning and preparation.

(3)   Have clear goals, good questions and the patience to listen.

(4)   Negotiators create value. Clearly identify the shared interest. Listen rather than talk whenever possible.

(5)   Have a contingency plan or plans.

(6)   Sit in their chair for a moment. Identify their weaknesses. Who has the most to lose? How do you gain leverage? If you feel you are being treated unfairly, let them know. If you feel you are being treated appropriately, acknowledge such.

(7)   Give strong consideration to asking for more than you need.

(8)   Before you take command of the situation (initially), be sure you know the situation and the expectations, then 'open'. If you do not have the information, let them open.

(9)   On negotiating an individual salary, be aware of standard norms for salaries.

(10)   A collaborator likes to negotiate. A compromiser does not like to negotiate. An accommodator is somewhere in between. Physicians are frequently 'avoiders'. Be an assertive business person! Dominate the situation! Avoiders are bad leaders. They avoid conflict. They create problems by avoiding them. It is important to delegate wisely and have a follow-up report with recommendations. If you are caught off guard (in the hallway) suggest sitting down and discussing – the 'come and see me' approach.

(11)   Consider agreement versus commitment.

(12)   Apologies are fine (individualized based on circumstance).

(13)   Establish a reputation for reliability and integrity. This is critical.

(14)   Have high expectations – 'be greedy'.

The atmosphere should be one signifying 'your word is your bond'. Do not share everything you are thinking! Be a good listener. Think on your feet, be self-confident, be persuasive, be interested in the problem. Listen, do not interrupt. Do no worry about the 'small things'. Be proactive and not reactive. Stand up to competitive people. This is important! If it is not going well, say 'time out'. Get mad when

appropriate, but do not lose command of the situation. Regroup and determine your options. Clearly 'revisit' shared interests and build on them. Provide an atmosphere allowing the hostile party to vent. Try to be first on the agenda. Watch out for the loudest voice. There is no such thing as fairness; it is a perception; it is a relationship factor. Be sure that the individual does not feel they are 'being taken for a ride'. Be careful of 'side deals'. Just say 'No'!

Leadership Skills in an Office Setting: 'How to Motivate People'

2

Joseph Balestreire

The Great Man

Leadership and ethics: the modern organization

'The master of the art of leadership comes with the mastery of the self. Ultimately, leadership is a process of self development.'

James M. Kouzes and Barry Z. Pozner. *The Leadership Challenge.*
(Copyright © 1997 Jossey-Bass, Inc. This material is used by permission of Jossey-Bass, Inc., a subsidiary of John Wiley & Sons, Inc.)

Gaining insight into your personal values, preferences and behaviors provides valuable knowledge as you begin your journey to develop as a leader. This chapter provides guidance to help you create a personal definition of leadership, a strategy for the development of specific leadership skills and behaviors and an implementation plan to practice, perform and reflect on the development of your leadership skills and behaviors.

A picture of leadership

To begin to create a picture of leadership, let us take a look at typical leadership styles, the skills of effective leaders and the difference between managers and leaders. The article 'Wagon masters and lesser managers' by J. S. Ninomiya, *Harvard Business Review*, March–April 1988, cites seven typical leadership styles:

(1) Godfather	Demands complete control of their organizations and total loyalty from their employees
(2) Ostrich	Loves the status quo and fears discord, always hopes problems will go away and would rather stick their head in the sand than face unpleasantness of any kind
(3) Do-it-yourselfer	Wants to handle everything themselves, especially the most challenging assignments
(4) Detailer	Wants to know everything their employees do in detail
(5) Politician	Tells us what we want to hear
(6) Arbitrator	Is successful in large groups and possesses a deep understanding of human behavior, has a weakness for compromise at the wrong moment, is too friendly
(7) Eager beaver	Like the beaver who builds dams to interrupt the flow of water, they create ever greater workloads and disrupt the flow of work in organizations

The article goes on to list the skills of effective leaders:

(1)	Decision-maker	Is decisive
(2)	Listener and communicator	Knows employees and senses culture and group dynamics
(3)	Teacher	Taps the potential of all employees
(4)	Peacemaker	Is a conflict resolver
(5)	Visionary	Sets goals and direction
(6)	Self-critic	Admits mistakes
(7)	Team captain	Uses consensus
(8)	Leader	Is a good 'wagon master', gets the wagons to Oregon and keeps everyone in high spirits

The Politician

The Bill Gates Wannabe

☞ *Exercise: Self-image – The ideal self*

Like Ninomiya, each of us has an image of the perfect leader. We may not be very conscious of this ideal, but it exists at some level of awareness. Every leader is telling a story he or she values. As a leader, you must ask yourself two questions:

- What is important to you?

- How do others know this?

The power of vision: If you can visualize it, you can create it, you can have it

The power of a positive vision of the future is essential for providing meaning and direction to the present. Meaningful vision empowers us to solve problems and accomplish goals. It is important to distinguish between mission, vision and values.

Mission   Why do we exist? This should include a description of your practice, the products and services you provide, and your patient population.
- What products and services do we provide?
- Who is our customer?
- Why do we provide these services?
- Where and how are services provided?

The Eager Beaver

Vision

A vision is a picture of the future that is created in the imagination and motivates action. It answers the question, what do we want to create? A vision differentiates us from our competitors. It energizes and excites people. A vision statement is a collection of words, created collaboratively, that summarizes what an organization is intended to look like. An effectively communicated vision:

- Creates a shared and meaningful purpose
- Inspires passion and interest
- Guides decision-making and strategy
- Conveys values

Values

How are we going to work together (behaviors) while pursuing our vision?

Meaningful vision empowers us to to solve problems and accomplish goals. According to Joel Barker in *Discovering the Future: The Power of Vision* (Charterhouse International Learning Corporation, publisher), the following are key characteristics of a shared vision:

- Developed by leaders
- Shared and supported
- Comprehensive and detailed
- Positive and inspiring
- Makes a difference

The Master of All He Surveys

☞   *Vision exercise*

Visions often take a while to shape in your mind. They may take even longer to formulate into a vision statement. Visions, like any distant object, get clearer and clearer as we move toward them.

Write your image of your future as a leader by answering the following questions. As leader, what would I be doing if:

- I was completely successful?

- I felt work was satisfying?

- I was seen as effective by others?

- I could see contributions as a result of my work?

Leaders as role models

Leadership is a very personal thing. How it influences others is very public. Think back over your career. Have there been one or more individuals who have been professional role models for you? The following questions will help you develop specific details about your role model:

- What did the role model do to encourage you, build your self-confidence and recognize your achievements?

- How did the role model show you that he or she cared about you as a person?

- What values were apparent in the role model's attitudes and behaviors?

- What was it that made this person credible as a leader?

- What impact did this style of leadership have on your performance and progress? On the values that are important to you?

- How did this experience influence the kind of leader you are today?

Leadership competencies/self-assessment

Assessing our leadership competencies is key to developing a plan to improve leadership performance. The following is a list of common leadership competencies and self-assessment criteria.

Exercise

Rate each criterion on a scale of 1 to 5, 1 representing a developing opportunity and 5 a strength.

Competency	Criteria	Self-assessment Developing → Developed				
Developing commitment to a shared vision: inspiring a sense of purpose by sharing the organization's vision of the future	Communicates and reinforces the mission, vision and values	1	2	3	4	5
	Describes his or her vision of the future to direct reports and others	1	2	3	4	5
	Explains how an individual's and department's work relates to the overall (organization's) objectives	1	2	3	4	5
Empowering: creating an environment in which employees have ownership of their jobs and are able to achieve job expectations	Asks for ideas about what to do and how to do it	1	2	3	4	5
	Enables people to make their own decisions	1	2	3	4	5
	Gets others to feel a sense of ownership for the projects they work on	1	2	3	4	5
	Supports people when mistakes are made	1	2	3	4	5
Encouraging innovation: generating and recognizing creative processes or solutions to work-related situations	Constructively challenges the way we do things at work	1	2	3	4	5
	Initiates discussions to stimulate new ideas to improve what we do	1	2	3	4	5
	Supports individuals who have new approaches to problems	1	2	3	4	5
Informing: providing people with the information they need to do their jobs successfully	Communicates and consistently administers hospital policies	1	2	3	4	5
	Gives people access to the information they need to make appropriate decisions	1	2	3	4	5
	Relays information personally or through other means in a timely manner	1	2	3	4	5
Judgement: selecting the most appropriate course of action	Determines when a quick decision is necessary and when the decision can wait	1	2	3	4	5
	Determines when and how often to monitor people's work	1	2	3	4	5
	Makes sound decisions based on facts	1	2	3	4	5

Continued

Competency	Criteria	Devel-oping	$\rightarrow$	Devel-oped
Leading by example: setting an example by behaving in ways that are consistent with the organiza-tion's vision and values	Remains visible and accessible to direct reports and others	1 2 3 4 5		
	Shows interest in what others are doing by listening and talking to them	1 2 3 4 5		
	Uses practices that consistently model the organization's values	1 2 3 4 5		
Performance management: devel-oping objectives with direct reports and monitoring progress toward goals	Communicates clear goals	1 2 3 4 5		
	Discusses and reaches agreement with individuals and teams on how they will achieve goals	1 2 3 4 5		
Promoting excellence: advocating and contributing to excellence	Demonstrates a commitment to excellence by following through on commitments	1 2 3 4 5		
	Establishes realistic, but high, expec-tations for self and others	1 2 3 4 5		
	Expresses confidence in the ability of others to do things	1 2 3 4 5		
Providing recognition: positively acknowledging the accomplish-ments of others	Praises people for a job well done	1 2 3 4 5		
	Takes the time to celebrate accom-plishments when project milestones are reached	1 2 3 4 5		
	Tells the rest of the organization about the good work done by individ-uals or teams within his or her departments	1 2 3 4 5		
Removing obstacles to perfor-mance: identifying work environ-ment factors that are constraining employees from performing	Provides people with the appropriate time to do their jobs	1 2 3 4 5		
	Provides people with the proper tools and equipment to do their jobs	1 2 3 4 5		
	Removes obstacles to improve per-formance	1 2 3 4 5		
Systemic thinking: having a wider or longer-range perspective of problems and situations; looking at the 'big picture'	Considers the impact of decisions on others in the organization	1 2 3 4 5		
	Considers the organization's vision and business objectives when mak-ing decisions	1 2 3 4 5		
	Understands his/her work, its opera-tion, and the interconnections with other functions and units	1 2 3 4 5		

The Visionary

☞   *Exercise*

Conduct a self-assessment of leadership competencies/skills and behavioral criteria to determine areas and opportunities for improvement. Based on your self-assessment, check your major strengths and development opportunities for each competency listed below.

Major strengths and development opportunities

Strength	Development opportunity	Competency
❏	❏	Developing a commitment to a shared vision
❏	❏	Empowering
❏	❏	Providing recognition
❏	❏	Encouraging innovation
❏	❏	Removing obstacles to performance
❏	❏	Leading by example
❏	❏	Performance management
❏	❏	Judgement
❏	❏	Informing
❏	❏	Systemic thinking
❏	❏	Promoting excellence

Developing an action plan

Identify two leadership behaviors you will continue, based on your strengths, and two new behaviors based on your development opportunities.

Action plan

Strengths

1. _____

   _____

2. _____

   _____

Development opportunities

1. _____

   _____

2. _____

   _____

Ethics: building integrity and trust

Exercise

One of the most crucial leadership qualities in life and business is establishing yourself as a trustworthy person and having integrity. Describe in three sentences or less, what integrity means to you.

*The Nominally
in Charge*

Qualities that inspire trust

Recent studies show that people would rather follow individuals who they can count on, even when they disagree with their viewpoint, than those they can agree with but who change their minds. A leader's consistent pattern provides security and builds trust. This pattern must reflect strong moral and ethical values for trust to blossom fully. Leaders generate and sustain trust by exemplifying the following:

Constancy   Whatever surprises leaders themselves face, they do not create surprises for the group. They maintain continuity and security.

Congruity   Leaders 'walk the talk'. There is no gap between the theories they espouse and the ones they practice. Their morality is found in their behavior.

Reliability   Leaders are there when it counts; they are ready to support their co-workers in the moments of truth.

Integrity   Leaders honor their commitments and promises. They are ethical in their relationships.

Respectful communication and trust

To eliminate fear from our relationships so that work can proceed smoothly, we must learn to communicate respectfully, even if we disagree with someone. Respectful communication has these five vital qualities:

The Saint

(1)   It seeks to know and be known. It is based on the intent to learn about the other person and to have that person know us.

(2)   It is honest and encourages honesty.

(3)   It honors the other's right to have his/her own point of view, which may be different from our own.

(4)   It shows empathy for the other's feelings.

(5)   It seeks common ground and focuses on areas of agreement or commonality as the basis for exploring areas of disagreement.

Personal code of ethics

Exercise

Take an honest look at your own code of ethics. This is an opportunity to scan your belief system to discover your values, ethics and code of behaviors. It is one thing to hold a set of moral values and another to live by them. The true test of integrity is the consistent expression of a code of ethics in action.

How will I know if my actions are ethical?

My ethical code

1.

2.

3.

4.

5.

6.

7.

The following factors may help you to decide whether you are making the right choices:

- Are my actions consistent with my ethical code?

- Does my action give the appearance of impropriety?

- Will the action bring discredit to me or anyone with whom I work?

- Can I defend my action to my peers, employees and the general public?

- Does my action meet my personal code of behavior?

Applied Law for the Non-Attorney

3

Joseph S. Sanfilippo and Steven Smith

In the current era of medicine, healthcare professionals are increasingly called upon to be knowledgeable with respect to the legal system. With the exception of an individual who pursues a legal degree, most healthcare professionals often do not have even basic knowledge with respect to legal terminology.

Understanding the terminology, especially with respect to office practice, will allow the healthcare professionals to be not only better informed, but also, ideally, aware of regulations and regulatory agencies that have an impact on the practice of medicine. Terms such as *res judicata*, 'the thing is decided', or *stare decisis*, 'let the decision stand', may play a role if a suit is filed with which a physician or other office personnel are involved.

We include this information to help the physician or allied health professional realize the sources of law that are dealt with when a suit is filed and a summons served. Knowledge and awareness of the task of proving negligence or harm in turn may be the concern at hand. If an office employee inadvertently administers the wrong medication, who is responsible? Does the potential for criminal versus civil action exist? What types of contract are pertinent to practice management? These questions are addressed. Fundamental information for all healthcare professionals is provided.

One must realize that one basic source of law is common law, which is derived from judicial decisions and has its origin in English common law (Table 1). Malpractice cases are tried on common-law principles unless a specific statute governs the point in question. Other types of law include: statutory law, which is a result of federal and state legislature decisions; and administrative law, which is prescribed by 'administrative agencies'.

Table 1 Basic tenets of tort law

Preservation of peace between individuals
Culpability
Deterrence
Compensation

A number of concepts should be mastered with regard to the legal profession, including the following definitions.

Tort	One party asserts that the wrongful conduct of another has caused harm
Res judicata	'The thing is decided', which cites previous court decisions with respect to the matter in question
Stare decisis	'Let the decision stand': when a lawsuit involving an identical or similar situation is filed, it should be resolved in a manner that reflects the initial decision
CMMS	Centers for Medicare and Medical Services (formerly Health Care Financing Administration): a principal operating component of the Department of Health and Human Services. It oversees Medicare and Medicaid programs
FcoA	Federal Council on Aging: composed of 15 members who deal primarily with the elderly. It provides recommendations to the President, the Secretary, the Commissioner and Congress with respect to federal policies regarding the elderly
NIA	National Institute on Aging: a segment of the National Institutes of Health designed for the 'conduct and support' of biomedical, social and behavioral research and training related to the aging process and specifically related diseases The priorities of the NIA include Alzheimer's disease, understanding aging, frailty, disability and rehabilitation, health and effective functioning, long-term care for older people, special older populations, and training and career development as applied to the aged

Tort law

A tort is a civil wrong other than a breach of contract committed against an individual or his or her property. The basic tenets of tort law include:

(1)   Preservation of peace between individuals;

(2)   Culpability – to find fault for wrongdoing;

(3)   Deterrence – to discourage the wrongdoer or 'tortfeasor' from committing a wrong;

(4)   Compensation – to indemnify the injured person for wrongdoing.

Statistically, one claim finds its way into the tort system for every eight cases of injury caused by medical malpractice; furthermore, only 50% of claimants ever receive compensation. Overall, 16 times as many individuals actually suffer injury due to negligence as receive compensation through the tort system[1].

The three basic categories of tort law are: negligent tort; intentional tort; and torts in which liability is assessed irrespective of fault (for example, manufacturers' defects) (Table 2). An intentional tort would include assault, battery, false imprisonment, invasion of privacy or infliction of mental distress. There must be 'intent' in that the wrong-doer realizes that harm will result; a wilful act is involved.

Table 2 Three basic categories of tort law

Negligent
Intentional
Liability irrespective of fault

Negligence is a tort, or civil or personal wrong in which it is an unintentional omission or commission of an act that a reasonably prudent person would or would not carry out under the given circumstances (Table 3). In essence, it is a departure from the standard of care.

Table 3 Types of conduct

Malfeasance
Misfeasance
Non-feasance
Malpractice
Criminal negligence

Types of negligence include:

(1)   Malfeasance – execution of an unlawful or improper act;

(2)   Misfeasance – improper performance of an act, resulting in injury, for example administering the wrong medication, inflicting a burn on the patient;

(3)   Non-feasance – failure to act when there is a duty to act, for example not ordering the appropriate diagnostic test or prescribing the proper medication;

(4)   Malpractice – negligence or carelessness of a professional person;

(5)   Criminal negligence – reckless disregard for the safety of another.

There are two basic degrees of negligence. The first is ordinary negligence, i.e. failure to do what a reasonably prudent person would or would not have done. The other is gross negligence or wanton omission of care.

The four elements that must be present to qualify for negligence and thus for a plaintiff to recover damages are (Table 4):

(1)   Duty to care – obligation of reasonable care to plaintiff;

(2)   Breach of duty – failure to adhere to obligation or conform to required standard;

(3)   Injury – actual damages occur;

(4)   Causation – the injury was actually and proximately caused by breach of duty and thus the injury was 'foreseeable'.

Table 4 Four elements of qualify for negligence

Duty of care
Breach of duty
Injury
Causation (proximate cause)

Standard of care The conduct expected of an individual in a given situation: this must be exercised in accordance with what a reasonably prudent person would do, acting under the same or similar circumstances.

Proximate cause/causation The fourth element necessary to establish negligence requires that there be a reasonable, close and causal connection between the defendant's negligent conduct and the damage that the plaintiff sustained. Proximate cause refers to the relationship between a breached duty and the injury. The breach of duty must be the proximate cause of the injury.

Foreseeability This is the reasonable anticipation that harm or injury is likely to result from an act or omission to act. The true test of forseeability is whether anyone of ordinary prudence and intelligence would have anticipated the danger to others caused by his or her negligence.

In the category of intentional torts, assault and battery must be considered. Assault is the infringement of the mental security or tranquillity of another. Battery constitutes a violation of another's physical integrity. The former is a deliberate threat coupled with the ability to do physical harm to another, but no actual contact is necessary. The latter, by definition, involves intentional touching of another's person in a socially impermissible manner without the person's consent.

False imprisonment From the medicolegal perspective, a patient who does not actually have to be constrained, but is constrained, would qualify under the category of 'false imprisonment'. An individual who is physically confined, and provided with reasonable grounds to fear that force, which may be implied by words, threats or gestures, will be used to detain them or intimidate them without legal justification, also qualifies under this category.

Defamation of character This is defined as false oral or written communication to someone other than the defamed person that tends to lay open that person's reputation to scorn and ridicule in the eyes of colleagues and others in the community. Within the category of defamation, libel results from the written word and slander from the spoken word.

Fraud This includes an intentional misrepresentation that could cause harm or loss to a person or property. If, for example, one knows that there is no foundation for believing a statement to be true and makes it anyway to the detriment of the patient, that healthcare provider can be held liable for fraud.

Criminal aspects associated with the medical profession

A crime is defined as a social wrongdoing and is punishable by law. Crimes are classified as either misdemeanors or felonies. A misdemeanor is an offense punishable by less than 1 year in jail and/or a fine. Examples include petty larceny and driving while intoxicated. A felony is a more significant crime, such as rape or murder, punishable by imprisonment in a state or federal penitentiary for more than 1 year. Drug abuse and child abuse fall under the auspices of criminal law.

Child abuse Failure to report child abuse constitutes a misdemeanor. The healthcare professional may be held liable accordingly.

Criminal negligence This can be associated with a healthcare professional when there is evidence of gross deviation below the standard of care expected to be provided by a reasonably prudent individual under similar circumstances.

Falsification of records This constitutes grounds for criminal prosecution. It represents a deliberate intent to defraud and conceal the truth. Kickbacks are punishable under criminal law. These would fall under three specific categories: inflated billing where the invoices exceed the actual price of the goods purchased; false billings; and phoney items submitted along with regular invoices, with the concept of being deliberately misleading.

Patient rights

Patient abuse is the mistreatment or neglect of an individual who is under the direct care of a healthcare professional and/or organization. The abuse can be physical, psychological, medical or financial. In one sense, long-term abuse and neglect is more commonly seen with respect to nursing home patients than acutely hospitalized patients. Elder abuse is less likely to be reported than is child abuse; victims are often 75 years of age or older. A majority of states have statutes or adult protective services laws that require mandatory reporting of elder abuse.

Forcible administration of medications can be a criminal act. For instance, a case was reported in which the patient's chin was held and the medication poured down her throat[2].

Contracts

A contract is defined as a written or oral legally binding obligation between two or more parties. The purpose of a contract is to enable the participants to be specific in their understandings and expectations of one another.

Types of contract include the following:

Express This is an oral agreement or written agreement: it is obviously always best to have the agreement in writing. Some oral contracts may not be considered by the court.

Implied This is based on the conduct of the parties for which implied authority is conveyed.

Voidable This is a contract in which one party but not the other has the right to escape from the legal obligations under the contract.

Executory This is a contract in which something remains to be done by one or more parties.

Executed This is a contract in which all the obligations of the parties have been fully performed.

Enforceable This is a valid, legally binding agreement. If it is breached by one party, the other will have an appropriate legal alternative.

Contracts for reality, goods or services

In this category, goods include all things that are 'moveable', with exceptions such as money and securities, which raise particular concern and rules. Service contracts exist for professional services, some management agreements and relationships with health maintenance organizations.

Elements of a contract include: the offer or communication; consideration and acceptance. Contracts require competent parties.

Independent contractor

An independent contractor is an individual who agrees to undertake work without being under the direct control or direction of another. The independent contractor is personally responsible for any negligent acts. In general, the healthcare facility has limited liability for injuries resulting from negligent acts or omissions on the part of truly independent physicians. There is no liability on the basis of *respondeat superior*, ('let the master answer'), here meaning that the employer is responsible for legal consequences of the acts of the servant or employee who is acting within the scope of his or her employment.

Employment contracts

This category includes the employee handbook which is strongly recommended in an office setting. It provides the terms of an employment contract and, ideally, each employee reads and signs such a

document. The healthcare provider must keep in mind the potential legal consequences of each provision within the employee handbook since he/she may be held accountable accordingly.

Anti-trust

Restraint of trade falls primarily under the purview of the Department of Justice and the Federal Trade Commission (FTC), which are responsible for enforcing federal anti-trust laws. Civil provisions of such include the Sherman, Clayton and Robinson-Pattman Acts[3]. Efforts to avoid monopolies are the underlying concept with respect to anti-trust laws. Many states also have anti-trust laws.

Medical staff

There are legal responsibilities of the medical staff with respect to the practice of medicine, diagnosis, treatment and prescription in particular. The healthcare organization for which the physician is working must ensure that:

(1)   The medical care of each patient is supervised by a competent and qualified physician;

(2)   Appropriate physician coverage is provided when the primary physician is not available;

(3)   The physician reviews each patient's total program of care including medications and treatments;

(4)   Progress notes are current, signed and dated;

(5)   All orders are signed;

(6)   Patients are seen by a physician on a regular basis.

The physician must be aware of the legal aspects with respect to the practice of medicine. It crosses the spectrum of tort law, criminal law, contracts and anti-trust laws. In addition, hospital responsibilities of office personnel should be clearly understood by all parties involved.

References

1. The Robert Wood Johnson Foundation. The tort system for medical malpractice: how well does it work, what are the alternatives? *Abridge* Spring 1991:2
2. 560 N.Y.S. 2d 573 N.Y. APP. Div. 1990
3. Sherman, Clayton, Robinson-Pattman Stark Laws

Suggested reading

Pozgar GD, Pozgar NS. *Legal Aspects of Health Care Administration*, 6th edn. Gaithersburg, MD: Aspen Publishers, 1996

US Department of Health and Human Services. *Task Force of Medical Liability and Malpractice*, no. 3. Washington, DC: USDHHS, 1987

United States Food and Drug Administration. *We Want You To Know About Today's FDA*. Washington, DC: FDA, 1974

Hospital Association of New York State. *Restraints and the Frail, Elderly Patient*. New York: HANYS, 1990:23

The silent epidemic: crime in hospitals. *Good Housekeeping*, September 1994:107

Witkin G, Friedman D, Guttman M. Health care fraud. *US News World Rep*, 21 February 1992

Weiner PI, Bompui SH, Brittain MG Jr. *Wrongful Discharged Claims 98*. 1986

American Medical Association. *Opinions and Reports of the Judicial Council*. AMA, 1996

It's Not a Plan Without a Business Plan

4

Stephen K. Klasko and David B. Toub

One of the most frustrating aspects for physicians attempting to enter the 'foreign world of business' is understanding the framework, nomenclature and 'road maps' necessary to obtain money in any business-oriented project. It would be similar to an MBA trying to enter the field of medicine without understanding how to use a prescription pad or stethoscope. In essence, the business plan is a high-level view of a venture that also describes past, present and future activities. Since the business plan is the ticket of admission to the investment process, the ability to express oneself clearly and in business terms is crucial.

A business plan is a 'living document' that allows a medical group the opportunity to reflect on where it was, where it is now, where it is going and how it might get there. Because of the fluid nature of this, we often speak of the business planning 'process', which includes so much more than just the final document. In fact, the business plan gives the medical group, often consisting of people of varying personalities and talents, an opportunity to reach a consensus on a direction for the future[1]. For a medical group this process takes time and commitment, an investment usually well rewarded by giving the group a competitive edge with regard to information about itself and the environment in which it exists.

Once the commitment is agreed upon, identifying the team becomes crucial. For medical groups, the core group will usually consist of physicians, administrators, nurses and other office/hospital personnel, as well as the appropriate marketing individuals. The nature of this group as well as the complexity of the project will then determine what external resources are necessary, such as business consultants, attorneys, accountants, finance experts and information systems experts.

The next step, often underappreciated, is gathering the data necessary to understand the environment in which this project exists. For healthcare, that would include both global and local assessments. What is the impact of managed care on this plan? What about the Balanced Budget Amendment of 1997? On a local level, are there any new insurers or providers who would have an impact upon this plan, positively or negatively? Without an appropriate assessment of the environment, it will be impossible to perform a scenario analysis, a key aspect of a healthcare business plan. This aspect of the data collection should be quite specific, to include percentages of patients utilizing the service in managed care plans, Medicare, Medicaid, indemnity plans and so on. It also is important to know in what markets you will compete, what niches can be developed, what the competition in the area is doing, and any unique services or technical know-how that sets you apart from others. This concept, called competitive differentiation, is crucial in convincing investors that your project is the most worthwhile (Table 1).

Table 1 Competitive differentiation

In what markets will you compete?
Niche identification
Competition in area
Unique services
Technical services

This is a good checkpoint in the process. You should not go forward unless certain questions have been answered in your environmental assessment (Table 2).

Table 2 Environmental assessment

Where is your patient base?
What referral sources do you have, which are solid and which at risk?
What are the long-run as well as short-term goals of your practice and this project?

Once the questions outlined in Table 2 are answered, your homework moves to the next phase, namely assessing the financial aspects of the healthcare industry as applied to your practice and this project. In this phase, it is necessary to be able to interpret the income statements of the practice to this point, which represent the revenues and expenses historically and provide the profit or loss status of your practice over time. The balance sheet can be interpreted as a current 'snapshot' assessment of the practice's (and your) financial condition. It is certain that any potential investors will review your practice's (and your) status with a fine-toothed comb, so be prepared to explain the strengths and weaknesses of your financial health. Cash flow statements are discussed elsewhere in this book and are also often used as a prognostic guide (Table 3).

Table 3 Financial aspects of healthcare indexes

Practice revenue and expense (historical)
Profit/loss statement
Balance sheet
Cash flow statements
Strengths
Weaknesses

Now you are ready to start writing. While there is no absolute 'generic' business plan, most plans contain common features such as an action plan, a mission statement and an executive summary (Table 4).

Table 4 Business plan

Executive summary
Mission statement
Human resources
Operations
Finance
Marketing

Just as a radiologist will approach a chest X-ray in a methodical fashion, writing a business plan also requires a set structure. The first portion should describe the organization and what it wants to accomplish, i.e. its mission. The middle portion of the plan analyzes the business environment, the organizational resources needed to accomplish the mission and how the business intends to grow. Much like a traditional head-to-toe approach to the physical examination, the middle portion of a business plan follows the typical business units of an organization. In other words, this portion analyzes the organization and the plan in terms of human resources, operations, finance, marketing and other business divisions. Finally, the third portion of the plan describes what actions will be necessary to complete the project successfully and an approximate timetable for their completion.

According to the Massachusetts Institute of Technology (MIT) Enterprise Forum[2], the key requirements of a funding plan are:

(1)   It must be arranged appropriately, with an executive summary, a table of contents and chapters in the proper order;

(2)   It must give a sense of what you hope, and more importantly expect, to accomplish 3–7 years into the future;

(3)   It must explain in quantitative and qualitative terms the benefits to the user of these services;

(4)   It must portray the partners as a team of experienced managers with complementary business skills;

(5)   It must contain believable financial projections, with the key data explained and documented;

(6)   It must be easily and concisely explainable in a well-orchestrated oral presentation.

Most important, the business plan should be a document that can be relevant for up to 5 years, depending on the changes in healthcare and your specialty. The plan should be reviewed and refined annually to ensure relevance to your market[3]. Composing a business plan will allow you to focus on certain details that are vital for the success of your practice. For example, if efficient billing mechanisms, such as electronic billing, are necessary for the success of this project, how will you deal with that issue? How will you prepare for technological advances in your specialty? What new patient categories and markets do you plan to pursue? How many nursing and other ancillary personnel are required for the project?

The document arising from the business planning process is organized into categories according to Table 5.

Although the executive summary appears as a summary at the front of your business plan, it is the last component that should be written. This should be brief (no more than one or two pages); there is often a temptation to rewrite the entire business plan. It should serve as an overview with respect to your practice and the project, what it is currently and what your plans are during the business plan life cycle. Vision, mission, goals and objectives should be succinctly conveyed.

The practice overview will provide information that sets you apart from the competition. A reader should be able to understand your practice and what differentiates it competitively, based on this section.

Table 5 Business planning process

Executive summary
Practice overview
Corporate values
Corporate vision
Business environment
Market trends
Areas for market segment growth
Patient-related activities, i.e. a consumer-oriented practice
Competition in these segments
Healthcare systems in general, e.g. third-party payers
Managed care
Growth strategy
Competitive advantage
Action plan
Final overview
Annual review

A mission statement should be considered as the starting point of the business plan. It is a concise statement that defines the practice's or project's purpose, and reflects the long-term vision. Most important, it should cover these topics: what the group does, for whom they do it, why they do it and how they do it[1] (Table 6).

The body of the mission statement could best be defined as a strategic assessment or a situational analysis, and is a comprehensive review of the environment, the local market and the internal operations of the group. A valuable method for evaluating and planning this part of the business plan is the 'SWOT' analysis – strengths, weaknesses, opportunities and threats – and is an honest description of the pluses and minuses of your existing or proposed practice. This is usually contained

within the initial third of the business plan as part of the environmental analysis. The SWOT analysis should contain a description of how you will correct any weaknesses and counter any threats.

Table 6 Mission statement

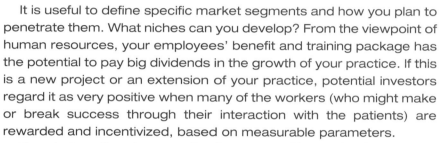

What do we do?

For whom?

Why?

How?

It is useful to define specific market segments and how you plan to penetrate them. What niches can you develop? From the viewpoint of human resources, your employees' benefit and training package has the potential to pay big dividends in the growth of your practice. If this is a new project or an extension of your practice, potential investors regard it as very positive when many of the workers (who might make or break success through their interaction with the patients) are rewarded and incentivized, based on measurable parameters.

Knowledge of cost accounting becomes of increasing importance when determining whether to purchase new products, adopt new technology, acquire satellite offices and so on. 'Rightsizing' personnel to accommodate demand while minimizing overhead is an art form which often requires outside consultation. In order to make these decisions, many questions must be asked, including:

(1)   What future competition do you foresee?

(2)   Will there be room to accommodate market expansion?

(3)   How will your information systems serve you best?

(4)   What are your financial and strategic goals?

The body of the report often concludes with a marketing analysis. Assuming that your needs analysis has been appropriate and that the patient demographics have been analyzed, and that an action plan has been established to profit from those trends, the next step is letting people know about it. Start by asking your committee to 'imagine it has no patients and to give its top three ideas for patient acquisition given the existing local market conditions'[1]. This might include any staff training to enhance customer services, information from patient surveys and any other special services that help differentiate you from your competition.

The final part of the business plan allows the reader to understand specifically your targets (goals) and benchmarks for achievement (objectives) (Table 7).

Table 7 Goals, objectives, strategies and tactics

Goals: Targets   Challenges
Objectives: Benchmarks   Measurable parameters   How these support the goal
Strategies: How to achieve goals and objectives
Tactics: Specifics

Goals should be attainable and specific, but challenging. Unlike goals, objectives are specific and measurable indicators that can predict your future success. An objective needs to support a goal and be measured by an operational indicator. For example, some of the goals and objectives in a departmental business plan include[4]:

(1) Facilitate the career development of all physicians in a manner that also encourages active participation in departmental activities;

(2) Develop a comprehensive clinical and laboratory research program;

(3) In concert with the low-risk obstetric program, implement a home-visit program for mothers and newborns after a 24-hour inpatient stay;

(4)   Expand inpatient and outpatient financial tracking systems to subset data to reflect service lines: obstetrics, benign gynecology.

Strategies and tactics indicate how you intend to achieve your goals and objectives. Strategies are general and tactics become more specific. Going back to our business plan[4]:

(1)   Develop a mechanism to assess routinely the professional satisfaction of physician and key support staff;

(2)   Work with an interdisciplinary team to define program content incorporating primary care and prevention, assessment and screening, evaluation and counseling, immunization and diagnostic/treatment services;

(3)   Develop a 'customer-focused' women's health education and wellness program for businesses.

Although the business plan is written, the work is far from over. Presentation of a business plan requires not only a clear understanding of what is between the pages but also some preparation as to what the audience is looking for. Upon presentation of our department's first business plan, replete with overarching goals and lofty objectives, our chief financial officer brought us all back to reality with a simple question: 'If you were investing your own money in this department, what would you need to see that would make you feel better about your money?'

Finally, it is crucial that physicians understand the importance of delving into the business side of medicine if they are to be successful. However, entering the 'dark side' does entail some risks, especially with regard to their colleagues. The traditional physician view promotes, as an ideal, a strict boundary between clinical and business domains. That boundary used to serve physicians well. Now, however, like it or not, healthcare is a corporate enterprise. It can no longer afford to isolate quality from cost, and efforts to preserve a 'clinical/administrative split' serve only to keep physicians out of decisions in which their influence is sorely needed[5].

Allowing physicians, administrators and patients to be involved in determining the core direction for one's community provides the key answer. Which service lines are going through change and at what point are they in a product cycle (is it emergence, growth or maturity)? One must develop strategies accordingly. For core directions, the questions to ask are given in Table 8. Just asking and answering these questions makes all the difference.

Table 8 Core directions

What is our business (mission)?

In what areas have we done well?

In what areas do we lack the competence or resources to be effective?

What are the key environmental factors/trends affecting this area?

Who is our customer?

What does the customer value?

Do our competencies and resources match the needs of these customers?

What is our strategy?

What major activities have helped or hindered achievement of our results?

How effectively are we using our financial resources?

How should we prioritize our efforts?

How should we measure our results?

References

1.   *Business Plan Primer*. Pfizer Pharmaceuticals, 1997
2.   Rich S, Gumpert D. *Business Plans That Win $$$*. New York: Harper and Row, 1987
3.   Furlong MJ, Burns LA. Strategic business planning for the multispecialty group practice. *J Ambulat Care Manage* 1996;19:16–25
4.   Klasko S, Shaw M. Department of Obstetrics and Gynecology. *Lehigh Valley Hospital Business Plan*. Lehigh Valley Hospital, 1998
5.   Klasko S, Shea G. *The Phantom Stethoscope: A Field Manual for Creating an Optimistic Future in Medicine*. Franklin, TN: Hillsboro Press, 1999

Re-engineering your Practice

5

Joseph S. Sanfilippo

Is your practice a candidate for re-engineering? In one sense, is there a need periodically to re-evaluate the way you run your office? Is there reason to reassess the 'business aspect' of your medical practice? Re-engineering is basically defined as a 'starting over'. Specifically, it is the fundamental rethinking and radical redesign of business processes to achieve dramatic improvements in critical contemporary measures of performance such as cost, quality, service and speed of delivery. For instance, by increasing the number of personnel in your office, have the lines of communication decreased? If this is your impression, then your practice is a candidate for re-engineering.

Many of the principles that apply to the effective operation of a corporation also apply to a private practice setting. Practice management can idealize performance of the business aspects of a practice. It is predicated upon an individual who 'leads' the corporation and has a vision or concept of the future and where to head the practice. More specifically, the practice leader or team of directors should focus on the items listed in Table 1.

Table 1 Practice focus

Vision
Mission
Goals
Objectives

As stated above, 're-engineering' can be readily defined as 'starting over'. This may require deleting from one's mind the more traditional notions of how a practice should be organized and run. Many of the organizational and operational principles and procedures prerequisite to running the business aspect of your practice require foresight with respect to the changing environment, competition and positioning, to enable a competitive advantage over other practices. The concept of competitive advantage is developed in the chapter on 'Strategic management'.

To start the re-engineering process, the following is suggested. Determine the bottlenecks in your practice (Table 2). Begin at the front desk; perhaps request that an individual known to you calls in for an appointment.

Table 2 Re-engineering assessment

(1)   Are there glitches at the entrance point?

(2)   How are patients treated?

(3)   How is our billing and coding?

(4)   What about collections entry and follow-up?

As one re-engineers the practice, it is important to have the employees buy into the vision, goals and objectives. The vision should look to the future of the healthcare professionals' practice. The mission statement should address the questions posed in Table 3.

Table 3 Mission statement

Who are we?

What do we want to be?

How do we get there?

The re-engineering process should include being cognizant of how the practice will compete now and in the future. What steps can be taken to be and stay 'a step ahead'? You must ask yourself whether you are willing to take risks and if so, to what extent, and what is the potential gain? Are you taking advantage of the talents of employees in the practice and their ingenuity? What processes work in your particular office setting? This should be approached from a historical perspective. These are concepts that must be initially evaluated and periodically 'revisited'.

Who is involved in the re-engineering process: physicians, the office manager or all employees? External environment effects and constraints imposed on the practice must be considered. What effect does managed care have on the practice? Is our practice growing? Are we cost-effective in providing services? Who is in charge of the re-engineering process and who periodically reassesses various aspects of the process? Should we consider an outside consultant? Would this be a cost-effective approach? Can such individuals help to identify problems within the practice? If the physician heading the practice is adept in developing cost-accounting or providing a pro forma for a new service or personnel recruitment, this is most useful. If not, one should be able to outsource cost analysis. Financial assessment is illustrated in Tables 4–6.

Table 4 Income statement

Revenue from services rendered	$	_____
– Variable costs	(–)	_____
– Fixed costs (e.g. rent)	(–)	_____
– Depreciation	(–)	_____
EBIT	$	_____
– Taxes (average 34%)	(–)	_____
Net income	$	_____

EBIT, earnings before interest and taxes

Table 5 Projected operating cash flow

EBIT	$	_____
+ Depreciation	(+)	_____
– Taxes	(–)	_____
Operating cash flow	$	_____

EBIT, earnings before interest and taxes

Table 6 Projected total cash flows

Operating cash flow	0	Year 1	Year 2	Year 3
$ ____	$ ____	$ ____	$ ____
Change in net working capital	(−)	(−)	(−)	(+) Recover original capital invested
Capital spending	(−)	(−)	(−)	(−)
Total projected cash flow	$ ____	$ ____	$ ____	$ ____

By estimating the net working capital required for each year of operation and the projected depreciation of the equipment involved, the cash flow predicted from the project is determined from the operating cash flow, capital spending and the addition to net working capital.

Net present value (NPV) is a measure of the additional value accrued by undertaking this investment. If one adds a new procedure to the practice, the obvious question to ask is will it increase profit? If so, what is the investment in start-up costs?

A physician who plans to have his/her practice in the forefront must be an innovative leader making a concerted effort to 'stay a step ahead' of the competition. The patient must come first, and perhaps the re-engineering process should begin with the front desk, which is often an impediment to success. The front desk should be viewed as the public relations focus of the practice ('internal marketing'). All employees are ambassadors of your practice. The manner in which telephone calls are answered, courtesy and willingness to help remain paramount. Will the patient experience frustration if they receive a recording, channeling them to press additional buttons? If this is the most feasible method of proceeding, is there a mechanism by which an 'operator' can come on line (periodically) in a facilitating manner to assist the patient?

Key questions in re-engineering include:

(1)   How can we do what we do more efficiently and effectively?

(2)   How can we do what we do at a lower cost, and perhaps 're-engineer' the process?

(3)   Why do we do what we do at all?

(4)   Is the way in which our employees proceed predicated in a manner that meets the patients' needs?

(5)   Do we have a first-class quality product (service)?

(6)   Is my office known for excellent service, and if not, why not; what are the problems that need to be corrected?

As the head of your corporation, you, as the re-engineering leader, can make it happen. You must be a visionary with an idea of what type of practice you or your board of directors wants to establish, and have it as an ongoing concept. In the business world there is a term 'going concern', which translates to: will we be in business in the future? This leads to a number of examples from the business world.

The next time you drive by Taco Bell remember that this, in essence, has been the brain-child of Joseph E. Martin, the Chief Executive Officer (CEO) of Taco Bell, a subsidiary of Pepsico, who introduced radical change in the face of a dire financial state to secure long-term success for Taco Bell. His approach was to begin with changing the employee mindset, to work for the customer, not for their boss. The second key point was to go to the customers and ask them exactly what they wanted. The response was not a bigger, better, fancier 'thing', as the corporate leaders and managers thought, but rather dedication to providing good food, served fast and hot, in a clean environment and at a price that is affordable. While this example does not fully demonstrate re-engineering, it does address total quality management, which is incorporated into the re-engineering process.

One other example of this is Xerox. Team spirit was tied to bonuses obtained for customer satisfaction. Their CEO reminded employees that 'customers pay your salary and don't forget it'. In the present case, the bottom line focuses on the patient, who is a customer, and all efforts must be channeled to providing quality care and a warm, friendly environment, for a successful practice.

The approach requires reinventing, and restructuring or re-engineering, your practice from a number of aspects, including individualism, self-reliance, willingness to accept risk and propensity for change as the most salient concepts. What is my competition doing? How can I stay a step ahead? In essence, the questions to ask at this juncture include:

(1)   How can we do better?

(2)   How can we do it faster?

(3)   Can it be accomplished at a lower cost?

Perhaps Adam Smith aptly put it, from the industrial perspective, that 'we must break our work down into its simplest and most basic tasks

and refocus on the customer's best interest as the most important aspect of our mission'.

Examples from one practice

Dr Henry overheard a patient complaining that she was put on hold for an inordinate amount of time. The physician anonymously called in, seeking a new patient appointment. He indeed was a victim of 'hold', and witnessed a scenario that included, 'hello, this is the North Hills Medical Practice, can you hold?' and before he could say 'yes', he was placed on hold in such a manner as to reflect what appeared to be an automatic practice of the front-desk operator. The physician thought about this process and the frustration it causes, as well as the barriers to entrance into his practice.

He conducted a survey, asking questions of patients in his office relating to the front desk, the waiting time once registered, billing and collection personnel, and promptness regarding follow-up phone calls by his office staff. The physician then embarked upon evaluation of the office manager and her interaction with office personnel. The bottom line was that there was a clear need for better interpersonal skills and re-engineering of the practice.

The physician considered and employed a consulting group, who went through the practice with a fine-toothed comb and restructured each component of the practice. The physician's practice then witnessed development of a mission statement, which was displayed in the waiting room. On one wall hung a laminated newspaper article featuring the physician's interview with the local media. The displaying of such had not crossed the physician's mind before it was suggested by the consultants. The practice subsequently had specific goals and objectives established. A new computer system was introduced to accommodate appointments, as well as billing and collections. There was establishment of regular office meetings conducted by the office manager. A sense of 'team spirit' was developed. Ideas were sought from the office personnel regarding more efficient functioning of the office. A reward system was introduced for ideas that led to decreasing the overhead.

The result was an improved *esprit de corps* within the office environment. There was more efficient billing and collections, and sustained growth of the practice. In retrospect, it was felt that looking at the whole picture and re-engineering the process was far superior to a less well-coordinated mechanism of just focusing on one item at a time. Much of the re-engineering process took into account what the patient (customer) wanted, and included input from office personnel.

The latter led to a 'buy-in' to the process, since the employees were integrally involved in the re-engineering of the practice. The benefits included patient satisfaction, improved communication among office personnel and, clearly, overall increased efficiency in the practice.

Technological advances provided for your patients

The questions to be asked are: how can technology allow us to do the things that we are perhaps not already doing or to do what we do better and how can new technology introduced into our practice enhance and improve the quality of care?

For example, will the introduction of a new piece of equipment serve the practice well? We begin with identification of a need. This is followed by determination of equipment availability, and advantages and disadvantages of each alternative (competitive products on the market), and determination of costs for the procedure and estimated revenues. Should the equipment be leased or purchased? The learning curve for all involved must come into consideration. Details of interpretation of results obtained from the new equipment and its clinical application are important. How will the equipment depreciate, and over how long a period will this occur? What is the life span of the equipment? Will additional personnel be required for this new technology to be introduced? Frequency of usage is another consideration. Will it be a source of new patients?

A cost-accounting or pro forma is then developed (see above).

Once these questions are addressed, a decision is made regarding the feasibility of proceeding, impact on the practice, and potential up- and down-sides, all of which are brought into consideration and put in proper perspective. The decision to expand services and introduce new technology should take into account the external environment (Table 7).

Table 7 Planning and decision-making should encompass the external environment: SWOT analysis

(1)   Do we have a competitive advantage?

(2)   How can we maintain our sustained competitive advantage?

(3)   What are our strengths? (S)

(4)   What are our weaknesses? (W)

(5)   What opportunities can be made with respect to the practice now and in the future? (O)

(6)   What are the threats to our practice? (T)

Healthcare professionals must also take into consideration any concern regarding 'ego' and how it interferes with communications. One must be willing to ask if there is an atmosphere in which no one is willing to make a suggestion to the physician or group of physicians, for fear that it would be taken in a negative vein and result in the employee who suggested such being fired. This atmosphere is detrimental to the growth of the practice, and one must consider whether this concern exists. Clearly, a foundation of good communication, team spirit and cost-efficiency are the prerequisites for success.

In the business world, once a corporation develops a competitive advantage, every effort is made to maintain that edge over competitors. This concept is termed sustained competitive advantage (SCA). As time has progressed, the term SCA is being replaced by opportunity creation and exploitation (OCE). With the changing business or medical care environment, it may become impossible to maintain SCA thus: practitioners must create a cycle of activity involving creation and discovery of new technology and apply it to their practice. Additional information regarding this topic can be obtained in *Strategic Renaissance* by Evan Dudik, AMACOM Publishers, New York City.

Contract negotiating as part of the re-engineering process

With respect to the signing of new contracts, the details must be understood by the appropriate personnel within the practice. The office manager, as well as the physicians, should understand the 'fine print'. Ideally, having an individual who co-ordinates signing of the contract to explain the details is in your best interest. This discussion should be documented for future reference.

Focus on the patient

Perhaps the most pertinent aspect of re-engineering revolves around the patient. Patient satisfaction remains the link to future success. This is 'social marketing', with the gold standard of profitability, and quality of care, delivered in a cost-effective manner. Here, the term 'discontinuous thinking' must be introduced. In essence, this means identification and abandoning of outdated rules and the fundamental assumptions that underlie current business operations within your practice. The real question to ask is: are we meeting our patients' needs? Do we have a high-quality product? Do we provide excellent service? Are we a fully integrated practice utilizing technological advances, such as in our method of billing and collections? Are our tools of the trade used appropriately? Do we provide a friendly environment for our patients? Do we pay our employees as a measure of their performance with respect to patient satisfaction?

Summary and conclusion

The take-home message includes the ability of the healthcare professional to re-engineer the practice, putting the wants and needs of the patient first, and correlating this with physician leadership regarding vision, mission, goals and objectives. There should be a willingness to embark upon periodic change within the corporation from both business and patient perspectives. All of the above should lead to enhanced financial rewards, first-class *esprit de corps* of your employees and proper positioning for the future to maintain a sustained competitive advantage.

Suggested reading

Dudik EM. *Strategic Renaissance*. New York: AMICOM Publishers, 2000

Hammer M, Champy J. *Reengineering the Corporation*. New York: Harper Business Publishers, 1993

Strategic Marketing Management

6

Joseph S. Sanfilippo and Jeroen Walstra

The Cash Cow

Introduction

Healthcare professionals, like all business people, must realize that marketing services require not only financial support, but also an investment of time and effort. Large corporations typically have a dedicated marketing and sales organization. Private medical practitioners, on the other hand, generally do not have the resources to dedicate personnel full time to those tasks. Often hospitals assist in the marketing of physicians in practice.

The American Marketing Association states that 'marketing is the process of planning and executing the conception, pricing, promotion, and distribution of ideas, goods and services to create exchanges that satisfy individual and organizational objectives'. This definition shows that marketing is a far broader activity than advertising or selling. Furthermore, this definition stresses the importance of beneficial exchanges that satisfy the objectives of both buyers and sellers, whether they are individuals or organizations. They are synchronized and work together to provide patient value. The tendency to 'box' functions, so that the reception desk does not talk with the nurses and billing does not communicate with the physicians, creates functional divides devoid of responsibility and interaction. Yet, interfunctional action leads to the fulfilment of value targets. Typically, a practice does not need to hire marketing experts. It is often easier to make a healthcare professional marketing-oriented than to hire a marketing person and get him to understand the medical practice. This chapter is designed to convey a strategic management component within a practice and to assist you in developing marketing strategy to enhance your practice.

Strategic marketing process

In the strategic marketing process, the organization allocates its marketing resources to reach its target markets. The approach is divided into five phases:

(1)   Situation analysis;

(2)   Strategy formulation;

(3)   Planning, budgeting and organizing;

(4)   Implementation;

(5)   Evaluation and control.

Table 1 SWOT analysis

Strengths

E.g. Prestigious reputation (brand name)
Reputation among patients
Technological expertise

Weaknesses

E.g. Lack of experience
Antiquated computer system

External opportunities

E.g. Growing market demand
Unique services

Threats

Changing demographics
Competitive practices
Managed care

Situation analysis

The strategic marketing process starts with the situation analysis. A number of controllable and uncontrollable elements warrant exploration in the marketing environment of a practice. First, there are changing demographics, macroeconomic trends, political actions, laws and regulations, technological developments, the competitive environment and external physical forces, such as the weather and earthquakes, which are uncontrollable factors. Second, the practice, the financial resources, the reputation, the relationship with patients, the capabilities of healthcare professionals and the culture within the organization are, to a lesser or greater extent, controllable.

An effective shorthand summary of the situation analysis is the 'SWOT' analysis. This is an acronym describing an assessment of the practice's internal strengths and weaknesses and its external opportunities and threats (Table 1).

In order to identify where the practice can find a competitive edge, the healthcare professional needs to study the environment and how the practice can interact with that environment effectively. The healthcare professional needs to understand:

- Where the practice has been recently

- Where it is now

- Where it is heading, considering the organization's plans, the external factors and trends affecting it

Marketing orientation

In order to be competitive, the healthcare provider needs to develop a 'market orientation'. The organization (practice) should be systematically and entirely committed to the continuous creation of superior value. A market orientation requires a patient focus, competitor intelligence and interfunctional co-ordination.

The practice needs to understand customer (patient) preferences and requirements and combine skills and resources of the entire practice to satisfy patients' needs, and understand what patient value is. How can we satisfy the needs of third-party payers (insurance companies)?

Strategic decision-making is of paramount importance for a successful practice. Knowledge of patients' wants and needs, a basic marketing approach, will serve to orient one's practice and facilitate establishing a focused course of pursuit. The business-focused practitioner will readily see the importance of strategic planning, development of a mission, and establishment of clearly defined goals and the means of measuring attainment of such goals via objectives. How does one provide a high level of satisfaction to the customers (patients)? Understanding the needs of the patient and other stakeholders is crucial in developing a market-oriented strategy that leads to highly satisfied clients.

The performance of a practice (corporation) is always relative to the competition. In order to differentiate the practice from its competitors, the service provider (physician or physician group) needs to understand whether and to what extent the patients perceive the alternative providers as 'alternative satisfiers'. Therefore, an analysis of strengths and weaknesses of those competitors must be done.

Strategic competitive positioning

The question here is: how does one position the practice to be at a competitive advantage? The practice can offer its services at a lower price and provide the same benefits as the competition, or offer additional benefits than the competition that more than offset the increase in price'. Specifically, strategic competitive positioning involves the following sources (Table 2).

Table 2 Strategic positioning: three specific sources

(1) Predicated upon unique services (variety-based positioning)
(2) Serves the needs of a specific group of patients (needs-based positioning)
(3) Segmenting groups of patients – accessible in different ways (access-based positioning)

This would primarily focus on seeking a competitive advantage based on one of three (generic) strategies (Table 3).

Table 3 Generic strategies

(1) Strive for overall low cost (third-party payer contracts)
(2) Create and market unique products that provide clear differentiation
(3) Have a special appeal to groups of patients, segments of the market, focusing on their differentiation concerns (menopause, urogynecology, etc.)

What unique procedures can you offer? Specific surgical procedures, for example, urogynecology, provision of the latest advances in specialty surgery or unique techniques having a primary focus on, for example, geriatrics or adolescent medicine, all address a targeted segment of the population. The sustainable competitive advantage is dependent on the opportunities in the environment and the strengths of the organization. Therefore, one needs to study the environment.

One of the major tools for gathering information during the situation assessment is marketing research. Marketing research includes collecting information about patients, total number of hospital beds or surgical procedures, number of practitioners, number of medical practices and their specialties in a particular area, demographic trends, competitors, third-party payers and the type of coverage provided, new technologies and new procedures (Table 4).

Table 4 External factor analysis

Patient information
Demographics
Hospitals
Surgical procedures performed
Number of medical practices and type
Third-party payers
New technologies
Qualitative and quantitative technologies
Healthcare reform plans
Government plans

Market researchers use qualitative and quantitative techniques. Qualitative techniques are employed to develop a theory, and are used mostly in the first or exploratory stages of the situation analysis. An effective method for a medical practice is the use of focus-group interviews. These are loosely structured discussions among 10–12 patients or other interested people to determine what they might be looking for in a new medical practice, procedure or technology. For example, a focus group would discuss how better to serve parents with children visiting the practice. Quantitative research helps with testing the theory. It is used more often in the confirmatory stage of research. In this stage, the researcher uses structures and questions to test the hypothesis about how patients, insurers or competitors might behave. An example of quantitative research would be to test different advertising slogans with regard to the level of interest for a new medical procedure.

Having completed the SWOT analysis, an organization often then considers four alternative growth strategies (Table 5).

Table 5 Four growth strategies

(1) Core business, focusing on the primary product line within the practice: market penetration

(2) New markets for existing services: market development

(3) New services for existing markets: product development

(4) New series for new markets: diversification

Growth strategies

Market penetration involves increasing sales of present products in their existing markets. This would equal new network sites for practice expansion. There is no change in the product line, but increased sales to present markets are possible through actions such as better advertising, more service outlets or lower prices.

Market development involves selling existing products to new markets. There is no change in the product itself, but distribution is expanded through reaching new target markets such as, for example, other metropolitan areas and foreign countries. The application is finding new demographic populations to provide medical services for a practice.

Product development involves selling a new product to existing markets. There is a change in the product itself, but it is sold to existing markets. The addition of new technologies into the practice is an example of product development.

Diversification Involves developing new products and selling them in new markets. This is a potentially high-risk strategy because new actions are required for both markets and products, i.e. a combination of the above.

Thus, to summarize, growth strategies have application to healthcare professionals in that they might consider expanding their practice into new geographic or demographic regions (market development), or introducing a new procedure into their practice (product development and/or diversification).

Referral strategies

Healthcare providers are interested in encouraging referrals. The following procedure is suggested. The first step is to determine what type or types of primary-care physicians should be the target of referral information efforts. If several types of primary-care physicians will be targeted, an analysis of the volume of referral by segments should be conducted, as it is possible that some segments may provide more referrals than others and will be more important to target. After the types of physicians to target have been finalized, the next step is to determine what information sources to use. Marketer-controlled sources are easy to influence. On the other hand, health services are not. Most health service systems are rarely accessible by physicians, patients and payers. Therefore, enhancing the provider's reputation in the eyes of those sources is the best way to achieve their support.

Educational programs in the form of seminars can be very effective in enhancing a provider's reputation (Table 6).

Table 6 Definition of sources

Source	Description
Marketer-controlled	
Directory	Hospital referral directory describing physician, facilities, services, etc.
Call service	Medical center or hospital referral call service
Representative	Hospital representative calling on physicians
Other material	Any other hospital-sponsored material
Newsletter	Newsletters, brochures or other printed material
Health services	
Physician referral	Fellow physician (other than specialist)
Specialist	Personal contact with the specialist
Patient	The patient or the patient's family
Payer	Patient's healthcare payer (e.g. patient's insurance carrier, HMO or preferred provider organization)

HMO, health maintenance organization

Strategy formulation

The main objective of strategy formulation is to help the organization gain a sustainable competitive advantage (SCA).

Gaining a sustainable competitive advantage as a healthcare provider is a formidable task. An important part of this objective is responding strategically to a continuously changing environment and the capabilities of the organization.

The task of identifying market segments is challenging (Table 7). After all, there are thousands of ways to divide up the market. An analysis will typically consider five, ten or more segmentation variables. To avoid missing a useful way of finding segments, a wide range of variables should be considered. The selection of the most useful segment-defining variable is seldom obvious. Variables include: sex, age, disease, procedure, ailment, benefits sought, lifestyle, usage level, application, geographic location, loyalty, insured or uninsured services and price sensitivity.

Table 7 Sources for market segregation

Patient information
Demographics
Hospitals
Surgical procedures performed
Number of medical practices and type
Third-party payers
New technologies
Qualitative and quantitative research
Focus groups
Questionnaires

Do not forget to segment healthcare payers. There are three major segments in most markets. First, are the major and national health maintenance organizations (HMOs); these companies will employ their own physicians and build their own delivery system if the physicians or hospitals do not accommodate them. Second are the mid-sized insurance companies and regional HMOs that are willing to provide hospitals with full-risk contracts in order to compete with the large payers. The third segment is Blue Cross/Blue Shield.

The choice of strategy also means a choice of product market in which the practice is to compete (Table 8). The scope of a practice is defined by the services it offers and chooses not to offer, by the patients it seeks to serve and not to serve, and by the competing practices it chooses to compete with and to avoid. Sometimes, the most important decision is what products or segments to avoid because such a decision, if followed by discipline, can conserve resources needed to compete successfully elsewhere.

Table 8 A strategy should:

(1)   Be patient-focused
(2)   Provide an analysis of the needs/wants (requirements) of patients and their preferences as applicable
(3)   Identify gaps in patients' wants, where efforts to satisfy them can be developed accordingly
(4)   Determine which patients' needs are not being addressed
(5)   Continue patient-satisfaction analysis
(6)   Create opportunities to increase efficiency

The competitive position in the market has consequences for how the practice should be run. In order to achieve the highest profitability, the operations must be as efficient as possible without compromising the planned competitive position. Areas to address are:

(1)   The allocation of resources within departments: both financial and non-financial resources such as people and equipment need to be allocated to functional areas.

(2)   The development of synergistic effects across departments: the creation of value by having departments that support and complement each other. Organizations that can create synergistic effects can establish an advantage over those that do not by being more effective and efficient.

(3)   The level of investment: although there are apparent variations, it is useful to address the issues outlined in Table 9.

Table 9 Level of investment

Invest to grow (or enter the market)

Invest to maintain current position

Harvest the practice by minimizing investment

Divest the practice and recover as many of the assets as possible

A useful method for deciding on the appropriate level of investment is use of the BCG/Boston Consulting Group matrix. This growth–share matrix is shown in Figure 1.

Market growth rate	Stars	Problem Children
	Cash Cows	Dogs

Relative market share

Figure 1 BCG/Boston Consulting Group matrix

The vertical axis indicates the market growth rate, or the annual rate of increase of the specific market or industry in which a given product line is competing. The horizontal axis indicates the relative market share. This is calculated by dividing the sales of the product line by the largest competitor in the industry.

The Stars have a high share of a high-growth market. From the financial perspective, they are the activities that are the 'winners' in the practice. The Cash Cows have the dominant share of a slow-growth market. These activities enable the practice to generate large amounts of cash to be used for company overhead and investments in other product lines. Problem Children have a low share of a high-growth market. These activities require a lot of cash in order to maintain market share, and the practice needs to decide whether further investment is justified. The objective is to convert them to Stars. The Dogs have a low share in a low-growth market. These activities do not hold promise to become winners for the practice and consideration for elimination should be given.

Keep in mind that the Stars provide the best long-term opportunities for growth and profit. The Cash Cows have a high market share and growth in the market; they generate cash in excess of needs. Dogs have a low or negative profit margin. Problem Children are cash guzzlers but may be promising in the long term.

Planning, budgeting and organizing

The next phase in the strategic marketing process is planning, organizing and budgeting. This part of the process focuses the organization's attention, resources and capabilities on the tasks and targets that are consistent with the strategy. It creates a mechanism for leadership to emerge for various strategic initiatives throughout the organization. The marketing plan needs to discuss in detail how to proceed with the service, in what location the service needs to be delivered and what delivery system to choose, how and to whom to communicate the provided service and what price to charge.

The marketing mix should make the above general marketing strategy work (Table 10). The approach should be consistent and coherent in the sense that the general strategy is recognizable in the strategies of product line, distribution, promotion and price (Table 10).

Table 10 Creating a competitive advantage using the marketing mix

Product:	Type of provided medical service
Price:	Fee
Promotion:	Advertising, personal selling, sales promotion and public relations
Place:	Location
People:	Includes relationship marketing or networking (patient contract)

An effective marketing plan typically requires a focus – a specific group of target-market customers toward which it is directed. This requires:

(1)   Segmenting the market;

(2)   Selecting target markets: having examined several alternative marketing options, the organization must select one or more target markets for which it will develop its marketing program;

(3)   Finding the right competitive positioning for the product or service, to make it superior to competitive substitutes.

Product line strategy

A medical practice provides, first of all, a service. The general characteristics are that: medical services are more intangible than tangible; the service quality is inconsistent; consumption and production take place at the same time; services cannot be stored; and services need to deal with idle capacity and peak demands (Table 11).

(1)   Intangibility is a unique feature of services in that the medical service cannot be 'touched, smelled, or seen before the purchase'[3]. A major need for the medical service is to make it tangible or show the benefit of using the service. One example is the St Francis Health System that advertises 'place your heart in the best hands in the region'. This phrase emphasizes service.

(2)   The service quality is inconsistent. Services are provided by people who have different capabilities and also vary in their job performance from day to day. Inconsistency is typically reduced by training and standardization of procedures within the organization.

(3)   Consumption and production take place at the same time. The consumption of the service cannot be separated from the deliverer of the service. The patient who undergoes physical therapy consumes the therapy at the same time as the therapist provides the treatment.

(4)   Services cannot be stored. This is less pertinent to a practice setting in that inventory carrying costs are more subjective and related to idle production capacity. Services need to deal with idle capacity and peak demands. Service providers typically lower the price and increase promotion when demand is low. When there are peak demands, 'demarketing' is generally the solution. Hotels typically have higher prices during the vacation season or during special events, and will lower their prices during down-times. The medical practitioner does not have this 'off-peak pricing' tool available, although staff and practitioner vacations may be scheduled during more 'idle' times. Therefore, his/her option is mainly limited to promotion and managing

the capacity of the practice. The practitioner may want to find alternative uses for idle office space. A number of physical therapists see not only patients, but also athletes who use weight equipment for training and muscular development.

Table 11 Physician's practice-specific characteristics

Directed at physical and psychological aspects of disease
Highly customized
Dealing with peak demand
Difficulty in evaluation, high in credence qualities – cannot easily be evaluated even after undergoing the process

Choosing the product line offered to the public is generally strongly influenced not only by the provider's core qualities, but also by healthcare payers. They have great discretion in deciding what services will and what services will not be reimbursed. Therefore, not only patient needs and benefits sought should be individually considered, but also third-party payer's requirements. In other words, the product line strategy is market- and payer-specific.

Location

The choice of location typically depends on the chosen generic strategy, the willingness of patients to travel for treatment and demographics.

If a low-cost strategy seems to give the most sustainable competitive advantage, a low-cost location and facility should be chosen. It may seem, though, that in some instances low-cost locations are not available, creating the idea that a low-cost strategy may not be feasible. However, be aware that cost is relative to the cost of the competitor. Obviously, it may be hard to find a low-cost location for a medical facility in downtown Manhattan. Yet, building owners do offer higher- and lower-cost locations.

A differentiation strategy should meet other specific needs of the patient. If, for instance, a family practitioner has many young families with children in the area, a practice may provide child care while the parent visits the doctor. This extra expense may add so much value to the practice that, as a result, the patient would never dream of going elsewhere. This extra expense may be added to the already high

costs of having a downtown location; however, this cost is relative to the competition. Therefore, the competition needs to be studied in order to find out what kind of spending they have allocated to their facilities.

The facility should be chosen in a location depending on the willingness of the patient to travel. Many top athletes are very willing to travel to receive treatment from a specific physician, to enable them to continue with their often lucrative sport. Certain organ transplants can only be performed in specific locations in the country. Some plastic surgeons have built up a strong reputation, and people travel large distances to be treated by them. On the other hand, most people want to have immediate accessibility to a family doctor for minor illnesses, a quick diagnosis or referral.

If the healthcare facility is strongly dependent on the local patient mass, an in-depth analysis of the demographic configuration in a particular area is needed. This will help to project and understand what type of services will be needed in the region for the near future.

Promotion and communication

Any professional service, including medical practice, needs to be actively promoted. It is dangerous to believe that a good service will sell itself (Table 12). The type of message and the media used should appeal to the patient. The tools for promotion are advertising, the referral process, educational seminars, public relations and publications.

Table 12 Promotion

Advertising
Referral process
Educational seminars
Public relations
Publications

Through promotion, the organization should communicate what the practice provides and what that means for the patient: in other words, how the patient benefits from the features of the practice. For example, as noted above, if a practice has a child-care facility, it means that the parent can take their child to the facility where he/she can play. The benefit is that it is convenient, since no special arrangements need to be made with grandparents, friends or a sitter. Second, it may save a patient money.

Advertising   Typically, print advertising in magazines and newspapers helps to position the healthcare facility. Choosing the positioning concept is an important first step in developing the positioning strategy. It should be linked to patient needs. The concept can be functional, symbolic or experiential. Functional positioning deals with solving problems or relieving burdens. Words used include 'care', 'health', 'treatment', 'cost', 'payment method', 'insurance' and 'exams'.

Symbolic positioning deals with the internally generated needs for self-enhancement. Examples include 'appearance', 'cosmetic' and 'care of self'. Experiential words address emotional and sensory stimulation, and deal with feelings and experience. Examples include 'fear', 'pleasant atmosphere', 'rewarding' and 'happy'.

A study of dentists advertising in the *Yellow Pages* revealed that the functional approach, which emphasizes benefits such as health, restoration and payment options, is by far the most popular. They may feel that a straightforward, functional advertisement is the most professional and, therefore, the least likely to generate peer disapproval. Dentists are less likely to use appeals directed toward symbolic or experiential needs. The standard for evaluating such claims rests upon the consumer alone. There is no objective, professional standard of care or service. The study showed, however, that dentists who use some type of positioning in their advertisements enjoy greater productivity than unpositioned dentists. The dentists who use a combination of functional and experiential or symbolic positioning have the highest performance rate.

Many healthcare organizations appeal to the need for safety and security in their communication. Slogans such as 'choose your healthcare as if your life depends on it', and 'you are in good hands with Dr Smith', appeal to large audiences.

Referral   The referral sources for a practice are essentially in two categories: marketer (practitioner)-controlled and health service sources. The latter are related to the traditional healthcare delivery systems, and include word-of-mouth or hospital-related marketing.

The referral process is an important source for physicians to obtain new patients and the deliverance of optimal medical care. Previous research shows that primary-care physicians use external sources of information. These sources are displayed in Table 6.

Some practitioners send a 'thank you' note to people who referred a patient to them.

Public relations and publications Being recognized in publications such as newspapers and journals builds credibility, locally and often nationally, and provides a cost-effective way of promotion.

Pricing

The healthcare provider typically has little control over reimbursement.

Reviewing of contracts from third-party payers is paramount. Attention to the details of the contract must be emphasized. Ideally, a representative from the third-party payer should explain the contract and convey details to the physician or physician group. This discussion should be documented. Questions to ask include: how do contracts compare, specifically on reimbursement, for the same procedure from Blue Cross/Blue Shield, Aetna, Medicaid or Medicare? The next questions are: should I sign the contract? Is it reasonable? What segment of my practice will I lose if I do not sign? What new patient population will be brought into the practice?

Budgeting

Establishing the ideal marketing budget is a difficult task, since there is no precise way to measure the results of advertising, sales promotion or educational seminars. There are four main methods for setting a marketing budget:

(1) *Percentage of revenue budgeting* allocates money to marketing as a percentage of past or anticipated revenues.

(2) *Objective and task budgeting* allocates money to the task required to accomplish specific objectives, for example the introduction of a new service.

(3) *Competitive parity budgeting* matches the competitors' absolute level of spending or the proportion per point of market share. Since competitors may have different objectives, this method is weak.

(4) The 'all you can afford' approach to budgeting allocates dollars to marketing only after all other budget items are covered. This method shows a lack of marketing orientation and does not recognize the value of market research, customer-oriented product development or promotion.

The preferred method is objective and task budgeting. Nevertheless, other methods such as percentage of revenue and competitive parity budgeting can give valuable benchmarks.

Organizing for effective marketing

Most large organizations recognize line and staff positions. People in line positions have the authority and responsibility to issue orders to the people who report to them. People in staff positions have the authority to advise people in line positions, but cannot issue direct orders to them.

Organizations are typically arranged by product line, geography, and customer or market groupings. During the past decade, matrix organizations have become popular in larger companies. The medical practitioner should familiarize himself or herself with the first three organization types. A product-oriented organization can be structured using a co-ordinator per one or more provided services. For example, one co-ordinator can be responsible for all arthroscopies, one for ultrasounds and one for all angiographies. The co-ordinator will develop and administer marketing programs, analyze and report on progress, administer budgets, oversee revenues and product development, and train personnel. The advantage of such an organization is the greater product knowledge that co-ordinators develop (Figure 2).

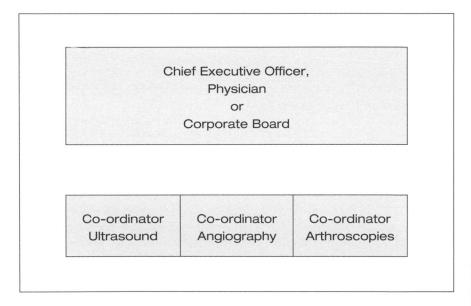

Figure 2 Product-oriented organization

If the practice has various locations, especially when they are far apart, the organization may opt for a geography-oriented organization. This will keep travel expenses and time under control. Managers may have responsibility for a greater variety of provided services and patients than in a product-oriented organization. The increased efficiency, as a result of reduced travel, may outweigh the disadvantage in decreased product knowledge (Figure 3).

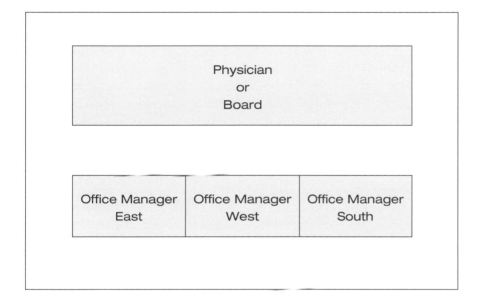

Figure 3 Geography-oriented marketing organization

The 'entrepreneur' health professional can develop a patient-oriented organization. The organization develops a greater knowledge and understanding of patients' needs. However, specific knowledge of the provided services may be lessened (Figure 4).

It is useful for the medical practitioner to be familiar with these organizational types.

Implementation

The marketing literature is filled with research and analysis to help readers develop marketing strategies tailored to the market place. However, when it comes to implementing strategies, the literature has little to offer and the self-help books are insufficient.

Many people who have been successful in mature, stable companies fail miserably when they transition to an entrepreneurial situation;

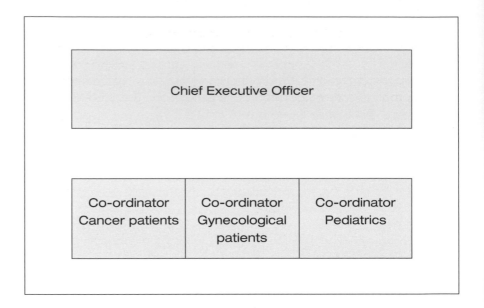

Figure 4 Customer-oriented marketing organization

clinicians must keep this point in mind. They typically fail for four reasons: they take too long to make decisions; they do not understand selling; they do not know how to make use of the resources they have to create market leverage; or they think about their marketing rhetoric more than their customers' reality.

Time management

Stephen Covey in his *Seven Habits of Effective People* gives a number of guidelines for managing time effectively and efficiently[1]. First, every activity should be driven by objectives or a mission. This helps you decide whether or not an activity is important. Activities are important when they lead to achievement of the mission or objectives. Second, some activities are urgent, others are not. Urgent are those activities that need to be undertaken immediately. Some activities are important, others are not. This leads to the model illustrated by Table 13.

Table 13 Time management[1]

	Important	Unimportant
Urgent	*Quadrant 1* Crisis Deadline-driven projects, e-mail, reports, pressing problems	*Quadrant 2* Some phone calls Some meetings Popular activities
Not urgent	*Quadrant 3* Prevention Planning e-mail Phone calls Family recreation Recognizing new activities	*Quadrant 4* Pleasure activities Time-wasters

The book suggests that the worker should spend most of his/her time in quadrant 3. This is the quadrant that is the least stressful and most productive. After all, some of the problems that become urgent and important (quadrant 1) may be avoided if more time is spent in quadrant 3. Obviously, in order to make the most efficient use of available time, the least amount of time should be spent in quadrants 2 and 4.

Once the entrepreneur understands what activities are important, he/she can plan time more efficiently. Many tools are available in the market place, varying from planners and calendars to fancy palm-top computers.

Evaluation and control

Evaluation and control is the final stage of the marketing process. It consists of comparing results with planned objectives for the marketing program, and taking corrective action if necessary (Table 14).

The measured quantified results are compared with the measurable goals set in the marketing plan. The measurable factors should include both efficiency and effectiveness measurements such as: gross charges, profitability, number of visits, visits/patient, number of new patients, number of complaints, number of patients lost, new product introductions and market share.

If the results compared with the objectives prove to be unsatisfactory, the entrepreneur–healthcare professional will need to find the cause(s) for the deviation, and formulate new plans and actions to solve problems and exploit opportunities.

Table 14 Evaluation and control in marketing

	Forecast	Actual
Revenues	$1 200 000	$1 300 000
Gross profits	600 000	280 000
Market share	10%	9%
New patients	83	96
Number of complaints	14	12
Number of patients lost	72	78
New services offered	1	0

Strategic marketing for the healthcare professional requires an understanding of the market in which we practice, both locally and regionally. What services does one offer? Are there niches to develop? That the customer (patient) comes first is an attitude that must permeate throughout the practice.

Practitioners can position themselves for growth through networking, good patient relations, use of the media and understanding of the marketing mix, i.e. product, place, price and promotion. Establishing a SWOT analysis will aid in strengthening the practice. Ideally, the practice should be focused toward competitive advantage and, once achieved, maintained in the form of sustained competitive advantage.

A summary

There are several dimensions to consider when we discuss strategy, including:

The strategic assets or skills that underlie the strategy and provide the sustainable competitive advantage
A strategic asset is a resource, such as particular equipment or a well-known name in a specialized field, that differentiates the practice in a positive way from the competition. A strategic skill is something that the healthcare provider does exceptionally well, such as plastic surgery after major trauma or breast removal, which has strategic importance to that practice. The strategy formulation must consider the cost and feasibility of generating or maintaining assets or skills that will provide the basis for a competitive advantage.

Strategic competitive positioning
How does one find competitive advantage, offering superior value and focusing on the patient, accomplished in such a manner as to have a relatively low overhead and thus an enhanced profit margin? This approach will allow the clinician to compensate for imposed financial changes associated with managed care or other specifics related to third-party payers. Strategic competitive positioning is key in this process. Strategic competitive positioning is the creation of an identity for a product, service or practice in the minds of the consumer (patient). It is a combination of the creation of a cost leadership, differentiation and segmentation.

Low cost, differentiation and segmentation are the three generic competitive strategies. In essence, all successful strategies will involve one of these choices:

Striving for overall low-cost leadership A low-cost strategy is based on providing equivalent benefits to the customer, but at a lower cost than competitive products. The success of generic drugs, for example, is based on building a sustainable advantage over branded drugs by offering the same product at a lower cost than the branded version. This can be applied to healthcare professionals if the decision is to gain market share by accepting third-party payer contracts which are lower than anticipated, but can be compensated for by increased patient volumes (market share).

Differentiation Many organizations struggle to get a sustainable advantage by differentiating themselves. For example, a university medical center indicates that they use the most sophisticated equipment in the area and seek technological leadership. A number of care providers in a metropolitan area provide so-called 'cubs' corners', where parents would take their young children while they visited the doctor. In other words, differentiators seek to provide unique benefits that more than offset a higher price for services, or offer lower prices than the competition for equivalent benefits.

Segmentation Segmentation involves aggregating prospective buyers into groups or segments, or prospective buyers who have common needs, and will respond similarly to a marketing action. Many successful small medical practices use segmentation strategies because of their limited resources. For example, some orthopedic clinics perform only arthroscopies. Some plastic surgeons limit their practice to cosmetic procedures for those who can afford it. Physiotherapists may choose to focus their efforts on sports injuries. Focus can be developed through 'niche marketing'. On the other hand, large hospitals provide a wide range of services and specialties.

Reference

1.   Covey S. *Seven Habits of Effective People*. New York: Simon & Schuster, 1989

Suggested reading

Powers L. *Modern Business Marketing: A Strategic Planning Approach to Business and Industrial Markets*. West, 1991

Fisher R, Ury W. *Getting to Yes*, 2nd edn. Penguin, 1991

Theory of Constraints: Application to a General Medical Practice

7

Mahesh Gupta and Louis Raho

Introduction

In the last decade of the 20th century, the healthcare industry was charged with various alleged failings, including rising healthcare costs, concern for patient errors and inefficient waiting times for services. In the March 1998 *Fortune* magazine report on customer satisfaction across industries, the patient-care service industry received the lowest customer ratings, and hospitals ranked in the bottom third. Like many other (service) industries, the healthcare industry is under tremendous competitive pressure to provide exceptional service and reduce costs simultaneously. This is the result of a number of powerful trends such as consumerism, aging population innovations in healthcare technologies and entrepreneurial healthcare managers. The continuing turbulent healthcare industry has undergone a significant transformation over the past decade. Its reformation has moved the industry toward health maintenance organizations (HMOs), preferrred provider organizers (PPOs) and integrated healthcare networks. Small private medical practices also face the unenviable task of adapting their practices in order to compete with complex provider networks.

Peter Drucker, a noted management expert, has said that the biggest problem that managers face is that the world in which they learned to manage no longer exists. Recently, a significant number of attempts have been made to demonstrate applications of new management philosophies (such as total quality management, business process re-engineering, activity-based management and theory of constraints) in addressing healthcare operations management problems. Applying new management philosophies in a healthcare setting is a challenge, which has not been easily met. However, an increasing number of healthcare practitioners are learning that these philosophies not only help improve the quality of care, but also help lower costs and improve marketability.

The purpose of this chapter is to introduce the basic concepts of theory of constraints (TOC), an emerging philosophy, and demonstrate how this philosophy can be applied to a private medical practice for physicians or allied health professionals. Such an entity can also be viewed as a part of a large medical complex (an HMO) providing primary care. An overview is provided of the theory of constraints, which attempts to answer three fundamental questions that every for-profit organization must address (Table 1).

Table 1 Three fundamental questions that every for-profit organization must answer

(1)	What is the goal of the medical practice?
(2)	What are the operational measures used by the medical practice to assess the goal?
(3)	Is the medical practice on a process of improvement to accomplish the goal?

What is the theory of constraints?

The theory of constraints is a relatively new and evolving management philosophy, which looks at a business as a complete and complex system where any number of components may interact with one another. According to the TOC, the complex systems are limited by one (or at best only a few) constraint(s). In general terms, a constraint can be defined as anything that blocks the system from accomplishing its goal. Thus, the performance of any system can be improved through identifying and managing the constraints.

As a result, therefore, the principle of the TOC can be applied in any healthcare setting, depending upon our definition of the system and its corresponding boundaries. We will define and apply the concepts of the TOC to a general medical practice.

What is the goal?

According to the theory of constraints, the ultimate goal of any for-profit organization is to make money now and in the future. This goal cannot be accomplished if two necessary conditions are not satisfied:

(1) To provide a secure and satisfying environment for staff now and in the future;

(2) To provide satisfaction to the market now and in the future.

Thus, the goal and necessary conditions can be viewed as a framework (see Figure 1). This framework proposes that the medical practice should focus on a process to increase revenues by providing quality services to a stream of patients, instead of looking for ways to

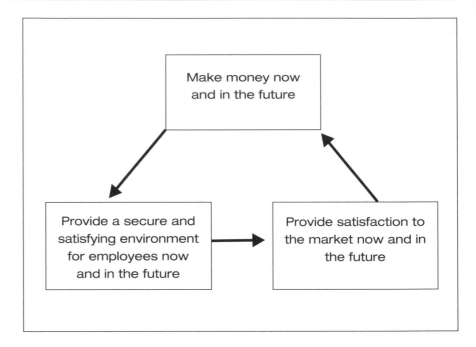

Figure 1 The goal and necessary conditions

cut costs (for example by laying off the staff). In fact, a medical practice should develop a mission statement to acknowledge this framework. (Also see Chapter 4 – It's not a plan without a business plan).

TOC guideline 1

A TOC-based mission statement suggests that, in the process of accomplishing the goal of making money in the short term as well as the long term, the two necessary conditions should not be violated.

What are the operational measures?

Owners of medical practices evaluate financial statements such as the income statements and balance sheets and calculate financial measures such as net profit (NP), return on investment (ROI) and cash flows (CFs) to determine to what extent the practice is achieving its goal of making money. However, these financial measures are not helpful for the managers and other staff members in deciding whether their decisions and actions would help the company turn a profit. The TOC proposes a simplified set of operational measures that help

managers and staff members judge the effect that their individual decisions make in their subsystems and how they affect the performance of the entire practice. Figure 2 depicts the relationships between financial and operational measures.

Throughput (T) is the rate at which the system generates money through sales (or patient care). In other words, throughput in this definition is all the money flowing into the practice through the variety of services provided to patients.

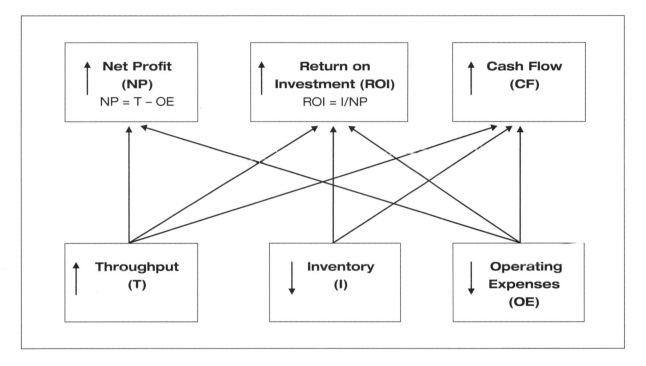

Figure 2 The TOC operational measures

Inventory (I) is all the money that the system has invested in purchasing things which it intends to sell (or provide to patients). In other words, all the money currently in the system is tied up in terms of computers, medical equipment, buildings, etc. and in raw materials and work-in-progress inventories. From a TOC perspective, the inventory should be valued at its purchase price to the company. In a conceptual sense, patients to be served, as well as patients in the process of being served, can be viewed as raw material or work-in-progress inventories. In this sense, the smooth flow of service to patients and a minimum patient waiting time are desirable characteristics, as is true in a manufacturing system, although such an inventory may not appear in the financial books of a medical practice.

Operating expenses (OE) are all the money that the system spends in order to turn inventory into throughput. In other words, OE include all the money going out of the practice such as wages, salaries and utility expenses.

TOC guideline 2

Thus, TOC-based operational measures express the goal in terms of throughput, inventory and operating expenses, an expression that suggests that the most productive managerial decisions should result in a simultaneous increase in throughput, a decrease in inventory and a decrease in operating expenses. The TOC promotes 'throughput world thinking', whereby an organizational culture is created to encourage innovative ways of increasing throughput and improving operational efficiencies, instead of spending time and effort on finding ways to cut or contain costs.

Is there a process for ongoing improvement?

The TOC has its greatest impact by directing healthcare managers (physicians or allied health professionals) to view the entire medical practice as a system (i.e. a set of interdependent subsystems), and then, by suggesting a focusing process of ongoing improvement. We describe a typical medical practice as a system, discuss the concepts of dependent events and statistical fluctuations, and apply the five focusing steps to improve the performance of a medical system.

A typical medical practice

Figure 3 characterizes a number of subsystems (i.e. stations or processes) and the typical patient flow in a medical practice. The patient arrives, parks and signs in with the receptionist. If the patient is new to the practice, he or she must fill out additional forms prior to being seen. Next, the patient remains in the waiting room to be called by a medical assistant. She measures the vital signs, and perhaps requests a urine sample, and subsequently escorts the patient to an available examining room to be attended by the physician (although occasionally a physician assistant or nurse practitioner may provide a segment of the care).

Parking Patient's arrival Process Number = 1 Average time = 5 minutes
Register and sign in Waiting room Process Number = 2 Average time = 5 minutes
Medical assistance Nurse's Aid area Process Number = 3 Average time = 10 minutes
Diagnosis Examining room Process Number = 4 Average time = 15 minutes
Payment Check out Process Number = 5 Average time = 5 minutes

Figure 3 A typical patient flow

The examination, diagnosis and/or treatment is provided. After the examination, additional medical assistance may be necessary (such as blood work, vaccinations, etc.). Finally, the patient takes care of any payments and/or paperwork related to his or her visit at the check-out station. It is important to note that, generally, a corresponding information flow takes place in parallel with the patient flow. On average, this information flow requires about 26–40 minutes from start to finish, assuming that all the activities are required. However, this time-in-system fluctuates for several reasons.

Dependent events and statistical fluctuations in a system

While the patient is going through this sequence of processes, many statistical fluctuations (SFs) may occur at any part of the process, which may in turn cause a process to take more or less than the average amount of service time. In a single independent process, the positive and negative deviations from the average service time can be assumed to even out. However, in a system of dependent processes, when statistical fluctuations occur in any part of the system, they generate significant time lags within the service system. As the deviations from the average service time accumulate, resulting time lags increase the load on the service system (i.e. the number of patients in the process), and the throughput (e.g. the number of patients served per hour) may be affected. Moreover, if there exists a process with limited capacity, it becomes the weakest link and, in effect, determines the throughput rate of the entire system.

Table 2 lists a number of examples of statistical fluctuations in various parts of a medical practice (described in Figure 3). It is also noted that these SFs cause a significant number of patients to take longer than the average service time, which increases the average time spent in the system and affects the number of patients able to be served. Furthermore, it is also observed that the physical examination, diagnosis and treatment (i.e. subsystem 4 in Figure 3) takes the longest amount of time (on average 10–15 minutes) and is the weakest link in the system. These statistical fluctuations further affect the performance of the weakest link and, therefore, the performance of the overall system.

Table 2 Examples of statistical fluctuations in a typical medical practice

Patient may not find parking and thus arrive late
New patient may take some time to do paperwork
Medical assistant may not be notified immediately because of preoccupation
Some patients may require more time for collecting vital statistics
Physician may not be aware that the patient is in examining room
It may take an unusual amount of time to retrieve and store patient information

TOC guideline 3

An organization can be viewed as a chain of interdependent events (or processes) where the performance of each event (or process) is dependent upon the previous event.

Five focusing steps of improvement to accomplish the goal (Table 3)

Step 1: identify the system's constraint(s) In general, a constraint can be defined as anything that prohibits the system from accomplishing its goal. Constraints can be categorized as physical constraints (for example scarce resources such as floor space, the number of doctors and nurses, or even the demand for the product or service) and policy constraints (such as ineffective policies, attitudes or behavior patterns). Policy constraints are usually far more damaging to the system, difficult to identify and difficult to overcome.

Table 3 Five focusing steps of process improvement

Step 1:	Identify the system's constraint(s), whether physical or policy constraint
Step 2:	Decide how to exploit the system's constraint(s). That is, get the most possible from the limit of the current constraint(s); reduce the effects of the current constraint(s); and make everyone aware of the constraint(s) and effects on the performance of the system
Step 3:	Subordinate everything else to the above decision. That is, avoid keeping non-constraint resources busy doing unneeded work
Step 4:	Elevate the system's constraint(s). That is, off-load some demand or expand capability
Step 5:	If in the previous steps a constraint has been broken, go back to step 1, but do not allow inertia to cause a system constraint

The constraint of the observed medical practice occurs at the physical examination, diagnosis and treatment process, i.e. process 4 (see Figure 3). This process takes from 10 to 15 minutes per patient (the highest process time among various processes). Moreover, the physicians are the most important, expensive and scarce resource and, therefore, this resource should be used to the fullest and never be idle.

TOC guideline 4

If an organization is viewed as a chain (or a grid of chains), then the chain is only as strong as its weakest link. There will always be a process in an organizational system that is the weakest and should be targeted for high-impact (in terms of operational measures, i.e. T, I and OE) improvement.

Step 2: decide how to exploit the system's constraint(s) From the goal and operational measurements' perspective, productive actions are taken to utilize the constrained resource fully so that throughput is increased, while inventory and operating expenses are decreased simultaneously. In general, in this step, the existing capacity of the constraint should be fully utilized and not wasted in performing services or other activities, which may not add value to the system by increasing the throughput (i.e. the number of patients served). Also, in this step improper policies and procedures for scheduling the constraint should be investigated, so that a smooth flow of patients to the constraint is maintained at all times.

In our medical practice example, we identified the physician examination, diagnosis and treatment process (i.e. process 4) as the system's constraint. The physicians complain that the flow of events leading to this process is choppy and inefficient, and they also claim to be chronically behind with their schedule. Our analysis of this process reveals the following problems:

Problem 1 For example, once the patient is placed in the examining room and is ready to be seen by the physician, the physician is often notified with a visual flag system on the door of each examining room. If the physician is in his or her office, he or she cannot see the flag on the door. Since the physician does not continually monitor the examining room door, immediate notification is impossible. The result might be an inefficient use of physician's time.

Proposed TOC-based solution: The practice should install an audible electronic system to sound a mild tone in the physician's office when a patient is ready to be seen. This change along with the visual flag system will allow physicians to be notified immediately.

Problem 2 After examining, diagnosing and treating a patient, the physician returns to his or her office to dictate a letter prior to seeing additional patients. The walking distance from examining room to physician office is significant and reduces the amount of time available for examining patients.

Proposed TOC-based solution: The practice should set up dictation stands, capable of holding several patient charts, in the examining rooms. The stands will cut down travel time between patient examina-

tion and dictation. Moreover, the medical assistant or office clerk can easily gather the charts at the dictation stand to return the information to the front desk, thereby creating a smooth flow of paperwork.

Problem 3 There are times when the scheduled patient has not arrived or is still in the pipeline, because of several possible reasons (termed statistical fluctuations in Table 2). This may result in physicians sitting idle or otherwise not using their time engaged with patients.

Proposed TOC-based solution: It is oxtremely important to ensure that patients are scheduled efficiently and examining rooms are always occupied with the patients to be seen, so that the physicians are always busy seeing their patients.

The proposed changes should increase the physician time available to see the patients, and thus increase the throughput (i.e. the number of patients seen per hour) as well as reduce the work-in-progress inventory (i.e. the number of patients in the system). This step focuses on implementing high-leverage and high-impact changes and removing non-value-added activities directly from the constraint.

TOC guideline 5

Any time lost at the constraint is time lost to the whole system. Thus, efforts should be made to make everyone aware of the constraint and its effects on the performance of the system.

Step 3: subordinate everything else to the constraint In general, this step means that all non-constraint processes of an organization, by definition, have idle capacity (i.e. the capacity to serve patients more than the constraint process can); otherwise, they themselves would be the constraint. The non-constraint resources before the constraint should make every effort not to delay in any way the constraint resource, and the non-constraint resources after the constraint resource should process the product/service without any unnecessary delay.

Problem 4 Many patients arrive late, and all new patients are required to complete 5–10 minutes' paperwork before being seen by the physician. These events may result in a situation where the examination room is idle and the physicians are not fully utilized. This will also result in an increased load on the service system because the number of patients to be seen accumulates.

Proposed TOC-based solution: The practice should request patients to arrive 10 minutes early to find a parking space. If patients are chronically late, the office receptionist should find out the reason and offer any help with directions, for example. The practice should also post a sign in the waiting room that states: 'Please try to arrive on time for your appointment. We will do our best to see you as soon as you arrive. Unfortunately, one late arrival will cause delays for subsequent patients'.

Similarly, the office receptionist should ascertain the status of the patient over the phone during the appointment sequence. If the patient is new, the practice should include paperwork with the new patient's information packet. The practice may offer a 10% discount on the first office visit if the patient returns the paperwork prior to his or her appointment in a prepaid, preaddressed envelope. In addition, the office receptionist should estimate time needed for each visit based on the complexity of the case, and schedule a relatively complex visit after every three routine visits.

Problem 5 Once the patient is called in, he or she must walk with the medical assistant approximately 60 feet to the scale to be weighed in the current facility layout. This 60-feet walk takes approximately 20–25 seconds and probably longer for an elderly or very ill patient. Once the patient is weighed, they must walk in the opposite direction from which they entered the examining room.

Proposed TOC-based solution: If these non-constraint processes start causing a constraint process to stay idle, the practice should move the scale to the front (as there is ample space in the existing layout). This accommodation will reduce the distance traveled to approximately 20 feet and decrease the time to walk to the scale by 15–20 seconds. Moreover, this move also minimizes the backtracking, as the scale is now on the way to the examining rooms.

Problem 6 The communication system used to notify the medical assistant that a patient has arrived may well be neither effective nor efficient. Current systems often employ a switch located at the front desk. When a patient signs in, that switch is thrown and a light comes on in the laboratory, which notifies the medical assistant. This system requires the medical assistant to devote 100% of her visual attention to the light; otherwise, she may be neglecting her work. Also, sometimes the receptionist may simply forget to toggle the switch when a patient signs in.

Proposed TOC-based solution: Again, if these non-constraint processes start causing a constraint process to stay idle, excess capacity should be created on these processes. A tone or buzzer can be added to the light circuit so that when the switch is toggled as the patient signs in, a tone sounds to notify the medical assistant. Additionally, the practice can install three doorbell-style electric switches, each identified with a physician's name, at the front desk that would be easily accessible to the patient. The patient can hit the button to notify the receptionist and, at the same time, the medical assistant of his or her arrival.

TOC guideline 6

The organizational system must not be balanced by trimming the extra capacity on the non-bottleneck processes, since this will result in a system where each resource is a potential constraint and, thus, can affect throughput adversely. The non-constraint processes should be utilized (i.e. by making the constraint work smoothly) and not be activated (i.e. by staying busy all the time).

Step 4: elevate the system's constraint(s) This step means to increase the capacity of the constraint to a higher level and can be accomplished by incurring significant investment (i.e. inventory) or operating expenses. This step should not be confused with step 2 (exploit the constraint), in which attempts are made to increase throughput without spending significant amounts of money. Rather, this step should be viewed as a strategic decision to evaluate and determine whether the medical practice wants to add more capacity to the constraint, thereby increasing the capacity to realize the unmet market demand for the product/services. This is commonly done by making significant modifications to existing facilities or equipment and/or by adding more constraint resources. This step usually involves capital outlays in terms of increased inventory (i.e. investments in equipment or buildings) and operating expenses (i.e. wages and salaries for new personnel).

This step also implies a strategic move to create idle capacity at the current constraint and move the constraint to the next weakest link. In our medical practice example, it might involve expanding the practice (or hiring a new physician) and moving the constraint to the market (i.e. increasing the number of patient members).

Problem 7 The current office layout and the room assignments to the physicians as well as designated examining rooms do not promote efficient usage of physicians' time involved. The physicians spend an enormous amount of time just traveling back and forth between examining rooms and their offices. Moreover, there is not enough office space to add another office for an additional physician.

Proposed TOC-based solution: The practice may want to consider hiring a professional facility-design consulting group to redesign and expand the present office space. One may also want to add another physician to the practice as a part of the strategic plan.

TOC guideline 7

The managers must decide between the cost of making a change and the profits coming from the change. TOC-based changes are focused on the processes that provide true continuous improvement for the organization.

Step 5: if in the previous steps a constraint has been broken, go back to step 1, but do not allow inertia to cause a system constraint This step is to prevent inertia from stopping the process of ongoing continuous improvement.

In our medical practice example, the implementation of step 4 will elevate the constraint and move it to the market, i.e. more patients are sought to register with our practice. Thus, we have identified our new constraint and start the process again.

In a complex healthcare system, it is possible to elevate a constraint in step 4 and go back to step 1 for identifying the next physical constraint and restart the process. The five-step focusing process, summarized in Table 3, allows healthcare managers to implement a systematic and focused process of continuous improvement towards the organizational goal, i.e. to make money now as well as in the future without violating the necessary conditions of customer and employee satisfaction.

What are the conclusions?

In reality, there are many potential improvement projects which may make positive contributions towards the goal of the healthcare organization. We have shown that the TOC provides specific and highly effective ways of identifying the high-leverage and high-impact projects for a medical practice.

Where to find more information on TOC

Cox JF, Spencer MS. *The Constraints Management Handbook*. New York: The St Lucie Press, 1998

Dettmer WH. *Goldratt's Theory of Constraints – A Systems Approach to Continuous Improvements*. Milwaukee, WI: ASQC Quality Press, 1997

Goldratt EM, Cox J. *The Goal: A Process of Ongoing Improvement*. Croton-on-Hudson, NY: North River Press, 1992

Goldratt EM. *What is this Thing called Theory of Constraints?* Croton-on-Hudson, NY: North River Press, 1990

McMullen, Thomas B. *Introduction to the Theory of Constraints (TOC) Management System*. New York: The St Lucie Press, 1998

Acknowledgements

The authors wish to express their gratitude to Glenn R. Stout, MD and Mary Coleman, MD, Director of Clinical Services, for their insightful comments and many significant improvements to the text.

Strategies of Office Management: Perspectives of a Physician

8

Arthur Boerner

Personnel management

The effectiveness of an office manager will be determined by the organization of the staff and the chain of command that is established. There are many ways in which this can be accomplished. One that has been found effective is to divide the office into three parts, each managed by a supervisor. They are:

(1)   The clinical department;

(2)   The patient relations department;

(3)   The insurance department.

These departments provide for all facets of management of a small to mid-size medical practice, and, as the size increases, these units may be subdivided into smaller components to increase efficiency. The management team is composed of the office manager, the supervisors and a representative from the physicians, who meet throughout the month to establish the active needs of the practice and allow for the flow of information up and down the chain of authority.

The office manager in a small to mid-size practice serves in a capacity similar to that of the human resources department of a major corporation. The hiring of employees rests with the office manager.

New as well as existing employees are an extension of the physician and need to complement the office environment. To this end the office manager should use peer interviewing to allow existing staff to help sift through the potential candidates. When the office manager is nearing a final selection, an interview with a physician in the practice should provide information for final selection or rejection. One of the hidden benefits of peer interviewing is that employees may be willing to work harder and longer rather than settle for a substandard applicant.

Employment packages are established by the management team to be offered to full-time and part-time employees. One major business expense is the cost of hiring and training an employee. The longer you retain an employee, the more return you will see on your investment. In all probability, the higher the patient satisfaction rating you will receive, as the patients see familiar faces year after year.

It is important to note that, these days, the base salary for your area business is set by the fast-food industry, so your starting salary and benefits should be more than competitive. This will attract quality employees to your practice and your retention level will be higher, making your practice more cost-effective. The package can include any or all of the following: health insurance, dental insurance, disability insurance, paid sick leave, paid vacation that increases with length of

service, paid holidays including the employee's birthday, and retirement funding by means of either a 401K program or a pension and profit-sharing plan (vesting to be tied to the length of service). With employee commitment to your organization comes their responsibility to perform the prescribed duties. Job descriptions and duties, along with rules governing the office, should be provided in an office manual supplied to each employee when they are hired.

Termination of employment is also the responsibility of the office manager. This is a process that requires documentation, as well as prior written evaluation of the substandard performance of the employee. A new employee can be terminated without cause during the probationary period, which is usually 90 days. A full-time, benefited employee will undergo biannual evaluations, held by the employee supervisor, to point out any problems or weaknesses that need to be corrected, as well as provide an opportunity to praise an employee for a job well done. These evaluations are in written form, to be signed by the employee to document their understanding. Employees who are constantly falling below standards or constantly breaching the established rules are placing themselves at risk for termination. To terminate, a *paper trail* must be established. With proper documentation of the employee's lack of improvement, it is appropriate to place the employee on probation. It is critical to go through a period of communication so that the employee is clear about what the problem is, what they can do to correct it and the time limit set for such correction. The failure of the employee to correct the problem starts the final process. A meeting is held with the employee where you completely level with them, informing them that they are given this one last chance: 'If your behavior or performance does not change, you will be terminated'. A finite period of time is given for them to improve their performance, knowing full well that, if this does not happen, termination is inevitable. It is also a good opportunity at this point to give the employee an opportunity to resign. This way, they leave the office with a clean slate and a termination is not part of their record. The office manager is responsible for all documentation in this process, and in doing this will save the practice time and money in the long run. It is worth the effort necessary to create it.

The role of the office manager includes a strong working knowledge of all jobs performed in the office, as well as establishing cross-training for each full-time employee to fill a position in another department. This allows for effective function through illness and vacations, and creates a team effort reflecting the solidarity created by the office manager.

Each department is responsible for an intricate part in the running of an effective office. The clinical staff are responsible for the physical flow of patients through the office, and the hospital. They may also be responsible for tracking hospital-based laboratory information, scheduling and tracking tests that have been performed on the patient. Periodic review through the office manager will assure proper tracking documentation and allow for quality review of the practice. The patient relations department is the personal contact between the patient and the practice. This is a vital link in securing proper patient information, and helping to establish the practice's personality. It is important that this department is staffed with employees possessing excellent 'people skills'. It is an interesting fact that the majority of patient transfers out of a practice are the result of patients perceiving they were not cared for at a personal level.

The insurance department is the heart of the cash flow through the practice, and must be organized to process accurate, complete and timely claims. These insurance claims represent the total work done by the practice whether the practice is manned by a proceduralist or cognitive specialist. The role of the office manager is to have this team work together in an effective and co-operative manner.

Judicious use of external advisors

The authority given to an office manager will require that this person uses external advisors for the successful operation of the office. External advisors can offer free advice, want to sell you something (commission vendors) or charge a fee for their service. We all appreciate something for nothing, so free advisors should be utilized first when possible. A great source of free advice is your local hospital. (The prudent physician reading this chapter will realize that these services are provided with the cost of his or her annual staff dues.) The hospital provides educational programs in OSCHA and CLEA training, as well as cardiopulmonary resuscitation and advanced cardiac life support training for staff members and physicians. One of the most impressive educational programs is in the area of training in clinical documentation, coding and practice management. The accounting staff at most hospitals can review managed-care fees, as well as fee-for-service contracts, with the various insurance companies, to determine whether opportunities offered are cost-effective and whether there is an appropriate insurance mix within your practice. Hospitals also have the opportunity, legally, to provide net guarantees for new physicians, which include salaries and operating expenses if you are planning to bring a new partner into your practice. They will also make strong efforts in recruiting physicians with specialties to complement your practice. The hospital will have taken the initiative to upgrade office management staff to comply with regulatory changes, and, at the corporate level, will keep physicians abreast of new Medicare issues regarding fraud and abuse.

The next broad area of free support, and probably provided with the annual dues, includes the American Medical Association and the county and state medical societies. These societies represent the physician on a local, state and national level, and are available to your office manager for updates regarding issues of state and national legislature that may affect your individual practice. They are also helpful in reviewing and commenting on various insurance programs offered by the national vendors, regarding areas of risk for physicians. The office manager should monitor these communications and make the practice physicians aware of changes that may need attention.

Colleges or academies in the specialty of your practice can be most helpful. These can offer suggestions for patient management, handle issues of non-compliance and termination of patients in written form, and assist with patient education and areas of difficult current procedural terminology (CPT) coding.

Commission vendors are advisors who come into your practice and play an integral part, but their information usually comes with the purchase of a service or product. The first of these is the employee-benefit specialist, who provides health, dental, disability and life insurance, and can establish and manage your retirement. They can also provide personal assistance to your employees with investment plans such as college funding, or after-tax investment for savings, or in areas not covered by the employee benefit package that may be of interest to the employee.

Your business insurance agent will handle the property and casualty insurance for the practice. Incorporated in this will be a plan for workman's compensation, and property insurance, which will insure the building and its contents including equipment used in outpatient surgery or procedures, and vehicles leased to the practice. He or she can also provide overhead insurance to cover the running of the practice in the case of disability of a physician or key employee. There will be an insurance policy to cover liability for the physical structure of the practice and automobiles, and liability for each physician through a personal umbrella policy.

The professional liability insurance agents are key to the survival of the practice. They represent companies that provide malpractice insurance for the physician, employees and physician extenders, and additional benefits to defend sexual harassment claims. It is the responsibility of the office manager in all of the above three vendor areas to keep these programs up to date, and to make sure that all products are at the most cost-effective level.

Medical-supply representatives, pharmaceutical representatives and bankers complete the list of commission vendors available to the office manager. The office manager will establish a relationship with one or two medical-supply representatives to ensure that appropriate disposable, injectable and durable goods are available in the practice. These are usually commission vendors who will do their utmost to retain your business and provide you with the most cost-effective service. Pharmaceutical representatives are vying for a portion of the market share that the physicians and physician extenders create by the prescriptions they write. They will be available to the practice to provide samples, and to establish a supply of medication for indigent patients or those patients whose insurance may not cover services that are deemed necessary. The office manager needs to establish a strong relationship with these various vendors, to ensure adequate supplies of samples and to assist in patient compliance and patient satisfaction when finances become a problem.

Bankers do not receive a direct commission for involvement in your practice, but they generate a fee for the use of money through credit, checking and savings accounts. The physician and the office manager should realize that the flow of money from your practice through the local bank can be presented as an asset of the bank in their procurement of money from the Federal Reserve. It is a mutually beneficial program for the banker to act as an advisor, assisting your office manager in establishing corporate or business checking accounts, and a checking account to facilitate your retirement fund, a savings account, a line of credit floating at the prime interest rate, or the issuing of business credit cards. Bankers can also be of benefit in establishing direct deposit of the payroll, and creating online banking to increase the efficacy of your office manager.

The office manager will need physician input to justify the expense of fee-for-service advisors. This group includes the practice accountant, legal counsel, computer hardware and software support, and various business consultants. The accountant and computer support are essential in the day-to-day activities of the office. Once you find a good accountant and computer support advisors, stick with them; they are worth a great deal to the practice. Their average annual fee will be in the operating budget, allowing appropriate access by the office manager on an as-needed basis. Every office should be represented by legal counsel, from a firm large enough to cover your practice needs but small enough not to lose sight of your needs. Your principal legal counsellor should be well versed in business law and estate planning. An entire chapter of this book could be devoted to the types of business consultants that exist and what they can provide for your practice. Whether the issue is merging two practices or providing your staff with special skills, there are consultants to fill the role. The office manager may choose a consultant to solve a specific problem, and it is very important that you do your homework and be sure that what you are getting is cost-effective.

Technology support

Information technology is a vital component of your medical practice. Your computer system, in terms of both hardware and software, is the most vital component of information technology that exists in your office. This being said, you must be aware that any hardware or software package that you purchase is out of date within 6 months from the date of purchase. Be sure that the hardware is appropriately networked by a software package so that all of the computers in the office are interlinked and communicating. A free-standing PC should exist in the computer network with specific options for software to provide the proper support for a particular employee's job. (This subject is also addressed in Chapter 12.)

In choosing a software package, it is important that the following options should be available:

(1)   Module to schedule appointments, retrieve data and activate a general patient recall for various procedures or annual examination;

(2)   Capability of billing patients, billing insurance companies and submitting invoices electronically;

(3)   An appropriate format for establishing patient data that will ultimately, as technology progresses, evolve into a paperless record system;

(4)   Word processing, obviously, for the many letters and notes that must be written to communicate from the practice;

(5)   The largest component of your software package will be the retrieval of data through a reporting system. This should include a chronological report of your accounts receivable, giving you information on activity at 0–30 days, 31–60 days, 61–90 days, 40–120 days and more than 120 days. Productivity reports based on CPT codes should be available. These can be broken down in terms of the number of patient appointments or procedures covered by various CPT codes, as well as the dollars generated from this productivity. You should also be able to retrieve the percentage of your patient base represented by a

specific insurance company, which is important in deciding whether to renew or negotiate new contracts. This report can also generate the dollars produced by the practice through various individual insurance companies. The program should be able to report the various doctors referring patients into your practice, and the demographics of patient flow into your practice from various outlying areas. Finally, the computer should be able to generate reports on unpaid insurance balances for any specific insurance company or patient.

(6)   Your computer software package should also include inner office e-mail, and the capability of faxing via modem information to other outlying sources.

(7)   One of the additional conveniences the computer can provide is a printing of daily encounter forms with appropriate charges and CPT coding, along with diagnostic CPT coding for more accurate computer input, as well as a list of patients who are in various hospitals and who need to be seen either on consultation or in rounds.

The second large component of information technology is the telecommunications system that is in existence via fax machines, telephone system in the office and cellular phones, and radio-paging. Offices should be equipped with fax capabilities either through the telephone system or through your computer via a modem. This is an excellent way for the hospital to supply medical records and laboratory data to your office. The telephone system in your office is probably the most important link your patient has with your practice. It is important that this is up to date, providing all of the necessary services to make it user-friendly. Most modern practices use automated telephone systems. This is a user-friendly method that actually reduces the patient's time on the phone and helps to route calls more efficiently. The patient has access to a directory that allows them to contact the extension they need to solve a specific problem, whether it be an insurance issue, scheduling of an appointment or obtaining information regarding laboratory tests. Even with this system, there will still be the odd occasion that the patient is on hold. This may be an opportunity for you to play a marketing tape that will present information regarding your practice, or 'health tips' that are beneficial for your specific type of practice. Generic tapes are available for a minimal charge, and there are services that will create a tape on hold that is specific to your office, identifying information about the practice and pertinent health information. The growth of your practice will determine the number of lines needed into the office. As these increase, it is important to work with the company installing your system to create a

rollover feature. This ensures that each time the patient calls you and that number is busy, it will roll into a vacant line.

Cellular communication is important for practices that have doctors moving from point to point in the course of a day, who need to be contacted. The office manager can usually put together a package for cellular phones for the best price. These cellular phones may offer features of voice mail, which allows detailed messages to be left for the physician as well as access to e-mail. Digital pagers are another area of offsite communication that can be of benefit to the practice, and patients. One convenience you may offer your patients is the short-term use of pagers. A good example of this is in an obstetric practice, where the husband may need to be available. The companies that supply the pagers for the physicians and office members can also, at a minimal price, provide short-term leases for pagers for patients' families. It is also very cost-effective, when there is a need to put a message onto a physician's pager, to incorporate a paging system within your computer. In this way, the staff can send messages directly to the physician, saving time and money by not routing it through the answering service.

On the horizon is the great unknown of telecommunications, the Internet. Many physicians' offices already have or are contemplating the creation of their own website. This is limited only by one's imagination. Internet access through office computers allows constant updates from the insurance companies, for example, most of which have websites. Most office consultants feel that the Internet is an untapped area for marketing, and patient educational services. The office manager needs to be well versed in the various modalities of information technology and support.

Optimizing use of clinicians, medical doctors and extenders

Medicine today is practiced much more aggressively with regard to bottom-line cost, and productivity of the healthcare providers within a practice. Physicians, physician extenders, mid-level providers such as nurse practitioners, nurse midwives, nurse anesthetists and physician assistants, and support staff such as ultrasound and X-ray technicians, physical therapists, certified surgical assistants and so on, in providing good-quality healthcare can generate a fee. Each practice will have a unique mixture of professionals who generate income for the practice. It becomes the task of the office manager to utilize them to achieve the maximum level of efficiency and production, whether it is in the office or the hospital.

The office personnel are responsible for keeping clinical professionals on task, and utilizing the physical structure of the office to the maximum realistic capacity. Remember, 100% capacity of an office is 24 hours a day, 7 days a week. So, most of us are lucky if we can get close to 50% capacity. Looking at your office as a fixed cost, using creative scheduling that is patient friendly, such as late nights, early mornings and weekends, will allow more clinical professionals to work from the same space. When an office manager hears 'we need a bigger office', he or she should remember that bigger is not always better, but it is always more expensive. Your guiding thoughts should be created with flexible professionals in mind.

To answer the question of whether physician extenders/mid-level providers should be added to the practice, you must consider the balance between volume of patients, your special mix of insurance plans and patient convenience (to see patients when they need or want to be seen with minimal wait in the office or to get an appointment). For example, a practice in primary healthcare with a large health maintenance organization (HMO) patient base has found that the use of patient extenders can be extremely cost-effective. A different situation is that of a subspecialist, who may only need a mid-level provider for 1 day a week on a contract labor basis.

Once the decision has been made to explore the use of a mid-level provider, the biggest issue is cost versus production. If your practice is not yet generating the revenue to hire a full-time professional with benefits, consider part-time or contract labor. A part-time professional is paid on an hourly rate, usually without benefits, and is given an opportunity to move into a full-time position as volume increases. The other option of contract labor is the most cost-effective method for both parties. The mid-level provider in this arrangement is paid whatever he or she generates in gross receipts, minus the practice overhead. Most well-run practices have an overhead in the range 45–55%. So, for convenience in this example, let us choose a 50% overhead. In this way, the provider keeps 50 cents from each dollar generated and you are at much less risk. The major down-side to part-time and contract labor is a possible lack of loyalty to the practice and loss of this person to a more attractive offer. The majority of practices will choose to hire full-time, mid-level professionals, for a competitive salary that is appropriate for your area, with benefits.

Physicians and mid-level providers should be monitored by the office manager to ensure the appropriate levels of productivity to justify their salary and benefit package. Remember, all professionals must generate gross receipts that equal or exceed twice their benefit package. Keeping your professionals on track and focused on good cost-effective patient care will go a long way to keeping the practice productive. Every year this becomes a greater challenge in an environment where healthcare reimbursements are doing everything but increasing. Part of the solution is to have a management team in place who support a staff of professionals to keep production high and costs low, thus resulting in a profitable business.

Operating Strategies for the Business Manager: Perspective of a CPA

9

Joseph T. Donnelly

The myriad of activities, both clinical and administrative, that are conducted daily within a medical practice have dramatically increased over the recent decade. Contributing factors include compliance issues (managed-care organizations, evolving federal laws), relationship shifts caused by hospital acquisitions and affiliations, technological changes in treating patients and changes in patient expectations. The conduct of all activities supporting patient care must be clearly linked to fundamental, well-communicated operating strategies. This chapter explores several strategies for managers to consider.

The dictionary definition of strategy is 'a method for making or doing'. Inherent in this definition is a structure that organizes activities in a co-ordinated manner to accomplish key objectives. Too often, medical practices have been faced with so much cumulative change that work activities are set into practice in response to an issue that was never 'linked' to an overall strategy for the practice. Without operating strategies to guide the host of supporting activities, a practice can easily fall into disarray.

How does a medical practice develop key operating strategies? Fundamentally, it starts with a mission statement for the practice. A well-crafted mission statement will enumerate the value of the system in place and establish appropriate limits in the overall scope of the practice. Examples of elements that should be considered in a mission statement include: scope of clinical areas (single specialty or multispecialty), provider complement (physicians only or the inclusion of extenders), geographic territory served or hospital locations staffed, and the degree of focus on teaching and/or medical research (see Chapter 4 – It's not a plan without a business plan).

Operating strategies address how the practice functions to accomplish its mission. Operating strategies encompass matters such as the decision-making process, authority-to-act guidelines and the structure of work processes.

Decision-making authority

Quite often, this area causes many problems within a practice for one of two reasons: either the guidelines are unclear or all authority rests with one person. An appropriate strategy for a practice is to develop a decision-making matrix that delineates decisions made at the Board of Directors level from decisions made by management personnel. Furthermore, at the Board level, the matrix can outline those decisions requiring simple majority vote, supermajority vote and unanimous vote.

Examples of decisions reserved for Board approval typically include:

(1)   Adopting or amending a retirement plan;

(2)   Offering employment to new physicians or executive director;

(3)   Terminating physician employment;

(4)   Incurring bank debt or entering into office leases;

(5)   Capital expenditures in excess of a prescribed dollar figure;

(6)   Sale of the practice or its assets.

Consider a subcommittee or task force to encourage or narrow down the physicians and/or employees to a core group that has demonstrated competencies in an area or discipline, and advance recommendations to the Board for final approval. For instance, standing subcommittees for finance, human resources and quality assurance tend to work well if properly focused and correlated with individuals who have skills in those areas. Task forces work well for non-recurring activities (such as upgrading the information system) that, owing to their scope, require Board approval, but need not require congruent levels of time spent by all members of the Board of Directors.

Examples of decisions made typically by management personnel (either a physician leader or the executive director) include:

(1)   The choice of employee benefit programs;

(2)   The hiring/termination of clinical/administrative staff;

(3)   The selection of professional and business liability insurance programs;

(4)   The parameters of a quality assurance system.

Of course, there are a number of other areas in which decision-making guidelines should be defined. They should be outlined in a way that capitalizes on an individual's talent within the practice.

The overall goal is to give the practice a sense of self-direction, as well as to motivate personnel to be accountable and responsible for actions and decisions affecting the practice. In doing so, the sense of autonomy will strengthen physician and employee morale, not to mention the practice as a whole.

Authority to act

A natural extension of the decision-making structure is the enumeration of authority-to-act guidelines. Physicians, managers and employees can take necessary actions in a timely manner if the action falls within their decision-making realm, since their action presumably already fits with the established mission. Authority to act can present itself in many ways. A detailed budgeting process serves as a pre-approval vehicle with which to take action. Budgeting can and should address recurring features and non-recurring areas. Practices should strive to establish authority-to-act guidelines at the lowest levels possible within the practice to promote prompt, efficient activities. Management personnel, for instance, need not be involved in ordering routine medical supplies if the expenditure falls within budgeting levels. By segregating non-recurring items in the budget, it allows for a higher level of approval, if needed.

Supporting the budgeting process is a strategy that can be put in place at the transaction level. Perhaps non-supervisory employees can place purchase orders or approve invoices up to a certain prescribed dollar amount. Management and physician levels can be established at higher amounts. The goal should be to place as much authority as possible throughout the entire practice. Most employees welcome the challenge and look for ways to improve their performance in an area of responsibility. An employee with the appropriate level of authority (coupled with a gain-sharing reward system) will be more likely to reduce costs below a budgeted amount.

Yet another example of authority-to-act guidelines relates to the development of a policy and procedural manual. This type of manual can encompass everything from staffing issues to fiscal policies. Taking the time to document the 'how-tos' of specific policies and procedures creates a powerful tool which can be used time and again. It also saves time and cost in circumstances in which the practice experiences turnover. All in all, its presence and subsequent use can lead to better organization, decreased costs and increased revenues.

Authority-to-act guidelines serve to reinforce the importance of the decision-making process. However, the actual tangible benefits that accrue to a practice come from the structure of its work processes, as guided by decision-making and authority-to-act guidelines.

Structure of work processes

Apart from the very large practices (more than 20 physicians), most practices require the administrators and physicians managing the operations of a practice to be called on to serve as Chief Operating Officers and Chief Financial Officers. The Board of Directors serve as the Chief Executive Officer. This is not a bad arrangement. Individuals need to focus on the multidisciplinary elements involved in wearing two hats. Briefly, this is accomplished by integrating processes that acknowledge that most activities within a practice have both operational and fiscal significance in their conduct.

Addressing work processes need not be overly formal. A practice can sample some of its activities, or develop informal mechanisms to identify work activities to track. Some ideas for addressing work processes include:

(1) Sample 50 EOBs that have rejected claims, and organize the reasons into 3–4 categories. Then trace the reason for rejection back to the root cause and attempt to identify a remedy.

(2) Compare the scheduling of clinical support staff to patient visits/procedures for several days, to look for excess capacity or periods of shortage.

(3) Require outsourcing services to report input/output data (time frames, volume, etc.), to enable you to manage the flow of information.

(4) Keep running lists of incidents in which any work needs to be repeated (obtain additional clinical supplies for a visit, redo a report or analysis) and trend out frequencies over time; trace back to the root cause and seek a remedy.

(5) Utilize information technology to support activities:
   (a) Acquire form-development software to design/redesign and print forms, eliminating the external vendor;
   (b) Transmit information to accountants and lawyers via e-mail files, saving on time and postage;
   (c) Use intranet to communicate a consistent message throughout the practice.

(6) Develop charts to explain job duties and the flow of information.

(7) Make an inventory of all management reports, survey all users and ask the minimum frequency to satisfy their needs, reducing unnecessary report generation.

(8)   Establish benchmarks, particularly related to clinical work units. Such data enable the practice to identify the degree of coding consistency, relative productivity and a calculation of efficiency gains or losses. Such an approach can lead to more sophisticated activity-based costing methods. In the realm of fiscal management, time should be devoted to the development of four major areas: revenue maximization, cost management, internal controls and cash management.

Revenue maximization

Within this area, an administrator must pay careful attention to the following:

Accounts-receivable management

It is a good idea to keep a close eye on the accounts-receivable (A/R) portion of the practice. Regardless of whether or not it is handled within the practice or by an outside vendor, A/R should be closely monitored. A list of all payers should be prepared, then analyzed to determine 'problem areas'. Look for timeliness of collections via an analysis of the aging A/R. This will alert the practice as to where more problem areas may lie. Once this information is compiled, it is a wise idea to share it with the entire practice. By giving physicians and employees the opportunity to view the practice's A/R reports, they are being given the opportunity to take an active role in shaping the practice's future.

Credit and collections

Although this section goes hand in hand with the accounts-receivable function, it is important enough to warrant its own focus. A medical practice should take a hard look at the credit and collections processes already in place. This is an area where, once again, if proper procedures are not followed, revenue can never be recovered once lost. Once a receivable reaches a certain age, more than 60 days for example, what type of procedures are in place to follow up on their collection? Are they sent to collection agencies or to the local magistrate? Are staff members given the responsibility of following up on denied and overdue claims? If the billing and collection function is done outside the medical practice, it is imperative to monitor the process. This is revenue that rightfully belongs to the practice. As discussed above, it should also be procedure to inform physicians and appropriate staff of the status of A/R and collections. This will enable everyone to take the initiative in becoming involved in the management of the practice.

Analysis of coding

An area lacking requisite focus in many medical practices is the use of accurate current procedural terminology (CPT) coding. It is important to remember that, if services provided by the practice are continuously being coded incorrectly, the practice can be losing out on a stream of revenue that can never be recovered. Even worse, the practice could be unknowingly processing fraudulent claims. Coding analysis should be guided by protocols established by the physicians within the practice.

To remedy this common problem area, the practice should continuously keep abreast of insurance and coding changes. What may cost money in the present will save twice as much in the long run. Both physicians and staff need to understand the importance of accurate coding. From time to time, a committee could be formed to monitor and/or audit procedure coding. If problems are discovered early, they can be remedied before revenues are lost forever (see Chapter 14 – Coding documentation and compliance).

Appropriateness of fee schedule

As discussed above, a fee schedule providing a breakdown of all fees associated with practice procedures is an important tool in the determination of turnover.

Cost management

The following areas must be examined when attempting to manage costs:

Benchmarking

There are many types of survey data available to medical practices. These data can be effectively used to 'compare' practice performance, revenue and expenses with those of similar types of practice.

While some may balk at the cost of additional data, in the long run, such information can be helpful in demonstrating to a practice where it stands against other practices in its field.

Financial planning

While the added expense of an accountant or financial planner seems extravagant to the practice, in the long run it could be beneficial to the profitability of a medical practice.

Employee costs

It is important for an office manager to review staff expenses. An area where expenses are especially noticeable is that of employee over-time. Overtime hours worked by staff members should be reviewed for appropriateness and validity. Some sort of overtime policy should be implemented in order to cut down on the unnecessary portion of overtime expense.

Medical supplies

Any practice can spend an inordinate amount on the purchase of medical supplies. It is a wise decision for the practice to review medi-cal-supply vendors carefully and do some 'comparison shopping'. Many extraneous expenses are liable to be eliminated through this type of exercise.

Budgeting

Any efficient medical practice will report that the implementation or overhaul of a budget is a necessary ingredient of a successful medical practice.

Purchasing procedures

This segment deals with the all-important question of 'who has the ultimate decision-making authority?' While, typically, the office man-ager handles the purchasing of supplies for the practice, it goes with-out saying that, perhaps, if the staff of the practice were involved with the ordering of supplies, certain costs could be eliminated. Sometimes, items are purchased and never used, and certain items are found to be lacking. Through group discussions, better methods of purchasing could be successfully implemented.

Internal controls

Every medical practice, regardless of size, should have a well-defined system of internal controls. This prevents any type of fraudulent activity and aids the practice in giving its members a sense of responsibility towards the practice. The following areas should be considered when implementing or evaluating a system of internal controls.

Cash handled by employees

Whenever cash is handled by any employee, it must be monitored. Often, owing to staffing limitations, the same employee will handle money as well as post the payment to this system. This is a prime example of an audit risk, for it would be very easy for an employee to collect money, yet not post it to a patient's account. Additionally, many practices require that any employee handling cash is 'bonded' through a financial institution. This further reduces the risk of embezzlement.

Segregation of duties

No single employee should be in charge of any activity that overlaps with another step in the process. As stated above, often the same employee who collects money posts it to patient accounts. Additionally, an employee who opens the mail should not be the same employee to post daily payments to any system. These examples clearly violate any segregation-of-duty rules or procedures that a practice might and should have in place. It is a much better idea to have different employees responsible for different duties.

Writing off bad debt

In any medical practice, it should be clearly defined who has the authority to write off debts over a certain age. If the receivables are deemed to be uncollectable, the practice should have a policy on who has the final word on writing off the bad debt. Once this is determined, a periodic review of patient accounts will uncover whether or not they are deemed uncollectable and written off when this is actually not the case.

Internal controls for billing practices and procedures

Controls should also be in place for the accurate handling of coding and billing. As illustrated earlier in the chapter, it is possible that a practice can unknowingly bill for inaccurately coded procedures. Thus, a careful review of a practice's coding history can eliminate denied and overdue claims. These reviews can be very effective in discovering errors. Errors can then be corrected.

Check-signing authority

A practice must determine who has check-signing privileges. Is it the entire governing body, one physician and/or the office manager? At any rate, checks should never be signed in advance just to keep 'handy'. This is a large risk; many auditors frown upon this, as anyone can take a blank check and use it for other purposes. Furthermore, it is important periodically to review cancelled checks and vendor checks for appropriateness.

Importance of reconciliations to source documents

Reconciliation to source documents is an imperative part of the internal control system. Some reconciliations useful to an effective internal controls system are as follows. First, it is always good to reconcile daily deposits (from deposit slips or the bank statement) to computer-generated reports of daily payments. It is also wise to compare daily patient visits (from a patient log or register) to collected co-pays. Finally, as mentioned above, it is always advisable that a practice should review its patient account ledgers and search for unauthorized write-offs.

Cash management

Cash management can be daunting at times. This is why it is often necessary to implement cash management procedures to follow.

Accounts-payable management

The practice should establish clear policies regarding how often to process payments for products or services. The practice should be mindful of terms that offer discounts for payment within a defined period, as often they are favorable and should be taken advantage of.

Investments

If cash builds up within the practice and bonuses are paid within defined time frames, consider investing in short-term instruments (bond mutual funds, CDs, etc.) to enhance the return.

Importance of bank reconciliations

Make certain that the cash account is reconciled monthly. Surprisingly, financial institutions make routine errors in processing deposits and checks. The longer you wait to identify a discrepancy, the harder it is to resolve.

Forecasting cash flows

Always have a good sense of the 'baseline' cash needs of the practice, and unusual costs projected over the next 60–90 days.

Customer Service Excellence

10

Joseph Balestreire and Joseph S. Sanfilippo

The level of customer (patient) service provided can be a critical factor in the success of your practice. Customers are not merely buyers of products and services. They are the most important reason behind the quality of services you provide. The level of customer satisfaction has a direct impact on the survival of your office practice. Knowing what customers want, need and expect will make it easier for you to provide a positive experience, shape customer expectations and measure your performance. This chapter explores what it means to provide excellence in customer service and offers a recipe for creating 'delighted patients'.

Lessons from the business world

What do customers want?

Customers (patients) want their needs and expectations to be met. Patients define their own needs and the treatment they expect from your office employees. They want a positive experience that they will be motivated to repeat. They will tell others how well their expectations are met. Patients want to believe that your office will stand behind the services it provides.

Customers want knowledgeable assistance. They want you to understand and be able to explain where to go and what procedure to use and why. They expect complete and accurate answers to their questions.

Customers want prompt, willing attention. They want you to answer the telephone quickly or to respond promptly and attentively to their presence. If you are busy with another patient, quickly have your staff assure new arrivals that you will be with them as soon as possible. Use a tone of voice and body language to show that you are willing to help.

Customers expect to be treated well. They expect you to be courteous and polite, respectful and considerate. Treat patients as individuals. Show understanding and empathy, especially when they have problems or are under pressure. Give them your undivided attention, which tells them that they are important.

Research tells us that:

(1)   The average business hears from only 4% of unhappy customers;

(2)   The average dissatisfied customer tells nine other people about their experience;

(3)   Ninety-five per cent of customers who have their complaints resolved will do business with you again;

(4)   The average customer whose complaint is not addressed complains to ten other people;

(5)   Customers whose complaints are resolved tell five other people about the quality of the service they received;

(6)   Financially, it costs five times as much to gain a new customer as to retain a current customer;

(7)   When you lose a customer, you lose your initial investment plus the stream of future benefits/cash flows;

(8)   Loyal customers in one area of service are good prospects for new service offerings you may develop.

Becoming a customer/patient-driven practice

In becoming a customer/patient-driven practice, you must stay one step ahead of the customer by anticipating their emerging needs and services. Internal and external customers must be routinely asked how you are doing, and their feedback must result in visible changes. As a leader, you must deal with customer feedback directly rather than making excuses.

Becoming a customer/patient-driven practice begins with having a deep understanding of what a customer is, who your customers are and what they want, need and expect (Table 1).

Table 1 Learning exercise: becoming a customer/patient-driven practice

Please answer the following questions:

What is a customer?

_____

_____

_____

_____

_____

_____

Examples

A person who benefits from our services

The most important person to us

Not dependent on us, we are dependent on them

The purpose of our work, not an interruption

A person who brings us his or her wants; it is our job to handle them

Who are our customers?

_____

_____

_____

_____

_____

Examples

Patients

Physicians

Other employees

Payers

Suppliers

What do we mean when we say customer service?

_____

_____

_____

_____

Examples

How we treat customers

Treating people with courtesy, dignity and respect

Looking for and recognizing customers, their needs

Meeting their wants, needs and expectations

What do our customers want, need and expect?

_____

_____

_____

_____

_____

How do we know this?

_____

_____

_____

_____

_____

Recipe for creating customer service excellence

If you can cook, then by following the recipe below you can create an environment of customer service excellence.

Step 1: decide your vision for customer service

(1)   Leadership establishes the vision for service excellence (using the Table 1 learning exercise questions as a guide) and delivers the message of the importance of providing outstanding customer service. The vision for service excellence must be delivered repeatedly and with passion.

Step 2: develop a shared vision with your staff

(1)   Identify your products and services. Identify the primary customer, their wants, needs and expectations, and establish your shared vision for customer service.

(2)   Define your customer service window (scope of your services).

(3)   Identify your customer service principles: behaviors that exhibit how you define customer service.

(4)   Using your customer service principles, conduct a gap analysis of office practices, processes and behaviors. Use this information to focus improvement in process and behaviors.

(5)   Apply customer service principles to how you manage – hiring and firing.

Step 3: discover the customers'/patients' vision for customer service

(1)   Ask/listen: discover the customers' vision, compare it with your vision, and identify expectations that fall within your customer service window.

(2)   Measure: measure outcomes and share results with staff.

(3)   Apply customer service principles to how you manage – part of the performance review process.

Step 4: deliver the vision + 1%

(1)   Implement systems and process improvements that focus on customer needs;

(2)   Conduct training to improve customer service skills and behaviors;

(3)   Measure results;

(4)   Apply customer service principles to how you manage – catch employees doing it right.

Special spices to add to the recipe

(1)   The most important ingredient is adding a passion for improved customer service;

(2)   Set the lead example;

(3)   Teach employees to under-commit and over-deliver;

(4)   Catch employees doing something right and make a big deal about it;

(5)   Make outstanding customer service legendary. Tell stories – a lot of them;

(6)   Creating outstanding customer service begins in the job interview; deliver a strong message regarding the importance of the customer.

The microwave recipe

(1)   Decide what you want;

(2)   Make a plan;

(3)   Take action;

(4)   Evaluate results: are you getting what you want? If not, change your actions.

In the competitive healthcare environment, customer service is quickly becoming the way in which organizations and office practices are able to differentiate themselves in the minds of the healthcare consumer. Knowing who your customers are, what they want, need and expect, and developing an action plan to achieve customer service excellence will be key in the future success of your office practice.

Suggested reading

Barker J. *Discovering the Future Series: The Power of Vision*. Burnsville, MN: ChartHouse International Learning Corporation

Kouzes J, Posner B. *Modeling the Way. The Leadership Challenge*. New York, NY: Jocooy Bass, 1907

Ninomiya JS. Wagon masters and lesser managers. *Harvard Business Review*, March–April, 1988

Marketing your Practice: Ethically, Effectively and Economically

11

Neil Baum

'All of us have the opportunity to market and promote our practices.'

Overview

The intent of this chapter is to provide the tools to attract patients to your practice and to manage them effectively and efficiently from the moment they call for an appointment until they exit the practice. Hopefully they will tell others about their positive experience with you and your practice (Table 1).

Table 1 What are the benefits of marketing and promoting your practice?

- Increase the awareness of all of your services to patients already in the practice and improve the efficiency of your practice

- Assist with marketing to your referring doctors and other non-medical referral sources

- Offer suggestions to increase your practice's communication with managed-care plans

- Provide techniques to measure the effectiveness of your marketing plan

Attracting new patients to your practice

The backbone of attracting new patients to your practice is to become visible in the community. There will be very few of us who will have the luxury of simply hanging out our shingle and waiting for the patients to knock down the door to get in. Most of us will have to make a very definite, planned, strategy to let the public know who we are, where we practice and what are our areas of interest and expertise. This will enable us to build our future practice. Marketing is just one element. We still have to be cost-effective, demonstrate excellent outcomes and provide outstanding service. But first we have to get the patients to call the office for an appointment. There is no short-cut to accomplishing this goal or objective. We have to become public speakers and write for local magazines and newspapers (Table 2).

Table 2 Promoting your practice

- Query letter to newspaper or magazines

- Eye-opening statistics

- Benefits to audience

- How editor can reach you

- Track it

- Follow-up phone call to editor

- Self-addressed, stamped envelope

- Seek aid of hospital public relations and marketing departments

Writing articles for lay publications

How many patients or referrals do you receive when you have an article published in the *New England Journal of Medicine* or the *Journal of the American Medical Association*? Your answer is most likely zero. Most of us enjoy seeing our name and our articles in peer-reviewed journals, but we might question whether the hundreds of hours of research, writing and rewriting are worth it. However, writing an article for a local lay publication takes only a few hours, and the results, i.e. new patients entering our practice, can be significant. For example, an article written on urinary incontinence (Appendix 1), which appeared in a senior citizens' bulletin, resulted in nearly 20 new patients, 15 diagnostic evaluations and three surgeries. One of the spin-offs was that five family members became patients, and seven additional patients were generated from the word-of-mouth promotion by the original 20 patients. Perhaps these statistics will whet your appetite sufficiently to consider writing articles for lay magazines.

An article written by you, or about you and your practice, that appears in the lay press will increase your visibility, your credibility and ultimately your profitability. The public grants you the label 'expert', when you have something published. The public is more likely to believe what you say and do, if you have it published first.

Selecting a topic

There is no shortage of topics in your area of practice that could be turned into an article for publication in a local magazine or newspaper. If you can provide interesting information, useful advice, a human-interest story or, best of all, a celebrity who will share his/her experience, you can be assured that some publication in your community will be interested in your article.

Do some research before you select your topic. Listen and watch the news and note which medical stories receive national attention. Look at national women's magazines, such as *Redbook, Family Circle, Ladies Home Journal* and *Self*. You will find that the local print media are interested in having local experts comment on these articles or provide a local angle to a national story.

You have to pitch in order to publish

The first step is a pitch or query letter to the health editor of the local paper or magazine. This is a short letter that describes the subject of your article, indicates the angle you will take and includes some information about yourself. The query letter is the equivalent of a sales pitch.

Address the query letter to the appropriate editor. If you do not know the editor, call the newspaper and ask for the name and address of the health and science editor of the paper or magazine. Do not send it to the main editor of the publication as he/she will most likely not make the decision and will pass it to an assistant or division editor, which means that your letter may not end up on the desk or in the hands of the best person to accept your article.

Most health and science editors receive dozens and sometimes hundreds of letters every day. Your query letter should be written in a way that makes a positive first impression on the editor. The letter should be a condensed version of your proposed article, with a clearly defined beginning (lead), a middle and an end. Try to find a 'hook' or unique beginning to attract the editor's attention. Begin with an eye-opening statistic, such as the number of people in the community affected with incontinence. The next paragraph could describe the benefits of the article to the readers, and, finally, conclude with your qualifications to write the article. Supply information on how the editor can reach you. Above all, limit your letter to one page. A 3–5 pager will not get read! Appendix 2 is a sample query letter to a newspaper on the use of collagen for the treatment of urinary incontinence.

Once you have sent the query letter, you must be prepared to track it. Unless you have a news-breaking story or medical discovery, a follow-up call is a necessary part of getting published. In many cases your query letter will not be looked at for weeks, so find out whether the editor received the letter and had a chance to read it. You might consider including a self-addressed, stamped envelope with the query letter to make it easier for the editor to reply. If, when you call the editor, he/she is 'still thinking about it', offer to provide additional information. Make the call short and do not be put off by the abruptness of editors. Most of them are under lots of pressure and the stress of meeting deadlines. If the editor does call back, make an effort to return the call to them promptly. If you are going to market and promote your practice, you need to inform your staff that a call from the media is to be considered similar to an emergency room call or a call from a referring physician, and that you will take the call or return it as soon as possible.

There is one caveat about query letters. Do not send out more than one query letter at a time. You do not want to be embarrassed by having two editors agree to publish your article and have to turn one of them down. This will guarantee closing a door for future articles or stories.

Do not forget that there are more places to publish your article or story besides the local newspaper. If you are targeting incontinent patients, offer to write articles for the local branch of the American Association of Retired Persons, local women's groups, diabetes associations, Junior League, church groups, service organizations and health clubs that have newsletters. Also, there are many city and regional magazines that will take articles on medical topics.

Writing an article that will be read

Now that the editor has agreed to publish your article, how do you write an article that will be read and will generate patients for your practice? There are several approaches you can take to accomplish this task. First ask the editor about the length of the article; most magazine articles are 800–1000 words. This works out to be three pages of double-spaced type. A newspaper article is usually a little shorter.

Of course, the easiest, but most expensive solution, is to have someone write the article for you. This easy way out is not necessary or advisable unless you have a very short deadline to meet. One of the best ways to start writing articles for lay publications is to tape record a conversation with an incontinent patient. You will find that what you say to one patient and the questions that the patient asks you can easily be translated into the written word, and will attract hundreds or hopefully thousands of readers. Usually the 3–5-minute discussion that you have with a patient will supply you with ample material for an article in most newspapers and magazines.

A resource for editing your article is the hospital marketing and public relations departments. Not only can they help you write the article, but they can help with the placement as well. Most hospital public relations and marketing departments know the health and science editors, and can furnish guidelines.

Other resources are the local colleges, universities and high-school English teachers. Professors and top college students can provide editing assistance for a very reasonable fee.

Getting more mileage from your masterpiece

One advantage of print media is that you can get additional marketing mileage from your articles long after they have been published. For example, the articles can be framed and hung in your reception area or examination rooms. You will find patients much more interested in reading articles that you have written than in looking at your diplomas and medical memberships. You can also make copies of the articles and include them as bill stuffers.

Take copies of your articles to a copy company and have them laminated. The cost is minimal, and laminated articles can be placed in your reception area and examination rooms. This allows patients to read the articles while waiting for the doctor.

One suggestion is that you have the original articles placed in a bound book in the reception area. Offer to provide copies to any patient who requests them. Finally, send copies of your articles to the local radio and TV stations and suggest that you be interviewed for a story on the subject. The advantage of print material is that it has a long shelf-life compared with radio and TV appearances, which only reach those who happen to be listening or watching.

In most instances, your first lay article will be the hardest to write and will take the longest to get published. But, like any skill, the more you practice, the easier it gets.

Creating powerful presentations through public speaking

An old adage says that the human brain starts working the moment you are born, and never stops until you stand up to speak in public.

However, that does not have to be the natural reaction to public speaking. There is no better way ethically to escalate your reputation than through the medium of public speaking. Unfortunately, our medical training does not provide us with the skills necessary to become good public speakers. According to the *People's Almanac Presents the Book of Lists*, 'most people fear speaking before a group more than sickness and even death!' The reason that people would rather die than speak in public is that they have not had the training and they are out of their comfort zone. However, this skill, like any other skill, can be learned, and with practice you can become competent, proficient and adept at getting up in front of others and getting your point across.

Attempts to have seminars that would attract patients with specific problems, for example, urinary incontinence, have not been successful. The social stigma of being incontinent is so great that it discourages men and women from attending such a meeting. However, if a newspaper announcement contains a coupon indicating where those who would like additional information can call or write, the response is better.

If you are comfortable talking to patients in a direct manner, then you can be a successful public speaker. The best speeches are those prepared well in advance. Giving a speech is not a situation in which you can 'wing it'. You cannot take the same carousel of slides that you use for a presentation to physicians at grand rounds and use the same material for a lay audience. To do so will bore and confuse your audience, and you cannot expect them to call your office for an appointment after the presentation. Your fellow physicians may tolerate and even expect a talk punctuated by technical charts, graphs, anatomical drawings, photos of surgical specimens and medical jargon. Lay audiences, however, expect straightforward explanations of complicated subjects, direct information, and suggestions for improving their health and well-being. Good presentations are crisp, clear and concise. Powerpoint presentations for lay audiences and for physicians have become increasingly popular. In today's fast-paced world of sound-bites, the audience expects clarity and simplicity (Table 3).

The outline for a talk to lay audiences is given in Appendix 3. Whenever possible, try to use visual aids as well as slides. Consider, for example, using a balloon and clothes pin as an analogy to the bladder and the sphincter, to demonstrate the normal physiology of the lower urinary tract.

First of all, you need an audience. Where do you look? Today the public is very much interested in health topics and wellness. Social, civic and professional associations frequently offer speakers and presentations on programs that accompany their regular membership

Table 3 Being a successful public speaker

- Decide on several topics
- Prepare, prepare, prepare
- Practice using a tape recorder
- Use good visuals and slides (read when held up to light)
- Know your audience
- Capture their attention
- Have reprints of pertinent published articles
- Tell the audience what you are going to tell them, tell them, then tell them what you told them
- Give audience goals and objectives
- Fire like a rifle – your point of view 'bull's-eye'
- Main points (two or three)

meetings. Some of the most common organizations are the League of Women Voters, the local parent–teacher association, American Association of Retired Persons, church groups and the Junior League. Your local chamber of commerce can furnish you with a more complete list for your community.

In contacting most civic, social and professional organizations, there are correct channels to follow. If you would like a speaking engagement at a selected organization, call and find out the name of the program chairperson. Let the organization know that you are available. Many programs are scheduled 6–12 months in advance, so take this into consideration when you contact an organization.

Before you contact the organization, decide on several presentation topics. Then send a letter to the program chairperson offering to talk on a topic that would be of interest to their organization (Appendix 4). This letter is very similar to the query letter about a written article, sent to an editor of a magazine or newspaper. Notice that each letter mentions:

(1)   Your qualifications to talk on the subject;

(2)   The length of your talk;

(3)   The content of the presentation;

(4)   The intention to call in a few weeks.

In your letter, discuss how common urinary incontinence is in the community. Discuss the potential benefits to the group and why they

should be interested in the topics, and why you are the one to make the presentation. Spend a few moments on the potential benefits to the audience. Not only will this get the attention of the program chairperson, but it will also form the basis of your presentation. Try to picture yourself as a member of the audience. Each member of the audience will be listening for 'what's in it for me?' When you can answer that question, you will have captured the attention of the meeting planner and then ultimately of your audience. The letter should also include your curriculum vitae, any articles that you have authored on urinary incontinence, the names of other organizations for which you have spoken, or any other materials that emphasize your expertise on the subject of urinary incontinence. Make a follow-up phone call 2–3 weeks after you send your introductory letter.

Know your audience

The more you know about your audience, the better you can tailor your presentation to their needs and the more likely it is that some members of the audience will become your patients. Before preparing your speech, ask the program chairperson for background information about your audience. It is important to know the purpose of the organization, how many people are expected to attend, how much the audience already knows about the topic of incontinence, who have been the previous speakers and what were their topics, the age range of the audience, their educational background, and possible areas of challenge or resistance if your topic is controversial.

The best way to learn about your audience and the goals and objectives of the meeting planner is to send a survey to the meeting planner (Appendix 5). This is particularly important if you are receiving an honorarium for the presentation, since you want to be sure that you truly understand the needs and wants of the audience. For example, if you are speaking on behalf of a pharmaceutical company, give the meeting planner and the pharmaceutical representative the survey and ask him or her to complete the survey and return it. By using this survey you avoid embarrassing yourself, or the pharmaceutical representative, if you review the questions before your presentation. You will also find that the meeting planners really appreciate this courtesy.

Preparing your speech

'Tell the audience what you are going to tell them, then tell them, and finally tell them what you told them', is the old adage about public speaking. It still holds true. All successful presentations have a circular structure (i.e. the end comes back to reinforce the beginning).

Begin your preparation by focusing on what action you want the audience to take as a result of listening to your speech. This goal or objective should be stated in the introduction, and should also be stated emphatically at the conclusion. Try to paint a word picture by referring to the fact that the number of men and women suffering from urinary incontinence in this community will be more than the capacity of the Superdome – a well-known landmark in my community. You might end your presentation by saying, 'Some of you here in the audience may be suffering needlessly from urinary incontinence. Call your physician or your urologist and get an examination so that you can enjoy the rest of your life!'

Once you have the beginning and the conclusion, you can fill in the middle and deliver a memorable speech that will motivate your audience to take positive action. In the middle portion of your speech, present two or three main points using illustrations, examples, stories, case histories or visual aids whenever possible. When talking about urinary incontinence, use a balloon to illustrate the bladder, and your fingers compressing the neck of the balloon will serve as the urinary sphincter. When you release your fingers from the neck of the balloon it will make a sound that produces a predictable giggle or laughter from the audience. Then remark, 'When it is a balloon leaking air, that's funny. But when it is your bladder losing urine, it's no laughing matter'. This visual aid clearly explains the functional anatomy of the bladder and the urethra better than any medical illustration.

If you support each main point with a variety of materials, anecdotes or visual aids, the audience will remain focused on your main goal or objective. If possible, include a personal story about yourself, a friend or a family member. This adds the all-important ingredient, the human touch. Mention any celebrities or historical figures who have suffered from the medical condition you are describing. If a well-known public figure has come forward and admitted that they suffer or are afflicted with the disease or condition, then you might want to include that in your presentation.

In this era of managed care, there is no better way to become attractive to the potential patients in the plan than to contact the employer or the company's nurse and offer to provide a 15–20 minute 'brown bag' presentation on an area of health and wellness. If you know your audience well and select your topic carefully, you can be

sure that there will be several people in the audience who suffer from the condition or disease, or they will have a friend or family member who needs your services.

Educating existing patients about your areas of interest and expertise

Attracting new patients to your practice is important, but do not forget the ones that you already have. When I had been in practice for only a very short period of time, I operated on a lady with kidney stones. Half a year later she came back with an incision on her abdomen, which she told me was from a bladder suspension carried out by her gynecologist. I asked her why she went to the gynecologist, and she told me that she was not aware that I treated patients for incontinence. At that time, I made a decision to ensure that all of my existing patients were informed of the services my practice offered, and what my areas of urological interest were.

Softening the bite of the bill and educating your patients at the same time

By including information and educational materials in your monthly statements, you have an inexpensive opportunity to provide your existing patients with information, news and data about your practice. You can include notices to your patients about new programs, support groups you are conducting, talks you have given or will be giving, or articles you have written. The bill stuffer is also an excellent opportunity to distribute your practice newsletter.

Now many practices have computerized billing that creates the statement ready for mailing in a special envelope, and it is not easy to insert other printed material. Most of the current software programs will allow you to customize a message on the statement. For example, when I wanted to tell my existing patients that I was trained to do the laparoscopic bladder suspension, I included this on my monthly statements. Several of my existing patients called and asked for additional information, and even made appointments to discuss it further.

One other benefit of bill stuffers is that patients are more likely to open a bill that they know will provide useful information rather than just a reminder that they owe you money. Include topics related to your practice, such as wellness, nutrition, humor and seasonal events. For example, in September of every year, we mention Prostate Cancer Awareness Month and provide details of the locations where the patients can receive a free PSA test and a rectal examination.

Extra! Extra! Read all about it

In the past 10 years we have seen a real boom in health and medical information designed for public consumption. More than ever before, patients want t o learn about health and fitness and the prevention, diagnosis and treatment of medical problems. At the same time, patients often complain that their physicians do not communicate effectively. One of the most frequent reasons that patients leave a practice is the doctor's failure to communicate. The average physician interrupts a patient discussing their present illness after 16 seconds! Patients and the public are very interested in receiving as much information as possible from their healthcare providers.

A newsletter will provide that information and will assist in improving communication with your existing patients.

While writing a quarterly newsletter can be a formidable undertaking, there are commercial newsletter services available. Many specialty organizations have template newsletters that you can modify to suit your practice. Usually, the first and last page can be customized. The Health Exchange (Medical Group Management Association, 104 Inverness Terrace East, Inglewood, CO 80112; (303) 799-1111) can provide you with all the materials to create your own newsletter and will send you samples of their newsletters for review.

Another possibility for creating a newsletter is to do it yourself. Information can be found at annual conventions or in specialty publications that can be easily modified as a newsletter for your patients. The only caveat is that it is necessary to 'translate' the medical vocabulary into layman's language.

Most physicians who have tried newsletters indicate that they will only use them for a year or two. The most common reason for abandoning newsletters is that there was inadequate return on the investment. Like any marketing tool, it is necessary to track the results. The newsletter can contain a reply card or a special telephone number, which is the same method used in conjunction with a *Yellow Pages* advertisement. Consider devising a code or system for distinguishing between new patients attracted to the practice and old or established patients who have returned for new procedures or evaluations. Each time a reply card is returned or the special phone number is called, your staff should enter this information into your computer. By tracking the data, rather than by using an intuitive guess, the number of patients who enter your practice can be quantified and a determination of the income derived can be calculated.

As with most marketing efforts, the results from a newsletter are not immediate. Do not become discouraged after you produce one or two issues. Successful marketing requires persistence, reinforcement and repetition.

Networking: the contact sport of the new millennium

All of us have patients who have had successful results after we recommend a treatment or perform a surgical procedure. You can use these success stories to help new patients who are undecided about a treatment, procedure or operation.

A patient network is similar to a support group, although it is not as formal. The medical profession ethically uses patients to discuss their experiences with other patients. The Ostomy Support Group is a good example of a successful group. New or potential patients who attend these meetings show better acceptance of their ostomy, and have demonstrated a better adjustment to their new lifestyle. The same situation is seen with those patients who are incontinent. Patients develop confidence and security when they hear first hand from someone who has already 'been there'.

Patients who have a medical problem and who have been helped are frequently willing to discuss their positive experiences with others who suffer from similar conditions. Several goals can be accomplished – patients discuss procedures to allay fears, and help others arrive at a decision with confidence and they help with your marketing efforts.

An example of how a patient network markets your practice is to encourage a patient considering a procedure or treatment to call another patient who has undergone a similar procedure.

Begin by collecting a list of patients who have agreed to talk to other patients. Try to match the two patients with regard to age, diagnosis and socioeconomic background. Designate someone in your office, usually your nurse, to contact the patient first. The nurse will ask the patient what would be the most convenient time for the new patient to call. The patient considering surgery is then given only the telephone number and the time to call. No names are ever exchanged, so neither patient's privacy is invaded. The patient considering surgery is given a sheet of instructions (Appendix 6) and a suggested script to follow, to make the call more meaningful. Tell the patient that, when they call, they should identify themselves as a patient of Dr [your name] and ask for the lady/man of the house.

Another spin-off from using this networking method is that patients who have benefited from the telephone conversation will volunteer to talk to new patients. They will usually say that they suffered from incontinence for such a long period of time and talking to a fellow sufferer helped them to make the decision to have the surgery or the procedure. As a result of the benefit of using the networking system, they are happy to volunteer to talk to any prospective patients. You can be sure that once you start using this system you will never have a shortage of telephone numbers to recommend to new patients (Table 4).

Table 4 Educate existing patients

- Include new procedures

- In monthly statements, use bill stuffers

- Work with patient advocacy groups

- Communicate, communicate, communicate

- Practice newsletter – include reply card or special phone number

- Patient network

Improving practice efficiency

Improving efficiencies has helped increase productivity in business and can be used in a practice without sacrificing patient care and satisfaction. The days of seeing a limited number of patients with high profits are gone. Currently, most physicians are experiencing the opposite by seeing high volumes of patients with low profit margins. To continue to offer good quality healthcare, physicians will need to utilize better the time spent with patients.

Do-it-yourself videos

One of the best ways of improving the efficiency of your practice is to use videos of you and your colleagues in your practice to explain subjects and topics to your patients.

We are living in an electronic and video age. Most homes have video cassette recorders (VCRs), and most Americans are familiar and comfortable with viewing videos or CD-ROMs. Creating a video or CD-ROM to educate patients is an easy and inexpensive method which has the additional benefit of creating a great marketing tool.

While one patient is viewing a videotape or CD-ROM of an operation, a procedure or a medical problem, you can be seeing other

patients. An effective video can act as a surrogate assistant, addressing and answering the most frequently asked questions about a particular procedure or treatment. Because a video uses visual images, you can provide patients with a better understanding of such subjects as anatomy, physiology and complex technology.

Videos serve as medical–legal documentation that you have explained a procedure and its potential complications. To make the medical–legal protection stronger, your patients should sign a chart or add a sentence to the consent form that indicates that the video or CD-ROM has been seen.

A video serves as a 'give-away' to your patients, their families or their friends. You can lend a videotape or CD to a patient so that a friend or family member who suffers from incontinence has an opportunity to learn about the evaluation and treatment of a specific problem. If that friend does not already consult a specialist, he/she is very likely to call your office for an appointment.

Subjects for videotapes or CDs include procedures or problems that you explain several times each day and operations or procedures that you do frequently.

To create your own video, begin with a script or story. This is simply a narration that accompanies the images on the video. You can begin by recording a discussion with a patient on the topic you are considering for a video. Next, have the discussion transcribed and use it as a guide or an outline for preparing the video script. As an additional source of ideas, review videos that are created by medical manufacturing and pharmaceutical companies. For most topics avoid substituting a commercial video by the medical manufacturing or pharmaceutical company for a personalized, customized video. Commercial videos are biased toward their products or equipment, and do not tell your story from your point of view. Also, a video of you conveys the impression of a personalized message.

Most videos contain a definition of the procedure or test; a description of how the procedure or test is performed; details of the necessary preparation; what the patient can expect after the procedure is performed; and details of the complications and their relative frequency. If your video is about a surgical procedure, it is important to include alternatives to the surgical procedure.

You can make notes on 8 x 10 cm cards, which can be used in place of a teleprompter. The only equipment necessary is a home video camera and a tripod. Most hospital audiovisual departments own all of this equipment, and will frequently lend it to you or provide you with assistance in creating the video.

Finally, you need to edit your tape. A personal computer can be configured to do editing, but most videos can be edited with two

VCRs. Keep the edited length between 7 and 10 minutes. Few videos should be longer than 15 minutes. Longer videos will not hold the interest of the patient and will also tie up your examination room or viewing area.

Offer the patient a written summary of each video after they have seen the tape. Always return to the room after they have seen the video to answer any questions. If you want to be sure that your patient understood the video, you can give them a short test on the material. Appendix 7 is an example of a test used prior to suprapubic endoscopic bladder suspension (Raz or Stamey procedure). This test should be included in the patient's chart should it ever be needed for medical–legal purposes.

The effective use of videos may increase the volume of patients by 15–20% without loss of patient satisfaction.

Color-coded prescription pads

We often have several dozen preprinted prescription pads in our examination rooms, and we will fumble around the drawer to find the correct pad or take the time to write an individual prescription. You can avoid the 'treasure hunt' for the correct prescription pad by having preprinted pads that categorize the drugs you use frequently. For example, the antibiotics you use can all be on one color-coded pad, drugs for incontinence on another color and miscellaneous drugs on a third pad. When you write a prescription, just circle the appropriate drug, add the number that you wish to dispense and circle the directions. The blank pad that you use for analgesics and other class III drugs can be carried in your lab coat. You can save 15–30 seconds each time you write a prescription by using this system. If you see 30–40 patients a day and write two to three prescriptions for each patient, that means a saving of 25–50 minutes a day just by using this system. Managing care now means managing minutes!

Ask your pharmaceutical representative to make these pads for you. Offer to place their drug at the top of your list. One other advantage of the color-coded prescription pad is that you will not get any calls from the pharmacist saying that he/she cannot read your writing!

Educational materials

Today our patients are much more medically sophisticated and also more interested in their health and well-being. We can easily fulfil this need or desire by providing educational materials on their medical

problems. This educational material will also reduce the number of questions from your patients.

Handouts may be prepared for your office, or, in some specialties, purchased. Additionally, some medical specialty groups are offering information on their web-sites and proprietary companies will help your practice develop a web-site at a reasonable price. Providing information in your office will make the work-up more efficient and provide information on procedures and pre- and postoperative instructions before evaluation or surgery. Patients who receive this information are usually more compliant, have a shorter postoperative course, and have fewer questions for the doctor and his/her staff.

You will also reduce calls and questions from your patients by providing them with information on the drugs you prescribe. In addition to giving them the prescription, give the patient information on the purpose of the drug, the common side-effects, the dosing instructions, the common drug interactions and when to take the medication, i.e. with or without meals. This information is available from *The Pill Book 2* or *The PDR Family Guide to Prescription Drugs*, and can be either photocopied or placed in a wordprocessor and then printed on your stationery.

You can assist your patients with educational materials prior to their first visit. If the receptionist asks about the nature of the visit before the first appointment, then a welcome practice package may be pre-mailed. In addition to a 'welcome letter', a practice brochure, a map of the location of the office (and parking information) and a recent newsletter, include an article on a particular medical problem. Also include a brief discussion of what is expected at the time of their first visit, such as the need for a urine specimen. This will reduce the number of patients that void prior to their appointment and must wait 20–30 minutes until they hydrate and can provide a specimen. If the patient is coming for a second opinion, or on a referral, the information needed to help make a medical decision can be brought, or forwarded prior to the appointment.

Preventing litigation

In the era of managed care, the ability to see more patients effectively is necessary to maintain income. Unfortunately, with less patient time, more litigation may evolve. One of the crucial areas that can be used to protect against malpractice is the use of detailed informed consents. Many states mandate that we list all of the complications and risks of the procedure in the consent. Some states (e.g. Georgia) have an informed consent template for common procedures which was generated by the state specialty societies. The necessity of doing this for all of the tests and procedures that we recommend or perform on our patients can be very time-consuming. You can make your practice more efficient by using pre-printed consents that contain the most common risks, complications and alternatives to treatment. Additional information on malpractice and risk management is available in *The Risk Management Handbook for Healthcare Professionals* (Parthenon Publishing, London, 2002)

Calling key patients at home

There is probably no better idea for improving the efficiency and marketing of your practice than by calling your key patients at home. Your key patients are: those who were recently discharged from hospital; patients who underwent outpatient procedures or surgery; patients with significant medical problems; and patients who are going to be admitted early in the morning for surgery (a.m. admits).

Your nurse can contact key patients and answer most of their questions which effectively triages the number of patients who you need to phone down to one or two. If your nurse tells a patient that you are going to call, give the patient an estimated time for the call so that the patient is at home and is not using the phone.

One of the benefits of calling your key patients is the wonderful response you will receive. Few things you do will be as much appreciated as home calls. You can almost hear the patient saying, 'I can't believe my doctor is taking the time to call me at home'. By calling your patients you can anticipate problems that may require an office visit before the next scheduled appointment, or admission to hospital if they are not doing as well as expected.

Finally, when you call your patients at home, you reduce the number of calls that you receive from them. If patients know that you are going to be calling, they are less likely to interrupt your office routine. Thus, if you spend just 5–10 minutes a day calling your patients, you will ultimately have more time with your family and friends. There is no better way to develop a reputation as a caring, compassionate physician than to call your patients at home.

Marketing to referring physicians

In the past, the traditional methods of obtaining physician referrals usually involved trial and error. Perhaps you went to school with another physician or you joined a group practice and got the overflow

patients. Doing an excellent job with every patient gradually generated a word-of-mouth method that would result in more physician referrals. Thus, slowly, usually after 2 or 3 years, a physician could build a reputation in the community. These methods worked in the past because there were enough primary-care doctors, enough patients and enough referrals to go round. Although the traditional system will work, there are effective and economically practical methods of streamlining the development of physician referrals and developing a specialty-based practice.

When referring physicians are surveyed about why they make referrals, they list the following in order of preference:

- Prompt reporting

- Teaching

- Gifts and entertaining

You must always keep your referring physicians informed about their patients' progress. When you see a patient by referral, follow this cardinal rule: never allow the patient to arrive back in the referring physician's office before your report. Nothing is more embarrassing to the referring physician than to be in the dark about what is going on with the patient. If a patient calls her ob–gyn doctor to talk about estrogen replacement therapy and medication to treat her incontinence, and that doctor has not received your report, you not only look bad in the eyes of the ob–gyn doctor, but the efficiency of your practice grinds to a halt. Now your staff has to retrieve the patient's chart, and you are interrupted to answer any questions that the ob–gyn doctor may have.

The usual communication between a specialist and the referring doctor is 7–10 days after his/her patient is seen. During that hiatus, the patient will often beat the letter back to the referring doctor. A technique for handling this is to use the 'lazy person's referral letter'. This requires no dictating, and guarantees absolutely that, 100% of the time, the letter beats the patient back to the referring doctor.

The three most important aspects of your referral letter are the diagnosis, the medications and the treatment plan. These ingredients are referred to as the 'buzz' words. These words are circled in the progress notes of the chart. For instance, a women is seen with a problem of mild to moderate stress incontinence after you recommend a trial of alpha-adrenergic agonists and Kegel exercises. You plan to see her back in the office and check on her progress in 2 months. These key words are circled in the chart. At the end of the day, the nurse goes through the chart after the patient's visit and looks for the key words you have circled. She calls up our 'boiler-plate' referral letter on the computer screen, which has blanks for completing (Appendix 8). The nurse types in the appropriate referring physician's name, the diagnosis and so on. The letter is printed and mailed that day or faxed directly to the physician's office the same afternoon that the patient is seen.

This type of referral letter delivers the essentials to the referring physician immediately. Whenever a referring physician receives a two- to three-page dictated report, he/she looks for the diagnosis, recommended treatment plan and the follow-up. The referring doctor simply does not have time to read a long report.

Now if the patient calls with any questions, the physician can answer them without having to contact you or your office for clarification. Furthermore, the letter can usually be generated without any dictating at all. For those who must dictate the traditional two- to three-page referral letter, you might consider underlining or using boldface print for the essential information, including your impression, the medications and your recommendations. Most referring physicians indicate that they prefer a timely computerized referral letter to a delayed three-pager. Some specialists are concerned that referring physicians are upset when they receive a computerized, impersonal form letter, but surveys of referring physicians indicate that they value timely information more than a delayed personal letter.

If you do not have a computer, you can still employ the 'lazy person's referral letter'. You can use photocopies of a typed letter with blanks in it. Simply fill in the blanks and send this to your referring physicians.

Niche marketing makes it possible to generate intraspecialty referrals, or referrals from colleagues within your specialty. For example, if you provide a service or procedure not provided by your colleagues, you can inform them that you do this and would be happy to work with them in the care of their patient. This concept of 'their' patient is very important in generating intraspecialty referrals. If the patient is sent to you, make sure that he/she is returned to the referring specialist.

The keys to keeping the referral pipeline from other physicians open are communication and education. It is important to let the referring doctor know that incontinence is an area of interest or expertise that you enjoy.

One method of keeping the primary-care doctors informed is to send a do-it-yourself newsletter about the latest developments in your specialty. After attending a (specialty) conference, you will have more than enough information for a short, one-page newsletter that educates referring physicians about the latest developments. Table 5 summarizes how to improve the efficiency of your practice.

Table 5 Improving the efficiency of your practice

- Do-it-yourself video

- Good medico-legal documentation

- Document viewing of video or CD-ROM

- Lend out videotapes or CD-ROMs

- Allows you to see more patients (15–20%)

- Color-coded prescriptions pads

- Educational materials

- Detailed informed consents

- Call key patients at home

- Market to referring physicians

Non-traditional referrals

We have the opportunity to communicate with other healthcare professionals who could be sources to referrals. For example, nurses and hospital employees are frequently asked whom they should see for various medical problems. Giving talks to the nurses both at your hospital and in the community can serve as an excellent method of letting these professionals know about your area of interest in the management of specific problems.

Pharmacists are another group from whom patients frequently seek advice. It is important to become an ally of the pharmacists in your community. Pharmaceutical representatives and medical manufacturing representatives are also a resource, not only for generating good public relations but also serving as referral sources for your practice. If pharmaceutical representatives see that you have an area of interest in a specific area, they will recommend your practice to other physicians, friends and colleagues. If you want to endear yourself to the drug representatives and other sales people who call on your practice, see them in a timely fashion. That is their 'hot button', and they really appreciate that you do not ignore them or keep them waiting.

One way in which to improve the efficiency of your time spent with pharmaceutical representatives is to request an agenda letter (Appendix 9). This letter asks them to inform you on the nature and length of their visit. You can then decide whether you want to see the representative about that subject, and can indicate that you accept their time frame. This method significantly focuses the representative's visit, and reduces the amount of time that you will spend with them to obtain information on their products. Recommendations with respect to building a practice are provided in Table 6.

Table 6 Building a practice

- Do an excellent job with every patient

- Prompt reporting to referring physician

- Circle key words on the chart

- 'Lazy person's referral letter'

- Include timely information

- 'Stat operative note'

- More marketing 'their patient'

- Communicate and educate

- Do-it-yourself newsletter to referring physicians

- Become an ally of the pharmacist and pharmaceutical representative

- See pharmaceutical representatives in a timely fashion

- Streamline communications with managed care

- Improve communication with gate-keepers and primary-care physicians

Appendices

*Appendix 1: **Manuscript from senior citizens' bulletin***

Dry is beautiful: treating urinary incontinence

Urinary incontinence affects nearly 10 million people of all ages and both sexes, yet the majority do not seek medical treatment. That is so unfortunate, since nearly 80% can be either cured or significantly helped.

What treatment is available?

Dietary changes are helpful for incontinence associated with urgency and frequency of urination. There are certain substances that are known bladder irritants. These include caffeinated and carbonated drinks, alcohol, citrus juices, spicy or greasy foods and products that contain artificial sweeteners. Many sufferers of incontinence will dehydrate themselves or restrict their fluid intake in an attempt to control incontinence. Rarely does this work, and often it will make the condition worse as the concentrated urine is more irritating and will result in more urgency and frequency of urination. The best solution is to drink 1–2 quarts of fluid – preferably water, but any liquid will do – spaced evenly throughout the day.

Bladder retraining is recommended for urgency and frequency of urination. Patients are instructed to use the bathroom on a set schedule, gradually increasing the time between urination until voiding can be controlled for at least several hours. Each person's bladder reacts to a certain volume before they appreciate the desire to urinate. Frequent urination actually reduces the bladder's capacity and will result in a life-style of making frequent trips to the rest room.

Exercise is helpful for both urgency and stress incontinence – loss of urine with coughing, sneezing, laughing, lifting or bending over. These are called Kegel exercises, and are named after the doctor who popularized them several years ago. These exercises are intended to strengthen the sphincters or muscles that help close the urethra or tube that transports urine from the bladder to the outside of the body. To locate the correct muscle, simply stop the flow of urine midstream while urinating. These muscles can also be identified by tensing the ring of muscles around the rectum while sitting or standing. You should be able to contract the muscles without contracting the muscles of the abdomen, thighs and buttocks. Once you can successfully squeeze and release the correct muscles, you can do the exercises as you go about your daily routine. Try to hold the contraction of the pelvic-floor muscles for 3 seconds. Then release the contraction for 3 seconds. Repeat this 3-second contraction and 3-second release three times in a row. Then do three sets of these three contractions a day. It will be necessary to practice this exercise for 3–4 months before any changes occur in the ability to control urination. You will also need to continue these exercises for the rest of your life.

Another method of building up the pelvic-floor muscles is to use pelvic weights. These consist of weighted cones inserted into the vagina. You hold the weight inside the vagina by contracting the pelvic-floor muscles. As the muscles become stronger, progressively heavier weights are inserted into the vagina.

There are several drugs that can be used to help control incontinence. Estrogen can be used in women who are deficient in this hormone, which is common after the menopause. As a result, stress and urge incontinence become worse. Estrogen can be given by mouth or applied as a cream directly into the vagina and on the outside of the urethra. There are many advantages and disadvantages of estrogen replacement therapy. Your doctor can be very helpful in assisting you to make the estrogen decision.

Other drugs, called anticholinergics, can be beneficial for urge incontinence. An example is oxybutynin or Ditropan®. This drug relaxes the bladder muscle and prevents it from contracting with only small volumes of urine in the bladder.

For patients with mild stress incontinence, alpha-agonists such as pseudoephedrine can be used to contract the sphincter near the bladder and the urethra. This drug cannot be used in patients with heart problems or high blood pressure, as it may make the blood pressure even higher.

Injections of collagen material that can be placed around the urethra to increase resistance to the flow of urine in patients with very severe stress incontinence are available. This treatment can be done on an outpatient basis, and the results occur almost immediately. Unfortunately, some of the collagen material is absorbed by the body, and reinjections of collagen may be needed if the incontinence recurs.

For those who fail exercises, medications and injections, there are surgical procedures that can be performed for stress incontinence. The most common is the bladder neck suspension. In this operation the bladder neck and urethra are resuspended to their natural anatomical position behind the pubic bone. For severe stress incontinence the urethra and bladder neck can be lifted by using a sling of synthetic material such as Dacron® or Gortex®, or the patient's own

tissue, and placing it under the urethra and attaching it to the abdominal muscles or the pubic bone. Finally, an artificial sphincter can be placed around the urethra, and attached to a pump and release mechanism in the labia. By compressing the pump mechanism the artificial sphincter is opened, and urine can pass out of the body.

Urinary incontinence is a terrible problem that affects the sufferer's quality of life. Today, with a better understanding of the cause of incontinence, no one needs to suffer the embarrassment of this treatable medical problem.

Appendix 2: *Sample query letter to newspaper editor*

Ms Meg Farris
Health and Science Editor
Times Picayune
New Orleans, LA

Dear Ms Farris,

I would like to have an opportunity to talk with you about writing an article on urinary incontinence, a condition that affects an estimated 70 000 individuals in our community, or the number of people that would fill the Superdome.

Unfortunately, because of myths and misinformation, only 10% of those individuals suffering from urinary incontinence are currently seeing a physician. It is not uncommon for those afflicted with this medical malady to become housebound and reclusive because of the social embarrassment. Urinary incontinence is also a common reason for admission to a nursing home. However, many of these patients who suffer from urinary incontinence can be helped, and most can be cured. Now there is a new treatment using collagen, a natural material derived from cow skin, that can be injected around the urethra, the tube that goes from the bladder to the outside of the body, to cure this problem. The procedure can be done on an outpatient basis and even in the doctor's office.

I could provide you with the opportunity to interview several patients who have been cured using this new technique.

I am enclosing some recent articles that I have written on this topic, and an article that appeared in the *Chicago Tribune*.

I'll be giving you a call next week to discuss your interest in writing this article.

Sincerely,

Appendix 3: Outline for talk to lay audience

(1) Goals and objectives:
    (a) Define urinary incontinence;
    (b) Discuss common causes of incontinence;
    (c) Review treatment of incontinence.

(2) Incidence:
    (a) Affects 10 million Americans;
    (b) Costs $10 billion annually;
    (c) Most who suffer have not received help from physicians.

(3) How do the bladder and the urethra work?
    (a) Anatomy of male and female urinary tract;
    (b) Explain normal urination:
        (i) storage;
        (ii) emptying.

(4) What are the causes of incontinence?
    (a) Stress;
    (b) Urge;
    (c) Overflow;
    (d) Neurogenic;
    (e) Mixed.

(5) How is urinary incontinence evaluated?
    (a) History and physical examination;
    (b) Laboratory tests;
    (c) Urological tests.

(6) Treatment:
    (a) Goals of treatment:
        (i) preserve kidney function;
        (ii) make the patient dry;
        (iii) achieve, as close as possible, a normal voiding pattern;
    (b) Treatment options:
        (i) behavior techniques:
            timed voiding;
            bladder training;
            pelvic-muscle exercises (Kegels);
            biofeedback;
        (ii) drug therapy:
            bladder relaxants;
            bladder outlet stimulants – alpha-adrenergic agonists;
            estrogens;

      (iii)   mechanical devices:
               pessaries;
               diaphragm;
               electric stimulation;

      (iv) surgery:
               open surgery;
               needle suspension;
               vaginal surgery;
               artificial sphincter;
               laparoscopic bladder suspension;

      (v)   mechanical compression:
               collagen;
               miscellaneous:
               diapers;
               catheters.

(7)   Summary:

Urinary incontinence affects millions of American men and women. Nearly everyone with urinary incontinence can be helped and many can be cured. No one needs to suffer in silence.

Appendix 4: *Example of 'pitch' letter to a local women's organization asking to speak on urinary incontinence*

[date]

[meeting planner]
[organization]
[address of organization]

Re: Presentation to [name of organization] on urinary incontinence

Dear [meeting planner],

Today, one in six women aged 45 and older is affected by urinary incontinence or involuntary loss of urine. Two in five women will wait more than a year to discuss this condition with their physician, usually because of embarrassment. Most women know very little about incontinence, and this includes women who suffer from incontinence.

Because this is such a common medical problem that affects so many women in our community, I would like to have an opportunity to speak to your organization on this topic.

I am a urologist in private practice in [name of city] and work at [name of hospital(s)]. I have an educational talk for women that will (1) describe the anatomy and function of the bladder, (2) describe the common causes of incontinence, (3) discuss the evaluation and (4) review some of the treatments available for women who suffer from this common condition. My talk is a slide presentation that is 20–25 minutes in length, and I would be available to answer any questions after the talk. I will also provide everyone in the audience with a hand-out that summarizes the presentation.

I am enclosing several articles that I have written on urinary incontinence, including an article that appeared in the [name of local paper or magazine] and a summary by The Bladder Health Council of the American Foundation for Urologic Disease on 'Women and incontinence; revealing America's hidden health issue'. I am also including a few letters of recommendation resulting from previous talks that I have given in the community.

I will give you a call in two weeks to discuss the possibility of talking with [name of organization].

Sincerely,

Appendix 5: Survey to meeting planner

(1)   What is the date of the meeting?

(2)   What time would you like me to arrive at the meeting?

(3)   Where is the meeting? What are the directions to the location of the meeting?

(4)   How long would you like me to speak?

(5)   Will you allow 5–10 minutes for questions and answers after my presentation?

(6)   Who will introduce me?

(7)   Would you like information that can be used in the introduction?

(8)   Can you provide a carousel projector and a screen?

(9)   How many people usually attend the meeting?

(10)   If I provide you with the handout for the members of the audience, would you make copies?

(11)   Who have been previous speakers at your meetings?

(12)   Could I bring a lady who had [the specific problem] but is now cured who would like to share her story with your group?

(13)   Is there anything else I need to know about your organization or group that will help me prepare for my presentation?

Appendix 6: *Phone call instructions for patient networking*

[name of patient],

Call [telephone number of patient who had the procedure] and identify yourself as a patient of Dr Baum's and ask for the man/woman of the house. He/she does not have your name and it is not necessary to give him/her yours.

You may ask any questions you want, regarding the procedure.

I suggest that you write down any questions you would like to have answered before you call.

Questions:

Appendix 7: *Test after viewing video on treatment of urinary incontinence*

Circle your response

(1)   Urinary incontinence is a common condition that affects women more than men.

True   False

(2)   Treatment options include exercises, medications, behavior modification and surgery.

True   False

(3)   The bladder suspension using the needles requires two small incisions on the lower abdomen.

True   False

(4)   One of the complications of surgical bladder suspension is urinary retention or inability to urinate.

True   False

(5)   The treatment for urinary retention is either the presence of an indwelling catheter or intermittent insertion of a small tube to drain the bladder several times a day.

True   False

(6)   Two very common complications after a surgical bladder suspension are bleeding and infection.

True   False

(7)   The bladder suspension is always successful and will not fail.

True   False

(Suggest large type because of the age of the patients.)

Appendix 8:   Example of referral letter template

Dear [name of doctor],

Re: [name of patient]

[Patient] was seen for a problem of

The pertinent findings on the physical exam were

I recommended

I will keep in touch with you regarding his/her urological progress.

Sincerely,

[your name]

Example

A patient, Jane Doe, was referred by Dr Bill Smith with stress incontinence and a hypermobility of the urethra and bladder neck. You suggest a trial of alpha-agonists, Kegel exercises and an appointment in 2 months.

Dear Bill,
Mrs Jane Doe was seen for a problem of stress incontinence.
    The pertinent findings on physical examination were a cystourethrocele.
    I recommended a trial of ephedrine 25 mg t.i.d. and a program of Kegel exercises. I will see her in two months.
    I will keep in touch with you regarding her urological progress.

Sincerely,

[your name]

Appendix 9: *Letter prior to appointment with a pharmaceutical representative*

Dear

There have been many changes that have occurred in healthcare recently that have impacted on my/our practice. As a physician, I/we are seeing patients who are more medically educated and demanding more of our time. Consequently, I/we have less time to spend with medical manufacturing and pharmaceutical representatives.

I want to continue to have a relationship with you and your company, but I want to make an effort to keep our visits short and focused.

I/we would appreciate an agenda for each of our meetings. Would you please include in the agenda what you want to talk about, what you want to know from me and my practice, and how long you anticipate the visit will take. I will approve the agenda and have my secretary make the appointment for you.

I will make every effort to see you on time and to end at the appropriate time.

Thank you very much for accommodating me/us. I believe it will help us both to be more efficient.

Sincerely,

Computers for an Office Setting: Management Information Systems and the Internet from a Clinician's Perspective

12

Stephen K. Klasko and Larry R. Glazerman

In 1951, Remington's UNIVAC I became the first commercially available computer. Fifty years later, it is the rare physician who does not have a computer on his desk in the office or in his study at home, and possibly a notebook computer in the back seat of his car. Indeed, although this was not known when most of us were in medical school, it will not be long before a physician will need to be computer literate to make rounds in the hospital, complete medical records and communicate with patients and staff. This has already come about in some forward-thinking areas of medicine.

In this chapter, the following common questions from colleagues are addressed:

- Why do I need a computer?

- What type of hardware and software should I buy?

- Where should I buy?

- How can I use the Internet most effectively?

Why do I need a computer?

It would be easy to say that if you need to ask that question (Table 1), you probably should not be reading this book. Since its invention, a

Table 1 Why do I need a computer?

Hardware	Where to buy
PC/Mac	Small store
Desktop/laptop	Superstore
Other hardware	Mail order
Printer	Internet
Modem	**Practice automation**
Scanner	Medical records
Software	Test tracking
Office	Patient communication
Word	Patient education
Excel	**Internet**
Powerpoint	Research
Access	Shopping
e-mail	Your own website
Accounting	
Others	
Graphics	
Video	

PC, personal computer

mere 20 or so years ago, the personal computer has become a staple of modern life. This little box that sits on your desk or floor has replaced the typewriter, calculator, slide projector and, at times, the telephone. The good and bad news is that is has forever changed the relationships between professionals (including physicians), support staff, patients (customers) and what we refer to as 'office machines'. Table 2 summarizes some of those changes.

Table 2 Changes in 'office machines'

	The Old Way	The New Way
Correspondence	Physician dictates letter into Dictaphone, hands tape to secretary. She transcribes it on her typewriter, hands physician rough draft. He makes corrections, hands rough draft back to secretary, who retypes entire letter with corrections.	Physician dictates letter into computer via voice recognition software or types letter on his/her own PC. The file is saved on network drive. Administrative assistant proofreads file on computer, suggests changes and saves corrected file. Physician opens file with suggested changes, accepts or rejects changes and sends final copy back to assistant. Assistant prints correspondence to be sent, electronically, as a fax directly from the PC, or, the old-fashioned way, on paper.
Medical records	Patient comes to office, staff finds chart (often misfiled) in rack, places patient in room, chart on door. Physician takes chart from door, looks at old records and sees patient. Physician makes notes (sometimes legible) on chart, sets chart aside for later dictation of note to PCP (see above). Physician writes slip to order laboratory and other tests.	Patient comes to office, staff pulls up his/her record on a computer terminal. Staff enters vital signs and chief complaint on terminal, places patient in room. Physician enters room with hand-held computer connected wirelessly to network, pulls up patient's file online; while taking history, fills in checkboxes for patient's answers to questions and physical findings. Physician also checks boxes for tests requested. Computer orders tests, printing requisitions, prints note for chart, prints letter for PCP.

Continued

Table 2 continued

	The Old Way	**The New Way**
Test results	Results delivered to office by US Mail. Staff opens envelopes, searches for charts, places results in charts to await physician review. Physician reviews results when he/she has time, gives stack of charts to staff, staff calls patients or sends letter about results.	Results delivered to office electronically. Physician logs on to computer, reviews results online (in conjunction with online charts), makes comments online, generates patient letters which are sent out either electronically or printed and sent traditionally.
Lecture slides	Lecturer prepares outline of talk on paper, submits to photography department who make Kodachrome slides 3 weeks later. Lecturer notices typographical errors and submits corrections. Receives corrected slides in another 3 weeks.	Lecturer prepares outline in presentation software, selects design scheme, prepares online slideshow. Goes to lecture with notebook computer and projector (together weighing less than 10 lb). Notices typos while rehearsing presentation, immediately makes corrections and presents lecture.
Communicating with kids in college (this is put in here just for fun)	Mom writes letter to son in college, mails it, anxiously awaits letter by return mail. Son checks mailbox once a month, gets letter, throws it on pile of dirty clothes, never to be seen again. Meanwhile, Mom gets frustrated, calls son on phone, gets no answer, is convinced son is roadkill.	Mom sends e-mail to son, who is always at his computer, which has a direct Internet connection. Son answers immediately. Alternatively, mom sends son instant message, and has live online chat with son. Mom and son are happy, even if son's answer is 'I'm busy. CUL8r' (shorthand for see you later).

PC, personal computer; PCP, primary-care physician

What should I buy?

Personal computers today come basically in two 'flavors': machines that run the Microsoft Windows® operating system (referred to as Windows machines); and Apple Macintosh® computers (referred to as Macs). In 1984, Apple was the first manufacturer to offer a WYSI-

WYG (what you see is what you get) interface or GUI (graphical user interface) with its Macintosh computers. (You may recall the 1984 Macintosh TV commercial that aired during the SuperBowl.) This was an innovation that radically changed the face of personal computing. In 1990, Microsoft Windows 3.0 duplicated the look and feel of the Mac on IBM and compatible computers. Both Apple and Microsoft have upgraded their operating systems several times over the years. For reasons beyond the scope of this chapter, Windows machines have proliferated in the corporate world, while Macs have major strongholds in education and graphic design. Each type of machine is described briefly below, along with some personal recommendations.

Terms you should know are summarized in Table 3. There are many other features to today's personal computers that can be found in any of several good books on the subject (see, for example, in Suggested reading).

Table 3 Terms you should know

Processor (or chip)	The brains of the machine. The processor actually does the work of the machine. The current processors from Intel are the Pentium series (Pentium II, III and IV). Processor speed is measured in MHz (or megahertz). Today's fastest processors work at greater than 1000 MHz (1 gigahertz).
RAM (random access memory)	This is where programs and information are stored while the machine is on. Information in RAM is lost when the machine is turned off. RAM is measured in megabytes (MB), generally the more the better: a machine purchased today should have at least 128 MB of RAM.
Storage (hard drive)	This is a large-capacity magnetic disk that is permanently installed in the machine. This is where information is stored when the machine is turned off. Today's hard drives are measured in gigabytes (1 000 000 000 characters of information), and usually come with 20 gigabytes or more.

Windows

The vast majority of personal computers in use in business today are running some version of the Windows operating system. These machines run on processors made by Intel, AMD and Cyrix, with Intel being the most popular. Personal computers purchased today will include Windows ME or Windows XP (for personal use) and Windows 2000 (for corporate use). Windows machines (which, in the past, were referred to as 'IBM compatible', since the first of them were made by IBM) are available from numerous manufacturers, including IBM, Compaq, Dell, Gateway and others.

Macintosh

Today's Macs use a PowerPC processor, which was jointly developed by Apple, IBM and Motorola. The current processor is dubbed the G4 and, in terms of sheer processing power, is slightly more powerful than the Pentium IV. Macintosh computers are made only by Apple Computer. Apple's current operating system is called OS X.

How do I choose?

(Note that the opinions expressed below are totally those of the authors, and are not shared by everyone, Including the computer-science major son of one of them!)

Before you decide what type of computer to buy, you need to know what you want to use it for. If your main goal is surfing the Internet, checking e-mail, playing some games and some basic personal productivity, such as word processing and managing your checkbook, either Windows or a Mac will serve you well (although even the above-mentioned son will admit that there are more games available for Windows). Graphic design and multimedia applications are better implemented in the Macintosh environment.

If, however, you want to connect to your hospital or office network, you need to do some homework. Many networks will allow access by either Windows or Mac with the correct software, while others will allow only Windows machines.

To summarize, IMHO (computer shorthand for 'in my humble opinion'), unless you are planning on doing heavy-duty graphics or video editing, we recommend Windows. The competition allows prices to be much more reasonable, there are more choices in hardware and software, and, like it or not, it is the standard in the corporate world. In general, it makes sense to stay with some of the major brand names, such as Dell, Gateway, IBM, Compaq and several others. You might find a lower price from a smaller manufacturer, and you might be happy, but the major players have well-oiled support staff and policies that will probably serve you better in the long run.

As a general rule of thumb, the obsolescence cycle of today's personal computers is about 3 or 4 years. The lesson here is that the top of the line today is the middle of the road tomorrow, and obsolete in a few years. Unless cost is a major issue, buy the largest, fastest, newest machine you can. It will not be very long before it is not the largest, fastest or newest any more, but you will be happy to have the extra speed, storage and memory for now.

Other hardware

Most computers today come with a modem built in. You should make sure that you get a 56-K (this refers to the speed) V.90 (this refers to the protocol that the modem uses for communicating) modem.

The only other essential piece of hardware is a printer. Printers today come in two varieties, ink-jet and laser. While laser printers offer slightly better quality and higher speed, ink jets are more affordable, especially for color. Printers from any of the major manufacturers, such as Hewlett Packard, Epson, Canon or Brother, will serve most purposes well.

Software

While hardware represents the nuts and bolts of the computer, it is the software, or programs, that makes it useful. Software represents the instructions that tell the computer what to do. Several types of software are important to the computing physician.

Probably the most basic software that you will need is a personal productivity package. These are available as integrated programs, such as Microsoft Works or ClarisWorks, as well as what are referred to as suites, such as Microsoft Office.

Microsoft Works is packaged with many personal computers and includes modules for word processing, spreadsheet, simple database design and a communication module, which can help you connect with online services. ClarisWorks, published by Apple for both Windows and Macintosh, includes similar modules.

The most common office suite is Microsoft Office, although others, such as Corel WordPerfect Suite, are also popular. Microsoft Office 2000, the latest edition, comes in several versions. The Standard version includes Word (a word processing program), Excel (a spreadsheet), Outlook (scheduling and contact management) and PowerPoint (presentation graphics). This is probably sufficient for most users, unless you need a database program. The Professional Edition of Office includes Access, a powerful database manager. There are several other variations of Office, described on Microsoft's web-site (http://www.microsoft.com/office/order/default.htm).

The main difference between the integrated programs and the office suites is simplicity versus power. The suites offer much more power and flexibility in the individual programs at the expense of some simplicity. You should try the software out at a store if possible before you buy.

Other important software that you will need includes an e-mail program and a web browser, both of which are essential for connecting to the Internet, as well as other software with specific functions.

Numerous e-mail packages are available from several manufacturers. Depending on how you access the Internet, some providers such as America Online (AOL), use their own e-mail program. If you use another Internet provider, you can use any one of several e-mail programs. One of the more popular is Eudora. This is available in a light version, which is obtainable online for free at www.eudora.com, and the Pro version, which is somewhat more extensive, with more features.

Web browsers basically come in two flavors, namely Microsoft Internet Explorer (commonly referred to as IE), and Netscape Navigator or Communicator. Both are available for free. Windows computers come with IE installed as part of the operating system. As a sidebar, anyone who has been following the major antitrust lawsuit against Microsoft will realize that the bundling of IE with the Windowed 98 operating system was a major issue in this case. Netscape Navigator is also available for free, either on disk or as a download. Neither of these browsers is clearly superior to the other; both have their strong proponents.

Several other software programs can be helpful with specific tasks. If you own a fax modem, a fax program is essential. Symantec has a program called WinFax Pro, which is outstanding. It is relatively inexpensive (less than $200), and full featured. As with most software categories, other options are also available. If you are interested in producing patient brochures and other literature, programs such as Microsoft Publisher or Adobe Pagemaker can help design and layout anything from sophisticated documents to simple brochures.

Further, if you have a video camera, it is now possible to use your computer to edit and add titles to your videos, both for home use and for presentations. Especially with the new digital video cameras, this can be done with no loss in quality, affording the opportunity to personally produce professional quality video. If you have any interest in this type of work, it is especially important to have an extremely fast processor, lots of RAM, and a large, fast hard drive. Digital video takes up quite a bit of hard drive space, and the transfer can be extremely slow with a slow processor and minimal RAM.

Where should I buy?

There are numerous options available for purchasing computers today. Computers can be purchased at electronic stores, super-stores, mail order, or over the Internet. If you are part of a large institution, it is possible that this decision will be taken out of your hands. If your computer will be on a large network, the network administrator may want control over the specifications and vendor. The advantage in a situation like this is that you will probably not have to worry about support, which will come from your institution. This is offset by what might be a slightly higher price.

Similar to other purchases, especially electronics, purchasing at a specialty store can be beneficial if you need advice and are willing to pay for it. Some of these stores have extremely knowledgeable staff, and support their customers well, although others do not. Here it pays to shop around.

If you are not afraid to 'get under the hood' so to speak, buying by mail order or online can be very cost-effective. Obviously, you can only buy online if you already have a computer to connect with, but many physicians are finding that they need several computers both at home and in the office. Many mainstream manufacturers have jumped strongly into e-commerce, with full-featured web-sites offering cus-tom building of systems, order tracking, and online customer service. Two of the best sites in this regard are Dell (www.dell.com) and Gate-way (www.Gateway.com). If you know exactly what you want, and are not afraid to tinker a bit, buying both software and hardware online can be quite rewarding.

Practice automation

One of the most common uses for computers in the physician's office in the recent past has been for billing, scheduling and practice man-agement reporting. The specifics of these systems are beyond the scope of this chapter. More information can be found in the annual summary of medical computer systems published by MD Computer magazine.

The Internet

Anybody reading this who is not at least superficially familiar with the Internet may have been living in a cave for the last 10 years. Despite what Al Gore has stated, the Internet was developed in the late 1960s by a cooperative group of research universities, in order to link their computers together and share data electronically. In the last several years, Internet access has become available in a large percentage of homes throughout the nation. Several things are important to understand about the Internet.

The main collection of computers linking the world is referred to as the World Wide Web (or web for short). Many institutions, such as universities and hospitals, have their own connections to the web, allowing access to anyone using a computer in the institution. In order to access the Internet at home, you need a contract with an Internet Service Provider, or ISP. These also come in many varieties. There are large national providers, such as AOL and Microsoft Network (MSN), as well as a multitude of local and regional providers. Your choice of providers depends on several factors, not only cost, but ease of access, technical support, and most importantly, how you choose to connect.

Traditionally, the most common method of home Internet access has been over a telephone line, using a modem. This is commonly referred to as dial-up service. The advantage to dial-up service is accessibility anywhere a phone line is present, and relatively low cost. Other methods of access have become popular recently, offering higher speeds, as well as the ability to be constantly connected to the Internet. The two most common high-speed access methods available to individual users are cable and DSL. Both offer similar advantages and speed.

Cable access uses the same cable that brings you cable TV. If your cable TV provider offers this, it can be a very cost-effective, speedy solution. DSL is a way of transmitting a much higher volume of information over telephone lines, and also allows continuous connections. Both of these methods are several times faster than dial-up access, but are somewhat more expensive. In addition, if you travel, you will also need dial-up access, since cable modems and DSL are obviously only good when you are at home. If either or both of these services are available to you, check out the different pricing plans and features before choosing between the two.

Today's physicians use the Internet in a multitude of ways, both as a source of information, as well as a marketing and patient education tool. In addition to the traditional uses for shopping, stock quotes, sports scores and the like, there are several medical-related sites that can be quite valuable. MDConsult (www.mdconsult.com), to which many hospitals and universities subscribe, has a wealth of reference information, patient information, and other content of interest to physicians in all specialties.

Many specialty societies and journals offer sites with access for both members and non-members. For example, the American College of Obstetricians and Gynecologists (www.acog.org) offers online registration for its postgraduate courses, searching of its journals and patient information materials, and other newsworthy items. The *New England Journal of Medicine* (www.nejm.org) also offers online access to its journal. In addition to these organizations, there are numerous independent sites that offer substantial clinical information. In my specialty, www.obgyn.net offers forums for both physicians and patients, which are wonderful ways to consult with colleagues about difficult cases, as well as an extensive reference section.

The next step beyond using the Internet as a reference source is having your own presence on the web with your own web-site. There are several ways to do this, as well as numerous ways that it can be used.

Many local ISPs will develop and maintain a web-site for you for a nominal fee. They often have in-house design staff who can layout the pages, produce the graphics and help with content development. In addition, there are companies that specialize in producing medical related sites. For an example of this, check out www.healthyme.md. For a sample of a site that they have developed, feel free to examine my practice's site at www.obgynttown.com. Companies such as this will typically provide medically related content for your review, and assist you with the marketing aspects of the site.

In addition, numerous specialty and local medical societies offer free web pages for their members. These can be a great source of exposure, especially if designed well. Check out Medem, which is sponsored by the AMA as well as several specialty societies (www.medem.com).

As more of us, physicians and patients, are becoming web-friendly, the uses of the Internet are growing exponentially. Many forward-thinking practices are using the Internet for secure patient registration, medical history taking, results reporting and other patient communication. As an example of what can be done, one of the most innovative sites I have seen is www.babypressconference.com. This site allows mothers who deliver at participating hospitals to have a live video press conference to show off their newborn to friends and relatives.

Several sites now offer online prescription writing with hand-held devices. These can either print out paper prescriptions or connect directly with pharmacies, check for drug interactions, and compare formularies. More information on these can be found at www.iscribe.com and www.ephysician.com. The possibilities that exist in this sphere are limited only by the imagination and resources of developers.

A final note

It is probably obvious that we could be characterized as the ultimate computer geeks. While that is probably true, we must add that we are not fans of automation for its own sake. We strongly believe that it is important to remember that we are a profession of people caring for people. There are several trends in automation that we do not like. For example, many practices today have an 'automated telephone attendant'. We are all familiar with the dreaded voice that tells us 'if you have pain on your left side, press 1…'; we have used systems like that in our office, and decided that despite the 'value' of not committing a person to answer the phones, there is definite value to hearing a live human voice on the other end of a phone line. The lesson we learned is that computers should be used to do what they do best, which is freeing up your people to care for patients, which is what they do best.

Suggested reading

Gookin D. *PCs for Dummies*, 8th edn. New York: Hungry Minds Inc., 2001

MD Computing Magazine. New York: Springer Verlag

Disciplining the Difficult Physician

13

Stephen M. Crow and Thomas E. Nolan

Introduction

> From the Oath of Hippocrates ... I will follow that system of regimen which, according to my ability and judgment, I consider for the benefit of my patients, and abstain from whatever is deleterious and mischievous. I will give no deadly medicine to any one ... Into whatever houses I enter, I will go into them for the benefit of the sick, and will abstain from every voluntary act of mischief ... While I continue to keep this Oath unviolated, may it be granted to me to enjoy life and the practice of the art, respected by all men, in all times! *But should I trespass and violate this Oath, may the reverse be my lot!*

Did Hippocrates mean it was okay to fire doctors? The most serious problem an attending physician or resident can demonstrate is a defect of character or a flaw in ethics. Breaches of ethics by medical doctors are well documented. Ethical lapses by doctors cover a wide range of situations and include: being belligerent, overbearing, and lacking civility; being deceptive with colleagues and organizations; engaging in sexual misconduct; attempting to sterilize a woman against her wishes; practicing medicine despite incompetence or a lack of credentials; accepting gifts from patients; involvement in conflicts of interest; dispensing outdated medications or dispensing drugs illegally; misleading juries by giving false testimony; misrepresenting research findings; engaging in fraud; evading malpractice data banks and not reporting mistakes and errors; abusing others verbally, psychologically and physically; abusing alcohol and drugs; falsifying information; and murdering patients.

Doctors are not the only people in healthcare settings who can do great harm. Examples of misconduct by other healthcare professionals abound and are great fodder for the lay press. But of all the professionals in healthcare organizations, it is particularly shocking when physicians, who have the greatest impact on helping the sick and injured, are identified as dangerous to patients.

A recent scenario involving Michael Swango may be an extreme aberration or an extremely good example of a defect of character. On July 19, 2000, Swango entered a plea of not guilty to federal grand jury charges that he murdered, attempted to murder and assaulted various patients entrusted to his care at hospitals in the United States and abroad. Commenting on the impending trial, author James B. Stewart noted that: 'This is not a case of mercy killings, but of a doctor charged with using his professional knowledge to become a serial killer. The most shocking part of the story is that he kept practicing even after he was convicted of the non-fatal poisoning by arsenic of co-workers in 1985, and after being investigated for murder at the Ohio State University Hospitals. He was still able to find jobs as a hospital doctor in South Dakota, New York, Zimbabwe, Zambia, and Saudi Arabia.'

Despite the preponderance of evidence against this physician, it demonstrates how difficult it is to muster the courage to fire someone, particularly a doctor. Euphemistically referred to as the 'disruptive physician', these rogues have a facility for getting along in life and in their profession by cheating, deceiving and taking advantage of people. Their behaviors include dishonesty, intentionally harming a patient, sexual harassment, altering research data and substance abuse. For years, a code of silence has protected rogue doctors by those who educate, train and supervise them in the delivery of healthcare, leading some to suggest that the ability of rogue doctors to go unchecked is a failure of the medical profession to police its own. Others imply that the increasingly competitive nature of healthcare and a lack of effective government control of Medicare and Medicaid disbursements may have created a culture of fraud and deception within the healthcare industry.

People expect doctors to be like Cesar's wife – above suspicion – even though they are probably no more ethical or unethical than society at large. Because of this halo effect, it is easy to see how a doctor who has a taste for mischief can satisfy that need. They have wealth and can afford to indulge themselves. Because they are the most respected professionals in this country, they are more likely to be excused for indiscretions by their constituencies. Relatively speaking, there are fewer consequences for bad behavior. Also, doctors tend to be brighter than most. This gives them the ability to charm, rationalize, intimidate, or otherwise manipulate others to forgive their foibles. Failing at wit, doctors have the mobility to change jobs and leave their pasts behind, or to move from job to job indefinitely as their unethical behavior resurfaces in each new healthcare organization.

We define rogue doctor as a practicing doctor or a person in training to practice medicine whose behavior consistently conflicts with what a reasonable person would expect from a doctor. The behavior can run the gamut from excessive personality conflicts to murdering a patient. Rogues can be found in every occupation in the work place, from garbage collector to President of the United States. An organization's best defense against rogues is to move them out of the organization quickly. Rogues do not change and they can do great harm, particularly in healthcare settings.

There are rogues in all professions. And historically, in many professions, people have been relatively immune from the consequences of their behavior – priests, lawyers, ministers, doctors and politicians. We suspect that until recently, rogue doctors were not confronted directly and booted out of the profession or their place of work. Instead, there was a code of silence that protected doctors who were either marginally competent or whose behavior took them outside the mainstream of medical ethics. Rather than dealing directly with these doctors, they were allowed to migrate from place to place in the hope that they would eventually acquire the requisite skills and/or professional ethics. We suspect this miracle rarely occurred.

Over the last 20 years, the legal environment in healthcare has changed radically, so much so, that any healthcare organization that would knowingly suffer an incompetent or rogue doctor on its staff, or did not disclose to a subsequent employer that the doctor was a threat to patient care is in serious legal jeopardy today. A residual tendency in some organizations is to protect doctors to the detriment of patients. While there may have been a code of silence for many years, it is impossible to remain silent any longer.

We offer a relatively simple, legally defensible protocol to remove rogue doctors, or other problem healthcare professionals or employees from organizations. In fact, the procedures we describe here have worked well in a variety of industries. As an arbitrator (S.M.C.) who frequently hears disciplinary cases and a human resource management professional who has managed and defended disciplinary actions for years, we find that the concepts and models followed by labor arbitrators are the simplest to understand and administer, and the easiest to defend. Although our suggestions flow from a management versus union perspective, the rules are all the same whether defending an action taken against a union or non-union employee, or an employee, on the lowest rung or the highest rung of the organization. Using labor arbitration contexts is the best way to understand how to fire an employee and keep him or her fired.

Fear of firing

Our reluctance to fire people can probably be explained in any number of anthropological, economic, psychological and legal frameworks that cannot be covered in detail here. It certainly is not the custom to report or fire doctors. According to a Health and Human Services report and contrary to federal law, 75% of all hospitals in the US never report adverse actions against doctors. There are several practical reasons why managers hesitate to fire employees. One is a lack of support – many managers do not fire employees because they fear that higher management will not support their decisions. Another is guilt. Some managers feel that before they became managers, they committed the same violations as their employees. Then there is the loss of friendship. Managers who allow themselves to become too friendly with employees may fear losing those friendships if any form of discipline is used. Also, there is the loss of productivity. Discipline, when applied properly, requires considerable time and effort. Last and most importantly with physicians is the fear of lawsuits. Managers are increasingly concerned about being sued for disciplining someone, particularly for taking the ultimate disciplinary step of dismissal.

If the healthcare industry is remiss in cleaning up the act of the few rogue doctors that cause the problems, the political sector will. Many people are calling for a more stringent federal data bank to monitor incompetent and criminal doctors. Established in the 1980s, the federal data bank has been an abject failure. More stringent federal control is unsettling to many in the healthcare field. The American Medical Association and its allies view federal control as the first step toward regulation of the profession by non-doctors.

In addition to the various fears of firing, we should add that a lack of know-how has a chilling effect on taking any form of disciplinary action. We find that most managers simply do not know how to fire an employee. This is particularly the case in healthcare settings where, until recently, there was no pressing competitive or economic need to remove employees who were not meeting standards of performance. We believe that the following sections provide a framework for giving managers the skills to take disciplinary action.

The protocol

The structure and the concepts within which an organization can move a rogue doctor out of the organization are most important. In reality, the structure and concepts hold great promise for improving the performance of *all* doctors in an organization. One reason is that it gives the doctors a clear understanding of what the organization expects. Due to their needs for achievement and professional socialization, doctors, maybe more so than other professionals, require feedback on what is expected and how well they are doing. They also need to be reassured that they are valued. An additional benefit of the structure is that the average or marginally performing doctor will improve or leave the organization since there are consequences related to the failure to meet expectations. There seems to be little question that the healthcare industry has a significant problem with marginally competent doctors and other healthcare professionals. In November 1999, the Institute of Medicine reported that medical errors kill up to 98 000 people a year.

Performance management system

A performance management system is a process used to identify, measure, evaluate, improve and reward employee performance. These systems are found in most organizations although many do a rather poor job of administering them. When performance management systems fail, it is usually attributed to a lack of upper-level management commitment. In practice, the performance management system charts the key expectations of the employees and appraises them periodically. From the appraisal, flow rewards and consequences. Here is where we depart from traditional systems. Rather than traditional rewards and consequences associated with appraisals – pay increase or no pay increase – we propose that the rewards and consequences in healthcare settings should derive their inspiration from the doctors' needs. Most managers are already familiar with how traditional performance management policies, procedures and paperwork operate. Here are our suggestions for how a performance management system would operate for doctors.

The performance management system is specific to doctors

Many organizations, because they value consistent treatment of the staff, opt for a 'one size fits all' policy and procedure for appraising performance. This does not work well with the medical staff – doctors *are* different. Just ask the staff of any healthcare organization. In addition, we are sure that most doctors would confirm and relish their unique status in healthcare settings. A performance management system for doctors should appeal to a high level of intellect. Expectations should make sense. Many appraisal systems do not make a lot of sense because they are based on expectations that are supported by traditions rather than measurable logic.

Then, there are the values of doctors. There is some evidence that doctors, more so than other professionals, have a certain set of identifiable needs. These values include a need for:

- Autonomy in medical decision-making

- The accumulation of wealth – a return on their investment in lengthy education and training

- A work location, usually urban, in close proximity to professional opportunities and quality-of-life conveniences

- Significant leisure time

- An absence of managerial intrusions in their decision-making

- Achievement

- Professional socialization

Doctors will be motivated to conform to organizational expectations with a performance management system that relies on rewards and consequences related to *their* values. Intuitively, if a doctor can fulfill most of his/her needs in the workplace, the organization should benefit by having a doctor who is motivated to meet expectations and will be loyal to the organization. On the other hand, if those needs are blocked by the organization due to a rogue doctor's failure to meet expectations, the organization can expect one of three *positive* outcomes. The doctor will either conform to expectations, leave the organization, or the organization will be in a strong position to fire him.

How does an organization link rogue behavior to consequences? Here are a few examples:

- We need teamwork here. If you continue to work in conflict with the staff I will have no choice but to exclude from you our team-based decision-making. And as your manager, I will have to closely supervise your work and limit your freedom to make decisions independently

- I have to be honest with you, the quality of your work makes me wonder if you will ever attain the skill level required to get a reasonable return on the money you have spent on your education and training

- I worry that at the rate you are going with your lack of profession-alism, we may have to dismiss you. And that will not be good for you or your family. Here you enjoy an urban setting that offers the best quality of life and professional network you could ask for

- The staff and I are really concerned about your propensity for being behind in your patient care and paperwork. We are taking up the slack. I'm afraid if there is not a turnaround soon I will have to ask you to give up some of your leisure time that you spend on the links and on your boat

- This is the third time we have discussed your frequent absences. The rest of us have to do your work when you are not here. Aren't you concerned about your lack of achievement as a phys-ician? Aren't you worried that the staff will build a wall around you to the extent that you will have no relationship or professional socialization with them?

This sounds cruel and unusual. However, when dealing with a rogue who has been taking advantage of people and hurting them for years, the only way to get his attention is to keep the pressure on. As men-tioned above, most of the rogues know that they do not have the wherewithal to change. And the majority will leave before dismissal. It will be a pleasure to fire those who do not. You will be fed up with them by then, and will have a bullet-proof case against them.

The performance management system is mission driven and captures the qualities that the healthcare organization and its stakeholders traditionally expect of doctors

It is important to communicate how the system supports the mission of the healthcare organization. Here is an example of a mission state-ment:

> 'The mission of the performance management system is to ensure that the medical staff is competent with respect to the knowledge, skills and abilities necessary to provide good healthcare, and that they demonstrate personal, professional and organizational integrity and behavior in the delivery of that healthcare.'

This mission statement captures the two realms of expectations for all employees. That is, the *performance* and the *behavioral* realms (see Chapter 4 – It's not a plan without a business plan). There is an easy way to understand the difference. If a doctor's work can be measured in terms of quantity and/or quality, it fits within the *performance* realm. Any other aspect of one's work is *behavioral*. Most of the rogue's problems are in the behavioral realm and can be categorized in many ways. We group behavioral problems as:

(1) *Low social intelligence* The doctor is not aware of the impact he/she has on others and behaves in a way that offends or puzzles patients or co-workers to the extent that they question his competence.

(2) *Poor work habits* The doctor either does not understand or chooses to ignore the traditional expectations in the workplace, for example, strolling in late for rounds, excessive absenteeism, not responding to an emergency room page, not fully prepared for surgery – has not done the homework needed for the case at hand.

(3) *Counter-productive personality traits* Personality traits that make patients and co-workers uncomfortable to the point that it negatively impacts on the doctor's credibility. For example, talking too much or too little, egocentric (what's in it for me?) rather than patient-centered (what's in it for them?), too laid back – no sense of urgency, perfectionist in all things rather than in the important things, low energy level, poor judgement, emotions that run amuck, overly argumentative, etc.

(4) *Neurotic tendencies* The doctor displays exaggerated ego defenses. For example, excessive rationalization and intellectualizations for mistakes, obsessive–compulsive to the extent that very little gets done, ruled by emotions rather than intellect, and extremely immature.

(5) *Pathological behavior* The doctor is losing his/her grip on reality. For example, substance abuse, erratic behavior, paranoia, sociopathic tendencies, problems with the police, etc.

(6) *Character (ethical) flaws* The doctor seems to have no moral compass. For example, lying, cheating, stealing, and a propensity to lie about or misrepresent situations – saying the patient was taken care of when, in fact, the patient was not treated in accordance with established protocols.

The performance management system is easy to understand and administer

Most systems are hopelessly time consuming and bureaucratic. There is no reason why the document of appraisal should be more than one page; it should take no more than 15 minutes to prepare and 15 minutes to administer. As mentioned above, doctors want feedback. It is part of their needs system. The appraisal should be done three to four times a year for these types of professionals. The appraisal setting should be private. The appraisal should strive to make the average and above-average performers comfortable. They need to be reminded of rewards for good work. The rogues should not be made to feel comfortable. They must be reminded of the consequences associated with their behavior.

Disciplinary action

Healthcare organizations need a framework for disciplinary action for doctors that will either require them to conform to standards or will serve as a legally defensible vehicle to discharge them. Traditional disciplinary action in the workplace is progressive. Progressive discipline is a systematic way of dealing with unacceptable employee performance or behavior over time by increasing the severity of penalties. The expected result of progressive discipline is that the employee will recognize he has engaged in unacceptable performance or conduct and will correct his future behavior. Progressive discipline has its origins in 20th century unionized industrial settings where labor arbitrators needed a framework for deciding if management had just cause to discipline union members. Progressive discipline for minor offenses, e.g. tardiness, takes the form of a verbal reprimand, a written reprimand, one or two suspensions without pay and discharge. For serious offenses, progressive discipline is usually accelerated to suspensions without pay (e.g. for insubordination) or discharge (e.g. for theft). If done properly, progressive discipline is defensible in court or other third-party situations such as arbitration.

The problem is that while traditional progressive discipline is effective in blue-collar applications, it does not always fit well with correcting the behaviors of higher-level managers and professionals. The major problem is the suspension without pay. Having a key surgeon off on a 2-week suspension for excessive absenteeism may hurt the hospital more than the surgeon. What is more, a suspension without pay is embarrassing and unlikely to foster a good working relationship afterwards.

Discipline without punishment is an attempt to address some of the problems of progressive discipline while ensuring that the process is still legally defensible. Discipline without punishment is a much-studied alternative to traditional disciplinary models. Of all the forms of progressive discipline the following protocol seems most appropriate for correcting behavior of doctors or working them out of the healthcare organization.

- Issue a verbal reprimand and get the doctor to agree to solve the problem. Tell the doctor what happens at the next step if he/she does not solve the problem. Arrange for another meeting within 1 or 2 weeks to check on the doctor's progress in solving the problem

- Should another incident arise within 6 weeks, issue the doctor a formal written reminder, a copy of which is placed in the doctor's personnel or credentials file. Get the doctor to agree to solve the problem. Tell the doctor what happens at the next step if he does not solve the problem. Arrange for another meeting within 1 or 2 weeks to check on the doctor's progress in solving the problem

- Give a paid, 1-day decision-making leave. If another incident occurs after the written warning in the next 6 weeks or so, the doctor is told to take a 1-day leave with pay to stay at home and consider whether or not the job is right for him/her and whether he/she wants to conform to the organization's expectations. When the doctor returns to work, he/she articulates his decision. If the physician decides he/she does not or cannot meet expectations, he/she is given a choice to resign or to be discharged. If resignation is opted for, then prepare the resignation letter immediately. If he/she refuses, them immediately dismiss the physician. If he/she decides to meet expectations, he/she must compose and sign an action plan detailing how he/she will solve the problem. Tell the doctor what happens at the next step if he/she does not solve the problem. Arrange for another meeting within 1 or 2 weeks to check on the doctor's progress with his/her action plan to solve his problem

- If the behavior persists within 6 months, the doctor is given a choice to resign or to be discharged. If they opt for resignation, have him/her prepare the resignation letter immediately. If they refuse, then dismiss them

Common sense, due process, and just cause

The burgeoning and dynamic legal environment of human resource management has had a number of effects on employee relations. One is that it has provided legal protection for those groups who have been the historic victims of employment discrimination. Another is an unintended effect, that is, the proliferation and ever-changing city, county, state, and federal civil rights laws that have had a chilling effect on taking disciplinary action against *any* employee, regardless of whether the employee is protected by civil rights laws or not.

The laws have become Byzantine to the extent that even if a person attained a clear vision of the fabric of the employment-related legal environment in the US, it soon becomes cloudy because there are changes almost daily. The number of new laws being adopted and the way current laws are interpreted by the courts, makes it virtually impossible to keep one's knowledge in this area up-to-date. At best, the human resource (HR) managers, who are the in-house employment legal specialists in organizations, know a few of the obvious specifics but only know in a general way how the total legal environment works. Most managers get lost in this legal labyrinth.

Here are the two main effects on local levels of the work environment. Many employers have become virtually paralyzed when it comes to taking disciplinary action against employees. And many employees believe that their 'rights' keep them immune from disciplinary action.

As to the legal environment – forget it. All that is required to rid organizations of rogue employees is a little common sense and knowledge of two simple concepts – due process and just cause.

Common sense

When discussing failures to meet expectations, keep it simple and stick to job-related facts. Do not offer theories about why employees are incompetent or out of the mainstream of expected behavior. For example:

- Your number of patient complaints exceeds the average

- You take more time to do procedure A than the other doctors

- When you fail to show up for staff meetings it shows an insensitivity to our mission

Do not undermine job-related problems with theories that open up suspicion of bias:

- Your number of patient complaints exceeds the average. Maybe you just don't understand how people are around here

- You take more time to do procedure A than the other doctors. This procedure is usually more difficult for women due to their lack of strength

- When you fail to show up for staff meetings it indicates insensitivity to our mission. Maybe you should increase the time you spend in psychotherapy

As viewed by arbitrators and HR professionals, the only theory that management can propose that will wash if a disciplinary action is challenged is that the employee knew what was expected but did not meet expectations because he either could not or would not. It has nothing to do with anything else – personality, color, creed, gender, religion, stress, psychosis, the work of Satan, *ad infinitum*.

Here is an example of the complexities of the legal environment and how straying from the 'not meeting expectations' approach can trap one. A communications manager was stunned when her employer fired her. She was floored to hear the reason – the employer was just trying to take some of the stress off her. In addition to holding down a labor-intensive, full-time job, the manager was taking care of her chronically ill husband and aged mother. Few people realize that the Americans with Disabilities Act prevents bias against people simply because they are associated with a disabled person as a caregiver, family member or friend.

When one considers the pressure of the manager's job coupled with the pressures of caring for her husband and mother, it is safe to say that, physically and emotionally, she was probably running on empty. And it is reasonable to assume that anyone in this position would be somewhat irritable at work, would require more time off, and that 'things would fall through the cracks' with respect to work duties. If that were the case, instead of dealing directly with those issues, the employer lied when the truth was better. The 'we are doing this in your best interests' is sure to embarrass, enrage or insult an employee's intelligence, and, as a consequence, it may motivate the employee to take legal action against the employer.

Had the employer stuck with the facts, their position would have been easier to defend if challenged. Instead they opened up a legal can of worms by suggesting that her problems were related to the stress associated with caregiving. Although it would have been cold blooded to fire her knowing that she was under a great deal of pressure like this, the firing may not have kindled legal action against the employer had they dealt exclusively with the job-related issues.

Due process

Due process means that an employee has been confronted with evidence indicating he/she does not meet expectations, that he/she is given adequate time to prepare for their defense by presenting evidence and witnesses on their behalf, and that they are given an opportunity to face their accusers. Strange as it sounds, in the past it was not uncommon for employers to fire employees over the phone, by letter or by the guard at the gate. And, in fact, there is no federal law that requires employers to give employees due process. However, it shows good faith when disciplinary action is challenged. Arbitrators tend not to support disciplinary action in absence of due process.

And, due process is simple – confront the employee with the facts, give them an opportunity to tell their side of the story, allow them to confront their accusers if they so desire, consider and respond to their point of view, and assuming that he/she offers no evidence to undue the accusation against them, proceed with disciplinary action.

Just cause

The concept of just cause asks a simple question: 'Did the employer have just cause to take disciplinary action against the employee?' Listed below are the tests of just cause. These tests represent the most specifically articulated analysis of the just cause standard as well as an extremely practical approach. Managers in healthcare settings need to 'pass' each of these steps before firing a doctor.

- *Notice* Did the employer give the employee forewarning of the consequences of not meeting expectations?

- *Reasonable rules and orders* Were the employer's expectations reasonably related to the orderly, efficient, and safe operation of the employer's business, and the performance that the employer might properly expect of the employee?

- *Investigation* Did the employer, before administering the discipline to an employee, make an effort to discover whether the employee did in fact fail to meet expectations? Healthcare organizations are not noted for their ability to investigate misconduct.

- *Fair investigation* Was the employer's investigation conducted fairly and objectively?

- *Proof of misconduct* Did the employer have evidence or proof that the employee did not meet expectations?

- *Equal treatment* Has the employer applied its rules, orders, and penalties even-handedly and without discrimination to all employees?

- *Penalty* Was the degree of discipline administered by the employer reasonably related to the seriousness of the employee's offense and the work record of the employee in his services with the employer?

Documentation

Most of us do a lousy job of documenting a case against a rogue. Here is what works: document and detail the truth on the appraisal form for the performance management system. There will not be many negative things to record on the doctors, maybe nothing, but the appraisal form on the rogue should read like a rap sheet.

Have a good, bad and ugly (GBU) folder on all doctors. Document any statement made about performance or behavior. On any piece of paper handy, make a note of the date and the time, the person's name, the statement made, and sign it. Ask the person who made the statement to make a note of their comments. If they agree, ask them to put it in writing. If the statement was bad or ugly, tell a manager you trust about the incident. Make a note of that conversation. Drop all notes in the GBU folder. All of this takes 15 minutes or less.

If the statement was good, give an 'attaboy' to the doctor. If the comment was bad or ugly, act on it quickly. Have a 'prayer meeting' with the employee and follow the script below.

Administering discipline

The following section provides an outline for communicating to a doctor who does not meet expectations. This protocol meets all the requirements of due process, just cause and good documentation. In short, if done correctly, any disciplinary action taken in the following manner should be legally defensible.

This action is taken when all else fails to get the doctor to conform to expectations. At this stage, the manager is not too optimistic and suspects that it is best for the doctor to move on. Three points need to be clearly communicated to the doctor:

- The doctor's performance and/or behavior is detrimental to the mission of the organization

- The doctor must improve immediately

- If the doctor does not meet expectations there will be disciplinary consequences

The manager should prepare – have a written script – and stick to it since most doctors will naturally try to get the manager off track with excuses, blame-games, etc. The setting for the protocol should be private. The demeanor of the manager should be positive and friendly yet concerned about the doctor's commitment. Copious note taking is required – it will be part of the documentation package.

The initial meeting

The manager needs to control the meeting and stay on track. This should take anywhere from 15 to 30 minutes. Anything beyond 30 minutes undermines the impact of the meeting and allows the doctor to take control. Typically, after 30 minutes, the doctor leaves thinking that all is forgiven. Here is the script the manager has prepared and uses to communicate to the doctor and record notes.

- Tell the doctor the specifics of what expectations are not being met. Give dates, times, people involved, and where the event(s) occurred

- Explain how the doctor's performance or behavior undermines the mission of the organization

- Ask the doctor for an explanation. This is due process. Take notes. Follow-up on anything that may require more investigation

- Tell the doctor that he/she must improve immediately otherwise disciplinary action may be required

- Tell the doctor to prepare a written action plan and have it for you the following morning

- Set a date to meet again to check the doctor's progress. Two to four weeks is optimal, sooner if the problems are of a serious nature, and immediately in the event of a re-occurrence

- Review notes, amend as required, date and sign

The Progress report meeting

The ground rules here are the same as the initial meeting. At this stage, one of two outcomes are likely – success or failure. Each requires a different approach.

Success

This is not the end of the story. Managers have to keep the pressure on since rogues tend to play the 'how long do I have to be good before I can be bad again' game. Expect no miracles. Rogue behavior is complex and hard to modify.

- Review the previous meeting and acknowledge there has been improvement

- Express concerns about backsliding

- Have the doctor explain how he/she will maintain their level of improvement

- Again, explain the consequences of not meeting expectations – disciplinary action

- Set a date to meet again to check the doctor's progress. Four weeks is optimal

- Tell the doctor that these progress meetings will continue until you are fully satisfied that the doctor is committed to the mission of the organization

- Review notes, amend as required, date and sign

Failure

The doctor has not made sufficient progress.

- Review the previous meeting and indicate that sufficient progress has not been made. Detail the specifics of re-occurring or new problems

- Ask the doctor for an explanation. Again take notes and follow-up on anything that may require further investigation

- Express concern that the doctor may not have the commitment to meet the mission of the organization and that he may be better off in another organization. (Note: do not miss an opportunity to accept a resignation at this point. If it is offered, have the doctor prepare and sign a letter of resignation in your office. Long hand is acceptable.)

- Tell the doctor that he/she must improve immediately otherwise disciplinary action will be taken for any recurring or new problems

- Tell the doctor to prepare a written action plan and have it for you the following morning

- Once again, set a date to meet again to check the doctor's progress

- Review notes, amend as required, date and sign

Disciplinary action

The ground rules are the same as before.

- Have a representative of management at this meeting to collaborate the content

- Review the previous meeting and indicate that, since sufficient progress has not been made, you must take disciplinary action. In this case, a verbal reprimand

- Detail the specifics of re-occurring or new problems

- Ask the doctor for an explanation. Again take notes and follow-up on anything that may require further investigation

- Express concern that the doctor may not have the commitment to meet the mission of the organization and that he may be better off in another organization. Again, do not miss an opportunity to accept a resignation

- Tell the doctor that he/she must improve immediately otherwise additional disciplinary action will be taken

- Give the doctor a memo detailing with specifics of the verbal reprimand – cases of poor performance and/or behavior, time, dates, place and people involved

- Tell the doctor to prepare a written action plan and have it for you the following morning

- Once again, set a date to meet again to check the doctor's progress

- Review notes, amend as required, date and sign, have the management representative date and sign the notes

Subsequent disciplinary meetings

These meetings take the same track as the above disciplinary meeting with exceptions as noted below.

Decision-making leave When the doctor returns to work, he/she articulates their decision. If he/she decides they do not or cannot meet expectations, he/she is given a choice to resign or to be discharged. If the doctor opts for resignation, have him/her prepare the resignation letter immediately. If he/she refuses, dismiss him/her. If the doctor decides to meet expectations, he/she must compose and sign an action plan detailing how he/she will solve the problem. Consider a 'barrage' technique at this point borrowed from interventions with alcoholics to break the tough nuts. A group of colleagues focuses on how the doctor's behavior harms the mission of the organization. Here, the group attempts to overwhelm the doctor with concerns to force him out of denial and to conform to expectations.

Dismissal If the problems persist, the doctor is given a choice to resign or to be fired. If he/she opts for resignation, have them prepare the resignation letter immediately. If he/she refuses, dismiss them with a letter you have already prepared.

Many managers question the logic of decision-making leave and opportunities to resign. Looking at it from a legal and psychological point of view, it is the best method. The suspension with pay shows compassion, an absence of malice, and it is non-punitive – read no damages. Plus, there is the psychological and legal impact of the written commitment. Theoretically, the doctor should be more motivated to follow a plan of his/her own making. And from a legal perspective, it is the equivalent of a smoking gun. The doctor in effect documents that he/she had work-related problems.

Giving a doctor the opportunity to resign leaves him/her with some dignity. Here the manager opens a back door and lets the doctor make a break for it rather than emasculating him/herself. It is face saving. The doctor can explain it to family and friends in a way that goes down better. 'I got tired of their crap and quit' as opposed to 'They got tired of my crap and fired me'. Since there is less pain, there is less likelihood of retaliating. If there is retaliation in the form of a legal challenge, the opportunity to resign can be viewed as an absence of malice.

Bird-dogging rogues

Keep in mind, the rogue's proclivity to get along in life by cheating, deceiving, and taking advantage of people is not a new thing – he/she has been like this most, maybe all, of their life. And because of that, he/she has mastered the art of getting away with their treachery by manipulating others into believing one of two things – that he/she is going to clean up their act, or, that he/she is going to get even if anyone causes him/her harm. Both of these are con jobs.

Since the rogue is good at his/her game of manipulation, he/she knows every dodge in the book. He knows how to say the things that give others false hope about their ability to change. They also know the buzzwords of employee relations law well enough to play upon peoples' fears of lawsuits.

The organizations that are truly successful with rogue doctors are those that, like a bird dog, unrelentingly stay on his/her trail until they are flushed out and shot. Shot in this case means he/she was forced out of the organization by resigning or by being fired.

The rogue doctor as contractor

Thus far, our focus has been on doctors as 'employees' of healthcare organizations. Now we address doctors as 'contractors' for healthcare organizations. In general, there are two types of doctors as contractors. One is the doctor who contracts directly with a healthcare organization, for example, a hospital. The other is the doctor who contracts with a practice that in turn has an arrangement (contract) with a healthcare organization such as a hospital. In either scenario, the doctor admits patients and utilizes the hospital's resources. In return, the hospital profits from having its beds filled and its resources utilized.

Is there a difference with respect to handling a rogue doctor who is a contractor as opposed to handling a rogue doctor who is an employee? The answer is – not much. In fact, both are contractors in a sense. One has an implied contract, the other has an explicit contract, and either contract can be terminated if the employee/contractor does not live up to the terms of the bargain. But the devil is in the details, and the imperative detail is the difference in consequences.

From the perspective of the doctor as a contractor, the unkindest cut of all is action by the hospital that limits or suspends admitting privileges, but the *coup de grace* is action that may threaten the doctor's credentials. This is the central difference in handling the contractor versus handling the employee. For the employee and the contractor, everything is the same up to the point of taking disciplinary action – the healthcare organization communicates expectations, evaluates performance, communicates variances from expectations, and tells the doctor that immediate improvement is required. However, once that is done, instead of implementing the classic progressive discipline protocol, the healthcare organization cuts to the chase: 'Unless there is an immediate improvement in behavior/performance, we will move to limit or suspend your admitting privileges. What's more we may have to take credentialing action against you.'

It stands to reason that a statement like this will have one of two effects on a rogue doctor – immediate improvement or immediate departure. That is because, most doctors' livelihoods are directly related to 'good' credentials that allow them to admit and treat patients. As such, hospital credentials are among the most important of doctors' 'possessions'. Additionally, doctors know that any adverse actions on their credentials are reported to the National Data Bank.

Because of the adverse impact on a doctor's livelihood associated with action that can lead to a suspension of a doctor's license to practice, healthcare organizations should seek legal counsel before taking action. As in Louisiana, where a doctor's license was suspended, lawsuits associated with limiting or suspending a doctor's right to practice can hamstring a healthcare organization's energy and resources.

Suggested reading

Aberhold L, O'Keefe N, Burke DE. Critical care for review process. *Personnel J* 1996;April:115–20

Baldwin DC, Daugherty SR, Rowley BD. Unethical and unprofessional conduct observed by residents during their first year of training. *Acad Med* 1998;73:69–74

Brand N. *Discipline and Discharge in Arbitration*. Washington, DC: Bureau of National Affairs, 1998

Campbell D, *et al*. Discipline without punishment – at last. *Harvard Business Rev* 1995;July/August:162–78

Daugherty CR. *Labor Arbitration Reports, 46 LA 359, Enterprise Wire Co*. Washington, DC: Bureau of National Affairs, 1966

O'Connor SJ. Motivating effective performance. In Duncan J, Ginter PM, Swayne LE, eds. *Handbook of Health Care Management*. Malden, MA: Blackwell Publishers, 1998

Wilmshurst P. The code of silence. *Lancet* 1997;349:567–9

Coding Documentation and Compliance

14

Rhona Ferguson

In the ever-changing world of healthcare, the provider of service must now assume the primary responsibility of procedural coding, documentation of that service to support the billed code, and assurance that the entire process will be in compliance with federal and local carrier rules and regulations. Although most practices employ someone to assign a procedure code to the services provided, it is the provider of that service who is ultimately responsible for the code selection. If your practice is audited, you will not be able to claim that you do not do the coding, and are therefore not responsible for any errors. When a contract is signed with a third-party insurance carrier, it is the provider of service who has agreed to abide by the rules of that specific insurance carrier, not the ancillary staff.

Staff members who are assigned the responsibility of coding in a medical practice should be considered a back-up system, a means of checks and balances. They should be able to review the documentation, compare the documentation with the codes selected by the provider and report any discrepancies back to the provider. An open line of communication from the provider to the coder is critical for reimbursement purposes. The coder should be able to suggest alternative codes that may be more appropriate for the documented service, or recommend that additional information be added to the documentation to support the code. Addenda to progress notes, diagnostic procedure notes and operative reports are appropriate and accepted by third-party carriers as long as those additions are added prior to the submission of charges to the carrier. If an addendum is added after the charge has been submitted, the insurance carrier may become suspicious of the intention of the provider. This may result in a more critical review of any future submission, and possibly a request for an audit of the practice. Any additions should be identified as such, dated and signed by the provider. Do not try to squeeze this additional information into the existing documentation.

Ongoing meetings should occur between the staff responsible for reviewing carrier explanation of benefits, the office manager and the provider. It is important to keep abreast of how the various carriers are recognizing the combinations of codes submitted, those services that are being denied and why, and what has to occur in the practice to address these issues. It is helpful to develop charge forms specific to office visits, surgical procedures and diagnostic services. This will encourage uniformity, especially in a multipractitioner practice (Table 1).

The office encounter form or superbill should be reviewed periodically to remove deleted codes and to add new codes that are appropriate for services provided by the practice. It is advised that practices do not utilize preprinted lists of diagnosis codes that carriers have deemed to be appropriate to justify the medical necessity of certain procedures. This encourages the inappropriate use of diagnosis codes for the sole purpose of ensuring that the service will be covered. It also arouses suspicion at the carrier level, because it is highly unlikely that every patient undergoing a specific procedure at 'Dr Smith's' practice has the same diagnosis. To make matters even more suspicious, the diagnosis happens to be on the covered diagnosis list. If the insurance carrier requests documentation to support the submitted diagnosis, the documentation must be present or you may be subject to a more extensive investigation. When the carrier performs a 'site review' of the practice, their suspicions will be confirmed when they note the preprinted lists of acceptable diagnosis codes taped on the wall.

Carriers consider services billed but not documented to be services that did not occur. It does not matter that a witness can attest to the fact that they personally observed the service being performed, or that it is part of a routine that is always performed without exception. If it is not documented, it did not happen. The same can be said for services that may be documented but, owing to sloppy or illegible handwriting, cannot be read. It did not happen! In years gone by, every attempt would be made to decipher poor penmanship, but that is a thing of the past because of the number of practices that are being reviewed: so many audits, so little time!

Table 1 Encounter form

PATIENT			DIAGNOSIS:		
Date of service					
1. OFFICE SERVICE	CPT	Modifier	**3. PROCEDURE**	OPT	Modifier
☐ New prob. focused	99201		☐ Impact serumen	69210	
☐ New exp. prob. focused	99202		☐ Breathing treatment	94650	
☐ New detailed	99203		☐ Nail removal perm.	11750	
☐ New comprehensive	99204		☐ Nail removal partial	11765	
☐ New comprehensive	99205		☐ Vasectomy	55250	
☐ Estab. minimal	99211		☐ Small joint inj.	20600	
☐ Estab. prob. focused	99212		☐ Intermed. joint inj.	20605	
☐ Estab. exp. prob. focused	99213		☐ Major joint inj.	20610	
☐ Estab. detailed	99214		☐ I&D abscess	10060	
☐ Estab. comprehensive	99215		☐ Rem. foreign body	10120	
☐ Consulation prob. foc.	99241		☐ Exc. benign lesion	11400	
☐ Consultation exp. prob. foc.	99242		☐ Simple repair lac.	12001	
☐ Consutation detailed	99243		☐ Inter. repair lac.	12031	
☐ Consultation comprehensive	99244		☐ Destr. 1 lesion	17000	
☐ Consultation comprehensive	99245		☐ Misc. surg proc.		
2. SUPPLIES					
☐ Ace bandage	A4660				
☐ Splint	A4570		John Smith, MD, PC		
☐ Suture tray	A4550		Family Practice 201 Kennywood Drive Anytown, USA Telephone 111-222-3333		
☐ Misc. supplies					

CPT, current procedural terminology; I&D, incision and drainage

Progress notes and operative reports

Each entry into the progress note, all operative reports and diagnostic procedural notes should identify the date of entry and the legible identity of the provider. Although a signature is not required to prove identity, it is advisable. The Health Care Financing Administration (HCFA) states that the absence of a signature will be looked upon unfavorably in an audit situation. Each page of the progress note should also identify the name of the patient and/or the patient's medical record number.

Each practice should be able to provide a list of each physician's signature and a list of 'home-grown' acronyms utilized within the practice. The absence of these lists may provide an auditor with justification to deny services based on the inability to decipher the record.

Health insurance claim forms

The most cost-effective method of claims submission is the submission of a 'clean' claim.

A 'clean' claim

- Has no coding errors, missing or inaccurate information
- Does not have to be reviewed by one or several different departments within the health insurance department
- Only 33% of all insurance claims submitted are clean claims

Many of the basic procedural coding concepts, necessary for clean claim submission, can be found within the *CPT Manual*. Information specific to each type of current procedural terminology (CPT) code can be found in the introduction to that section and throughout the subsections of the manual. Reviewing all of the instructions found in CPT will take several hours. If this review results in increased practice revenue and avoidance of a carrier audit, it will be time well spent. Keep in mind that the guidelines in CPT are just that: they are guidelines. This means that health insurance carriers can develop their own set of internal guidelines or policies, and do not have to adhere to those listed in CPT. If you follow the guidelines, as suggested in CPT, you will be using correct coding guidelines. Although the claim may still be adjudicated based on the carrier rules, it will not be viewed with suspicion.

Each major division in the *CPT Manual* represents a specific specialty. Coding from CPT does not have to be limited by the specialty that you practice. If you specialize in orthopedics and have performed a service that can be identified in the 'Integumentary' section of CPT, use the most appropriate code from the 'Integumentary' section. This is true for all specialties. Critical-care services are one set of codes frequently underutilized because practitioners believe that these codes are limited to critical-care specialists. If the patient meets the criteria for critical care, and the practitioner meets the criteria described prior to that set of codes, then the critical-care codes are appropriate. Do not forget to document the time involved in this service.

Evaluation and management services

Some procedure codes have a specific time element identified; this time element can be found after the semicolon in the description. The description usually reads 'first hour' or 'each additional 30 minutes'. If these codes are selected, the length of time involved in the care of the patient must be documented. If your documentation does not reflect this time, the service will be denied for lack of supporting documentation. In these specific codes, time is the only factor that differentiates the different levels of that particular set of codes. This time element is not to be confused with the average length of an evaluation and management (E&M) service.

Every E&M code, except the emergency department codes, describes the length of time that the physician 'typically' spends with the patient. Many practices erroneously select the level of E&M service based on the typical time mentioned in each code. The key components that determine the level of E&M service are history, examination and decision-making. Time is not a key component in the selection of E&M codes in the majority of circumstances. There are situations, however, when time does become key, and then the typical time described is the determining factor for the selection of the level of code.

When more than half of the visit is spent counseling the patient or co-ordinating the care of the patient with another healthcare provider, the typical time described in the visit code becomes the key determining factor in the selection of the E&M code. It is important to remember that the time spent in these cases is the physician's face-to-face time with the patient and/or family in the office setting. Ancillary staff time spent with the patient cannot be factored into these codes. For hospital visits the time is described as floor time or unit time. This is the time that the physician spends with the patient, writing on the patient's chart, reviewing any diagnostic reports, and communicating with staff and family about the patient.

Documentation, when time is the key component, must include the total length of the visit in addition to the amount of time spent in counseling or co-ordination of care, to prove that 50% or more of the total time requirement has been met. Documenting time does not have to be exact; it can be an estimation of time spent with the patient. A description of the type of counseling or co-ordination of care must also be documented. This instruction on key components can be found in the introductory section of 'Evaluation and management codes' found in the *CPT Manual*.

There will be some instances when the provider will have to decide if the selection of the level of E&M service should be based on history, examination and decision-making, or on the counseling and co-ordination of care. All three key components may justify choosing the level as well as the time spent counseling or co-ordinating the patient's care. This may happen in a complex case and is an option that is left to the discretion of the practitioner.

When selecting the E&M code based on the three key components of history, examination and decision-making, it is important to remember that the documentation has to support the level of service chosen. New patients, initial hospital visits and consultations all require that some level of history, examination and decision-making be documented. Documentation for established patients requires only two of the three key components. Which key components are chosen is dependent upon the situation and the condition of the patient. If the patient's condition is known from previous visits, and there is no justifiable reason to repeat a history, then the examination and decision-making components should be all that it is medically necessary to document. The same can be said if the course of treatment remains the same, then an interim history and examination would be all that is medically necessary.

History

Every entry must contain the presenting problem or chief complaint. The history includes the history of the present illness, a review of systems, and past medical, family and social history (Table 2). The development of the presenting problem from onset to the present is the history of present illness. An inventory of body systems obtained through questioning the patient is the review of systems. This inventory identifies signs or symptoms which the patient may be experiencing or has experienced. It helps to define the problem, clarify the differential diagnoses and identify testing needed, or serves as baseline data on other systems that might be affected by any possible management options. Review of systems is the most often overlooked history element in regard to documentation. The patient's personal medical history (the patient's past experiences with illnesses, operations, injuries and treatments), family medical history (a review of medical events in the patient's family, including diseases which may be hereditary or place the patient at risk) and age-appropriate review of patient's personal social history are included.

Table 2 History form

		Prob. foc.	Exp. prob. foc.	Detailed	Complete
H	**HPI (history of present illness)** ☐ Location ☐ Severity ☐ Timing ☐ Modifying factors ☐ Quality ☐ Duration ☐ Context ☐ Assoc. signs & symptoms	Brief (1–3)	Brief (1–3)	Extended (4 or more)	Extended (4 or more)
I S T O	**ROS (review of systems)** ☐ Constitutional ☐ Card/vasc. Resp. ☐ Muscle ☐ Endo. ☐ Eyes ☐ Integ. Near ☐ Hem/lymph. All/immuno. ☐ Ears, nose throat, mouth ☐ GI GU ☐ Psych. ☐ All others neg.	None	Prob. pert. (1 syst)	Extended (2–9 syst.)	Complete (10 or more)
R Y	**PFSH (past medical, family, social history)** ☐ Past history (the patient's past experience with illnesses, operations, injuries and treatments) ☐ Family history (a review of medical events in the patient's family, including diseases which may be hereditary or place patient at risk ☐ Social history (age-approp. review of past and current events	None	None	Pertinent (1 hx area)	Complete (2 or 3 hx areas)

The history does not need to be repeated at every visit, but can be referred to if indicated. When a reference is made to a previously recorded history, documentation must include the location of that history in the patient's chart, and a comment about any pertinent elements, the description of any new information or the notation that there has been no change in the information. If the condition of the patient does not necessitate a review of a previously obtained history, the history should be omitted.

Elements of the review of systems and past medical, family and social history may be documented by ancillary staff or contained in a patient information sheet completed by the patient. The practitioner must document that the information was reviewed, and revise or confirm the information recorded by others. The history of the present illness must be obtained by the practitioner and may not be obtained by ancillary staff. If the patient's condition prohibits the examiner from obtaining a history, the service qualifies as a comprehensive history if the circumstances are documented.

Examination

The examination can be documented at four different levels. A limited examination can be performed that focuses strictly upon the affected system or area. The second-level examination is expanded to include a limited examination of the affected system or area and other systems or areas. The third-level is a detailed examination of the affected system or area expanded to include a focused examination of other systems or areas. The fourth-level examination is a complete examination of the affected system and other symptomatic body areas or organs or a general multisystem examination.

Elements such as the patient's general appearance and a notation of vital signs are considered elements of the examination, and should be documented. Often overlooked, the documentation of these elements may justify a higher level of service. A comment on pertinent negative findings and why they are pertinent should be documented as well as the positive findings. The psychological state of the patient is also an element most often observed but missing from documentation (Table 3).

Table 3 Examination form

		Prob. foc.	Exp. prob. foc.	Detailed	Complete
EXAMINATION	**Body areas** ☐ Head, incl. face　☐ Chest incl. breast, axillae　☐ Abdomen Genitalia, groin, buttock　☐ Back incl. spine ☐ Neck　☐ Each extremity **Organ systems** ☐ Constitutional　☐ Ears, nose mouth, throat　☐ Resp.　☐ Skin ☐ Neuro Eyes　☐ Psych. ☐ Cardiovasc　☐ GI GU　☐ Musc. ☐ Hem/lymph./ immuno.	1 body area or system	Up to 7 systems	Up to 7 systems	8 or more systems

Decision-making

The medical decision-making process is the most often misunderstood and most difficult component to explain, of the three key components. The Federal Government, when reviewing documentation to support services, looks closely at documentation to support the thought processes of the provider. There are three categories contained within the decision-making component: uncertainty, data and risk. Only two categories need to be documented to qualify for a selected level.

Decision-making comprises the uncertainty of the prognosis, the amount of data that the practitioner must review or order, and the level of risk to the patient. Uncertainty refers to the uncertainty of the practitioner as to the outcome of the care. The number of diagnoses being managed, the complexity of establishing a diagnosis, the progress of the patient and the number of management options that need to be considered are all factored into the level of uncertainty.

Documentation in this area should include the progress of the patient. Has each condition stabilized, worsened, resolved or improved? The initiation of a new treatment, or a change in treatment, should be documented, and the reasoning behind the treatment. Referrals or consultations to request advice should be clearly documented as to the reason for the referral or consultation. If a diagnosis is not established, the assessment may be stated in the form of a differential diagnosis or as a 'possible', 'probable' or 'rule out' diagnosis.

For coding purposes, 'possible', 'probable' or 'rule out' cannot be used to select a diagnosis code. In the absence of a definitive diagnosis, the diagnosis code that describes the signs and/or symptoms should be selected. Because of advanced computerized record keeping, assigning a patient a suspected condition that may be ruled out at a later date can affect that patient's ability to acquire health and life insurance, and is difficult to remove. Your practice could be held legally responsible for the patient's insurance difficulties.

The amount and complexity of data to be reviewed refer to diagnostic tests ordered and the review of any information pertinent to the patient's condition. Any diagnostic test that is ordered or reviewed and the reasoning or thought processes behind the decision to order a test should be documented. A good habit to develop is to initial each lab report upon review. Information obtained from other sources such as old records, someone other than the patient, or the discussion of the patient with another healthcare provider should be noted. A notation of 'old records reviewed' or 'additional history obtained from family' without elaboration will not support a performed service. If old records were reviewed and their review was of no value, this should be documented.

The direct visualization or interpretation of an image, tracing or specimen previously or subsequently interpreted by another physician should be documented. This service is not separately billable as an interpretation, but does factor into the level of decision-making. Documentation should read 'films reviewed' or 'specimen reviewed' to indicate that the provider was not simply reading a report. Avoid using phrases such as 'X-ray shows' or 'scan indicates'; these indicate the review of a report as opposed to visualization of a diagnostic service.

Table 4 Assessment of risk

Number of diagnostis or treatment options			
A	B x C = D		
Problems to exam physician	Number	Points	Result
Self-limiting or minor (stable, improved or worsening)	max = 2	1	
est. prob. (to examiner); stable, improved		1	
est. prob. (to examiner); worsening		2	
new prob. (to examiner); no additional work-up planned	max = 1	3	
new prob. (to examiner); add. work-up planned		4	
		TOTAL	

Bring total to line A in final result for complexity

Amount and/or complexity of data to be reviewed

Data to be reviewed	Points
Review and/or order of clinical lab tests	1
Review and/or order of tests in the radiology sect. of CPT	1
Review and/or order of tests in the medicine sect. of CPT	1
Discussion of tests results with performing physician	1
Discussion to obtain old records and/or obtain history from someone other than patient	1
Review and summarization of old records and/or obtaining history from someone other than patient and/or discussion of case with another healthcare provider	2
Independent visualization of image, tracing or specimen itself (not simply review of report)	2
TOTAL	

Bring total to line C in final result for complexity

Final result for complexity

A	Number of diagnoses or management options	<1 Minimal	2 Limited	3 Multiple	>4 Extensive
B	Highest risk	Minimal	Low	Moderate	High
C	Amount and complexity of data	<1 Minimal or low	2 Limited	3 Moderate	>4 Extensive
Type of decision-making		Straight-forward	Low complexiity	Moderate complexity	High complexity

Level of risk	Presenting problems	Diagnostic proc(s) ordered	Management options selected
Min.	One self-limiting or minor prob., e.g. cold, insect bite	Lab tests/ven. CXR, ECG, EEG, UA, US	Rest, gargles, elastic bandages, superficial drugs
Low	Two or more self-limiting or minor problems One stable chronic illness Acute uncomplicated illness or injury	Physio. test not under str. Non-CV image w/o contrast Spfcl. ndl. bx Lab tests/art.	OTC drugs Minor surg. w/o id risk PT OT IVF w/o additives
Moderate	One or more chronic illnesses with mild exacerbation, progress or side-effects of treatment Two or more stable chronic illnesses Undx new prob. w. uncertain prognosis Acute illness w. syst. sympt. Acute complicated injury	Physio. test under stress Dx endoscop. Deep ndl. or incisional bx CV imaging w. contrast Obtain fluid from body cavity	Minor surg. with id risks Elective maj. surg. with no id risk factors Rx drug management Ther. nucl. med. IVF with additives Clsd. tx of fx or discl. w/o manipulation
High	One or more chronic illnesses with severe exacerbation, prog. or side-effect of treatment Acute or chronic illnesses or injuries that may pose a threat to life or bodily function status	C/V imaging w. contrast w. id risk factors Card. electrophysio-logical tests with id risk factor Discography	Elective maj. surg. with id risk factors Emergency maj. surg. Parenteral controlled substances Drug therapy requir. for toxicity Decision not to resuscitate or de-escalate care because of poor prognosis

CPT, current procedural terminology; undx., undiscovered; ven., venogram; CXR, chest X-ray; ECG, electrocardiogram; EEG, electroencephalogram; U/A, urinalysis; U/S, ultrasound; CV, cerebrovascular; art, arteriogram; Dx endoscop., diagnostic endoscopy; id, identification; card., cardiogram; OTC, over the counter; PT, physiotherapy; OT, occupational therapy; IVF, *in vitro* fertilization

The final element of decision-making is the risk component. This indicates the risk to the patient from their underlying disease process anticipated between the present encounter and the next, the assessment of risk involved in diagnostic procedures, and the risk during and immediately following any procedures or treatments (Table 4).

One of the determining factors that Medicare uses, when deciding which practices to audit, is the frequency of submission of the higher levels of E&M services. Higher levels are considered to be any level 4 or level 5 code. Data concerning the national average of submission of these higher levels of service specific to specialties are considered when a practice is targeted. If the specialty falls outside the national averages, an investigation or audit ensues.

Most practices should submit E&M codes that, when plotted out, result in a bell-shaped curve. The peak of the bell represents the majority of codes at levels 2 and 3, and the lower ends represent levels 1, 4 and 5. Some practices avoid the use of higher-level codes, preferring to code all services at a lower level of service, regardless of the complexity of the visit. The purpose of this practice is to avoid carrier scrutiny, but may have the opposite effect. It may trigger the insurance carrier to become suspicious of the practice. There should be a good mix of all levels of codes. Over-coding and under-coding should be avoided at all costs.

The process of learning how to select the correct level of service takes time to master, but will result in increased practice revenue. Repeated under-coding of an evaluation and management service by one level can result in a tremendous amount of lost revenue. Assume that all legitimate level 4 office visits are inappropriately coded at a level 3 office visit. The difference in reimbursement may be from $20 to $30 per visit, or an average of $25 per visit in lost revenue. Now, multiply that by 20 patients a day, times 5 days a week, times 52 weeks in the year. This is a total of $104 000 in lost charges per year, and only reflects one level of E&M service!

Some 'rules of thumb' for new and established services are shown below.

Some rules of thumb for new and established services

- New patients have not received any service from the physician or anyone else in the practice within the past 3 years

- When the provider leaves one practice and joins a new practice, or becomes a sole practitioner, any patient who follows the provider from the old practice can be billed as a new patient on the first visit

Hospital visit

An initial hospital visit may be used once per hospital admission, and only by the attending or admitting physician. All other physicians must use the appropriate subsequent hospital visit code or consultation code. Initial hospital consultations, when appropriate, may be used once per hospital admission, by each consultant. All services are considered outpatient services until the patient is admitted to the hospital.

When several evaluation and management services occur on the same day by the same practitioner, but in different settings, only one code should be billed. The type of service is determined by the setting that ended the encounter for the day. All of the elements during each encounter are factored or combined into the selection of the final level of service in that setting.

Consultation

Medicare changed the criteria for consultative services on 1 September 1999.

A service can be coded as a consultation if:

- It is provided by a physician whose opinion or advice regarding evaluation and/or management of a specific problem is requested by another physician or other appropriate source (unless it is a patient-generated confirmatory consultation)

- A request for a consultation from an appropriate source and the need for consultation is documented in the patient's medical record

- After the consultation is provided, the consultant prepares a written report of his/her findings, which is given to the referring physician

Payment may be made regardless of treatment initiation unless a transfer of care occurs. A transfer of care occurs when the referring physician transfers the responsibility for the patient's complete care to the receiving physician at the time of referral, and the receiving physician documents approval of care in advance. Transference of care, as described above, would rarely happen.

A physician in a group practice may request a consultation from another physician in the same group practice, as long as all of the requirements for use of the CPT consultation codes are met.

A request for a consultation must be documented in the patient's medical record. A written report must be furnished to the requesting physician.

A consultation may be billed for a new or established patient when a request for preoperative clearance has been made by a surgeon, as long as the criteria for consultations have been met.

Follow-up consultation codes are only appropriate in the inpatient setting. There are two situations when follow-up consultation codes can be used. A follow-up consultation code is appropriate when the criteria for a consultation have been met, and a second visit is required to complete the consultation. The consultant may have to obtain the results of ordered diagnostic tests, on a subsequent day, in order to develop an opinion and make a recommendation back to the requesting physician. A follow-up consultation is also appropriate when a consultation has occurred previously during the same hospital admission, and now the consultant is asked again for his or her opinion. This can be for the same condition that has not improved, or a new condition.

Second opinion

A confirmatory consultation code or second opinion is appropriate when the provider is asked to confirm a diagnosis, the appropriateness of recommended treatment or a surgical procedure. This can occur in any setting. When a consultation is initiated by a patient or family member, and not requested by another physician, the confirmatory consultation code would be appropriate to use.

Sick and well visit

It is appropriate to bill for both a sick visit and a well visit during the same encounter, whenever a problem is discovered during a routine examination. This may be a condition that is discovered by the practitioner during a routine examination, or a condition that the patient informs the examiner of during a routine examination. Because some health insurance policies do not recognize well visits or routine examinations as a covered service, the patient should be balance-billed for the well visit. This balance is not the total amount charged for the well visit, but is the difference between the provider's well visit fee and the sick visit fee. The co-payment, if applicable, is still collected during the office visit. The sick visit code should be submitted with a –25 modifier appended, which indicates a separately identifiable service. There should be a separate diagnosis code to identify the condition that justifies the sick visit code.

Preventive visit

Well visits or preventive visits are not problem oriented, therefore there is no chief complaint or history of present illness. The history contains a comprehensive system review and comprehensive or interval past medical, family and social history, as well as a comprehensive assessment/history of pertinent risk factors. Trivial or insignificant findings discovered during a well examination that do not require additional work and the performance of the key components of a problem-oriented E&M service are not reported separately.

When a patient is being seen for the first time for a well visit examination but has been seen previously for a problem-oriented examination, this first well examination is coded as a periodic preventive medicine evaluation, not as an initial preventive examination. All categories of initial visits must still meet the criteria of an initial visit before they qualify as such.

Modifiers

Modifiers are a useful tool to assist the provider in clarifying or defining circumstances that affect the description of the code. Modifiers are a two-digit qualifier appended to the end of an E&M code or any other procedure code and separated by a hyphen. There are certain modifiers that may increase the value of a service, allow for payment of a service when it would usually be denied or reduce the value of a service.

There are many modifiers used to describe various exceptions to the global package payment. Some are used with the E&M service codes, and others are used with the surgical procedure codes. All are indicated to alert the insurance carrier that the particular service is to be reimbursed separately and is not to be included in the payment for the surgical package. These modifiers are to be used by the physician who performed the surgical service. All other providers need not use these modifiers unless they are included in the global package reimbursement.

It is important to realize that, when reviewing a health insurance claim, the carrier often has to rely on the 1500 form alone, to justify the codes that are submitted. A 1500 form, for those who are not aware, is the claim form used to submit professional services. A UB92 form or a 1450 form is the claim form used to submit a facility bill.

When the carrier reviews a 1500 form, the provider needs to convey to the insurance carrier as much of the description of the encounter as possible with the use of procedure codes, modifiers and diagnosis codes. The provider needs to tell the carrier the complete story of what happened during the encounter, if at all possible, in the absence of documentation. There are some circumstances that do not permit the use of modifiers alone to support certain services. This necessitates the submission of documentation of those services.

Prior to 1999 each introductory section of the *CPT Manual* had a list of those modifiers that were appropriate for use within that specific section of codes. In the 1999 and subsequent *CPT Manuals* the modifiers have been removed from the introductory sections and are now contained in 'Appendix A'. The American Medical Association (AMA) has indicated that there was a misassumption concerning the limited use of modifiers, based on their appearance in these various sections of the manual, and that modifiers can be used in any section of CPT when appropriate. Individual insurance carriers may not agree with this new declaration concerning the use of modifiers.

It is important for the practitioner to become familiar with the different modifiers and how their use will affect reimbursement. Encounter forms or superbills should either have a space available to fill in the correct modifier, or a comment area that would allow the provider to describe the circumstances that can be expressed with the use of a modifier. Surgical charge slips should also contain an area that can be utilized in this same fashion. If the provider does not know the specific numeric selection for the specific modifier, he or she should at least know that a modifier does exist that better helps to describe the performed service.

Some important evaluation and management modifiers that may affect the global surgical period, thus affecting payment, are shown in Table 5.

Table 5 Evaluation and management (E&M) modifiers

Modifier	Description	Definition
–24	Unrelated E&M by same physician during post-operative period	When a physician provides a surgical service related to one problem, and then during the period of follow-up care for the surgery provides an E&M service unrelated to the problem requiring surgery
–25	Significant, separately identifiable E&M by same physician on same day as the procedure or other service	When a physician provides an E&M service that is above and beyond the other service provided on the same day, or beyond the usual preoperative and postoperative care associated with the procedure that was performed
–57	Decision for surgery	When an E&M service resuls in the initial decision to do surgery, usually within 24 hours of the performance of a surgical procedure

Surgical services

There are many modifiers used to describe various exceptions to the global package payment. Some are used with the E&M service codes, and others are used with the surgical procedure codes. All are indicated to alert the insurance carrier that the particular service is to be reimbursed separately and is not to be included in the payment for the surgical package. These modifiers are to be used by the physician who performed the surgical service. All other providers need not use these modifiers unless they are included in the global package reimbursement.

Surgical services are considered to be any service coded within the 10 000–60 000 series of CPT codes. Some of these services may not appear to be surgical in nature, such as fracture care and joint injection, but are held to the same coding principles as the more apparent surgical services.

Some important surgical service modifiers that may affect the global surgical period, thus affecting payment, are shown in Table 6.

Documentation guidelines for surgical services are similar to the documentation requirements of E&M services, in that the documentation must be complete, be legible and support the services that have

Table 6 Important surgical service modifiers that may affect the global surgical period

Modifier	Description	Definition
–22	Unusual procedural service	The service(s) provided is(are) greater than described in the most appropriate surgical procedure
–52	Reduced services	A procedure is partially reduced or eliminated at the physician's election
–58	Staged or related procedure by the same physician during the postoperative period	The physician performs a procedure that: (1) was planned prospectively at the time of the original procedure; or (2) is a more extensive procedure than the original procedure
–59	Distinct procedural service	The physician needs to indicate that a procedure or service is distinct or independent from other services performed on the same day
–62	Co-surgeon	Two surgeons (usually with different skills) may be required to perform the same surgical procedure
–76	Repeat procedure by same physician	An identical procedure is repeated by the same physician subsequent to the original procedure on the same day
–77	Repeat procedure by another physician	An identical procedure is repeated by another physician subsequent to the original procedure on the same day
–78	Return to the OR for a related procedure during the postoperative period	A procedure is performed during the postoperative period of the initial procedure, that is related to or a complication of the first procedure
–79	Unrelated procedure or service by the same physician during the postoperative period	When a procedure is performed during the postoperative period that is not related to the initial procedure

OR, operating room

been billed. Coding should be developed based upon the operative report, not the surgical charge slip. Often performed services are missed or billed when there is no supporting documentation in the operative note. There may also be circumstances when the provider does not submit certain procedures because he or she does not realize that the service is separately billable, but the documentation clearly supports the service.

The person performing the dictation must sign the transcribed procedural notes. A signature verifies that the content of the dictation is complete and correct. Any changes or corrections to the dictation should be noted, or an addendum may be written or dictated prior to billing of the services. Insurance carriers will view subsequent billing, based upon an addendum added after a claim has been submitted, with suspicion.

Signature stamps

Signature stamps may only be used when they are in the sole possession of the performing practitioner. Ancillary staff acting in the name of the practitioner may not use signature stamps. Attestation stamps are not acceptable proof of participation in a surgical service, since they do not provide information as to the detail of participation. The provider has to document the detail of that participation.

Operative report

The date of the procedure must be contained in the operative report. The report must describe in detail the surgical procedure, as well as giving a description of the anatomical site. Any medication or dye injected, the site of injection and dosage should be clearly stated. Documentation should note any specimens obtained and whether these were sent to pathology. Closure of the surgical wound, suture type for each layer and surgical dressing should be documented.

A physician's signature must be present on the operative report if that physician is documenting the service. A physician's initials are not an acceptable substitute for his or her signature. The operative report should conclude with the state of the patient upon departure from the operative suite.

Resource based relative value scale

It is important for physicians to understand the resource based relative value scale (RBRVS). The RBRVS bases physician reimbursement on the amount of work involved for doctors to diagnose and/or treat patients. Sometimes shortened to 'RVU', this system of reimbursement can be found in the edition of the Federal Register published in December of every year. This reimbursement methodology was developed to replace the customary prevailing and reasonable charge system. 'Relative' in RBRVS comes from determining the amount of resources (time, effort, supplies, nursing support, overhead, etc.) a doctor consumes to provide a service or procedure, compared with the resources needed to provide a different service or procedure.

Physician payment reflects

- Practice (skill, education, difficulty of procedure)

- Malpractice (percentage of malpractice insurance allocated to this service)

- Expense (cost or overhead)

When ranking procedural codes, the codes should be listed in order of their relative value units from highest to lowest. The procedures that have a higher 'weight' of difficulty, time and overhead should be listed before those with a lesser 'weight'. Payers follow a multiple surgery payment methodology, by which they reimburse the first procedure at 100% of their fee schedule allowance minus co-payments and deductibles, followed by the next highest at 50% and so on.

This methodology considers that any procedure following the primary procedure does not require preparation of the surgical approach; thus, the approach is factored out of any procedure that is not primary. The –51 modifier (multiple procedures) is appended to each procedure that is not the primary procedure. If procedures are not ranked correctly when they are submitted, payment may be less than expected. A procedure with a lower relative value unit will be paid at 100% of fee schedule if placed first, and the procedure with a higher relative value unit will be paid at 50% if not placed as the primary procedure. Many insurance carriers will not re-order the procedures to reflect their difficulty correctly.

The multiple payment methodology applies to surgical coding; other services are not affected by this payment methodology.

Add-on codes

CPT classifies codes as either primary codes or stand-alone codes, and add-on codes. These add-on codes are sometimes referred to as secondary codes or supplemental codes. Add-on codes are codes that must be used with a primary code and can never be used alone. These codes can be identified by the words 'each additional', 'list in addition to', and 'second' or 'third'. Reduction in payment has already been factored into the RVUs for these codes. When secondary codes are used, do not use the modifier –51. CPT instruction prior to a set of codes may instruct the provider to omit the –51 modifier. The reporting of the –51 modifier with these codes may affect reimbursement unnecessarily. If a modifier –51 is used with supplemental codes, some carriers may cut in half the value of a service that has already been reduced by the very nature of the intention of the code.

Supplemental codes frequently specify codes or ranges of codes with which they can be used. It would be inappropriate to use these codes with codes other than those specified. It is important to review carrier reimbursement to ensure that multiple surgical cutbacks have not been applied to the secondary codes. These codes should be paid at 100% of the payer fee schedule reimbursement. The *CPT Manual* has identified codes designated as 'add-on' codes in Appendix E, and codes exempt from modifier –51 in Appendix F. The codes in Appendix F have not been identified as add-on codes but are still subject to the same coding guidelines.

Family of codes

Codes contained within a coding family are subject to several different payment methodologies, depending upon the insurance carrier. A family of codes is introduced with a procedure followed by a semicolon. It is the placement of the semicolon that defines the common portion of the code descriptor. The intention of the use of the semicolon (;) in a family of codes is to conserve space. The code description preceding the semicolon defines the common portion of the family of codes. Following the common portion of the code descriptor is one to several indented procedure descriptions. The indented code descriptors define the service that is unique to that specific code. When reading the indented procedure, the base code is read up to the semicolon, dropping down to the indented procedure to complete the unique portion of the procedure. It may be necessary and appropriate to use several codes from a family to describe fully the service provided. Some insurance carriers have difficulty when addressing payment from several codes contained within the same family, and may attempt to deny one of the services as incidental to the base code. This is not appropriate, and such denials should be contested.

Some carriers will attempt to deny all codes from a family except the code with the highest RVU, proclaiming that duplicate payment for the base code will occur if more than one code is recognized. The provider should contest this denial. An argument in defense of payment for all codes within the family is that the –51 modifier appended to all of the procedure codes after the primary code eliminates this duplicate payment from occurring. Medicare has addressed this difficulty by choosing to pay several procedures within a family using the following methodology: the primary code is paid at 100% of fee schedule; any secondary codes and so forth are reimbursed at their fee schedule rate minus the fee for the primary procedure.

Some procedures within a family will never be reimbursed when submitted together, because they are considered to be mutually exclusive of each other. Mutually exclusive codes should not be used together because they are of procedures that cannot reasonably be done during the same session. CPT codes are mutually exclusive of one another, based on either the definition of the procedure or the medical impossibility/improbability that the procedures could be performed at the same session. These codes are not necessarily linked together with one code narrative describing the more comprehensive procedure.

Incidental procedures

- Are individual services that are part of a more comprehensive procedure

- Add little time or additional risk to the comprehensive procedure

- It is unnecessary to list every event common to the procedure as part of the description of the code

- Reflect normal principles of medical/surgical practice

- Some are common to virtually all procedures

- Some are integral to only a certain group of procedures

Some surgeons attempt to code for anesthesia services, such as the injection of local anesthesia, when performing a surgical procedure. Any anesthetic administration, when performed by the operating physician, is included in the reimbursement for the surgical service. This can also be said for the application or insertion of any device that is not permanent in nature. Payment for the removal of the device is included in the fee obtained for the insertion of the device. This is true of any device that is temporary in nature; however, permanent devices are separately billable when they must be removed.

Separate procedures

Separate procedures are services commonly carried out as an integral part of a total service, and usually do not warrant separate identification. These services are noted in CPT with the parenthetical phrase '(separate procedure)'. When this phrase appears before the semicolon, all indented descriptions that follow are covered by it. Separate procedures are considered an integral part of a more comprehensive procedure code; this usually applies to procedures within the same section of the CPT book.

Separate procedure codes can be billed when they are the only service billed on that date of service, or if they are billed in conjunction with procedural codes from another section of the CPT book. When separate procedure codes are billed with procedure codes from another section of CPT they are not an integral part of that other code.

National correct coding initiative/policy

The national correct coding initiative (NCCI) is Medicare's edit system. Mutually exclusive edits introduce each subsection, followed by edits for comprehensive codes. The manual consists of a table of codes divided into column I and column II. Column II lists all of the codes that cannot be billed with column I. Indicators in these tables provide additional information concerning the edits (see below).

Unbundling

Unbundling occurs when all of the component codes are submitted instead of the comprehensive code. Payment is usually greater when services are unbundled, and, because of this, payers are becoming more adept at isolating and rejecting claims that report unbundled services.

One form of unbundling or fragmentation is breaking a surgical service into its multiple components, and reporting each component separately, when a single code describes all services. A good habit to develop, to avoid unbundling, is to ask, 'What usually happens when this service or procedure is performed?' Services considered a routine part of a procedure or an inherent part of a procedure should not be listed separately for coding purposes. Another form of unbundling is billing for a global service, then breaking out each service included in the global package as separate charges.

Surgical global package

A surgical global package compensates the surgeon for all preoperative, perioperative and postoperative services that fall within the normal course of surgery. A normal package starts 1 day before the surgical service and varies, depending upon carrier, as to the length of the surgical package. Most insurance carriers allow separate reimbursement for any service that occurs due to a complication of surgery, or any service that is unrelated to the indication for surgery. Medicare includes all services, including complications, up until the next surgical service.

Unlisted procedure codes: '99' codes

Unlisted procedure codes also require the submission of documentation. Although many practices avoid the submission of these codes at all cost, they are worthwhile codes to use when appropriate. These codes, usually ending in the double digit '99', are found at the end of each section or subsection in CPT, and describe any procedure that has no procedure code. The use of the unlisted procedure codes always requires the submission of procedural or operative notes. The portion of the note that describes the service rendered for which there is no procedure code should be underlined in ink. It is helpful to note the unlisted code to the outside of the underlined procedure. This assures the provider that the insurance carrier will have no difficulty determining which portion of the service is being described by the unlisted code.

It is helpful also to provide information comparing this unlisted procedure with a similar procedure with regard to skill requirement, risk and time involved. This will assist the insurance carrier in determining an appropriate reimbursement methodology.

Audits/reviews

Insurance carriers develop their own internal guidelines, with cost containment in mind. Repeated submissions of incorrect code combinations, overuse of modifiers and high E&M services cause insurance carriers to mark or 'red flag' a provider in order to pull a provider-specific report. A review of this report usually results in a review or audit of that specific provider's coding habits, compared with the documentation to support those services.

Medicare is currently performing five different types of audits or reviews. Most practices have already been unknowingly involved in one of these types of audits known as a 'one chart audit'. This is a request for documentation to support one E&M service prior to payment by the carrier. Do not ignore this letter. Many practices feel that the reimbursement for one service cannot justify the time and money spent to send this documentation to the carrier. When the carrier discovers that their request has been ignored, an assumption is made that the provider either does not have the documentation to support the service or does not want the documentation to be reviewed. This triggers a larger audit.

The 'electronic claim submission' audit is performed to verify that a service was performed in your office. After this review you will receive a letter that indicates whether you have passed or failed. Do not be lulled into a false sense of security if you pass this audit. A pass score means that confirmation has been made that the patient was in the office and received services. It is not a review of your documentation, even though the letter may state 'documentation supports the claim as billed'. Passing this audit is not a guarantee that your documentation will stand up to a full-blown chart review.

Reviews

Focused medical review

- Includes eight records or fewer

- Documentation for same date of service

- Called an 'educational' review by Medicare

- Notified of results with recommendations to correct poor billing practices

- Audit failure puts provider on 'PAL' (provider audit list)

Comprehensive medical review (most serious type of audit)

- Includes 15 or more records

- Dates of service will span a period of 6 months

- Upon finalization of audit, Medicare will request refund of overpayments plus penalties

- If fraud is suspected, results of audit forwarded to Fraud and Abuse Unit of Federal Government

- Settlement of fraudulent audits may result in fines of $10 000 per claim plus treble charges

This last type of review is very serious. Legal counsel must be notified immediately, and a coding consultant should be contacted to assist in gathering the information requested. Send all information as instructed plus any information that supports the medical necessity of the care.

If there has been no payment for the service listed, do not submit the information. There will, most likely, be some repayment due back to the carrier. Do not make a repayment on monies never received. Keep copies of everything.

After the documentation is submitted you will receive a detailed report of the findings for each date of service. It is important to have your coding consultant review for any errors. Included in this report will be the overpayments for each service and the settlement fee. Settlement fees are determined based on two calculations. The first is based on the actual number of charts reviewed and the second is an extrapolation of the error percentages to your total Medicare patient population for the same time period.

You can request a copy of the worksheets used to determine documented levels of service. If your coding consultant can justify the level billed using Medicare's worksheet, you may be able to defend the submitted level of service.

Consultants and recommendations

Many practices avoid the use of consultants, for fear that the consultant will report their findings back to the insurance carrier or Federal Government. Consultants do not have a duty to inform the government or insurance carrier of their audit findings; they cannot, however, commit or further any acts that they perceive to be fraudulent or inappropriate. Carriers consider practices with compliance tools in place to be acting in good faith, and will accept this as a mitigating factor when determining culpability.

Understanding coding guidelines and compliance rules and regulations will result in increased practice revenue and will decrease the risk of costly fines as a result of a carrier audit. Read as much information concerning coding and compliance as you possibly can. Share the information with your practice staff. Subscribe to publications that will keep you current in coding and compliance. The codes, rules and regulations change constantly. Depend upon certified coders. Do not utilize 'self-proclaimed' coding experts. The number of years that someone has been coding may indicate the number of years that they have been coding incorrectly. There are many consultants who will tell you exactly what you want to hear, and it will sound almost too good to be true. It usually is.

Accounting Principles

15

Bates H. Whiteside

Introduction

Accounting information is used for decision-making in all types of organizations – business and non-business – as well as by both managers and individual citizens. This includes physician practices. Every person in society benefits from some knowledge of accounting since it is used wherever economic resources are utilized. Many decisions are made daily in our society that have economic consequences, such as whether our savings should be invested in a savings account in a bank, in government bonds, or in the shares of stock issued by a business corporation. We may feel that our savings can be quite safely invested in a savings account or in a government bond, but we are far less certain about the outcome of an investment in shares of stock. To make an informed decision, we need information about the economic activity of corporations that issue such shares, and this is where accounting enters the picture, since accounting is a primary source of information on economic activity.

Since economic activity includes the production, exchange and consumption of scarce goods, it is found everywhere in our society. Accounting is nearly as extensive. Accounting is needed to show what was accomplished and at what cost. This is true whether individuals, business entities or not-for-profit entities such as churches, governmental organizations and hospitals, use resources. Accounting is the process used to measure and report to various users relevant financial information regarding the economic activity of an organization. Accounting is a systematic or organized means of gathering and reporting information on economic activity. The information gathered is used by many internal and external parties, together with other information, for a wide range of decisions. Internally, accounting information is used by various levels of management personnel. External users include actual and potential shareholders, creditors and their professional advisors, employees and their unions, customers, suppliers, competitors, governmental agencies and the public at large.

Forms of business organizations

Accounting serves all forms of business organizations. There are three basic forms of organization for a business enterprise: single proprietorship, partnership and corporation. We will use the corporation as our sample business structure. The corporation is the most significant form of business organization but virtually the same accounting concepts apply to all three forms of organization.

Single proprietorship

A single proprietorship is an unincorporated business owned by one individual (healthcare professional) and often managed by that individual. A single or sole proprietorship is a one-owner business whose owner has not elected to become a corporation or a partnership – a sort of default option. Many small service-type businesses (such as physicians or other professional services) and retail establishments (such as clothing stores, antique shops or novelty stores) are sole proprietorships. There are no legal formalities in organizing such a business, and usually only a limited amount of capital (money) is required to begin operations. While there is no legal distinction between the business and the owner as entities, since the owner is responsible for both personal and business debts, there is an accounting distinction. The financial activities of the business such as selling services to the public are kept separate from the personal financial activities, such as making a payment on an automobile used exclusively for non-business purposes. The business is considered an entity separate from the owner for accounting purposes. For legal purposes the business and the owner are the same; therefore, the owner has no personal legal protection from general business creditors. A sole owner has unlimited liability, meaning that if the business cannot pay all of its liabilities, the creditors to whom the business owes money can come after your personal assets. Many part-time entrepreneurs may not know this or may not put it in their minds, but this is a huge risk to take. Obviously, a single proprietorship has no other owners to prepare financial statements for – although the proprietor should still prepare these statements as a check on how his or her business is doing. (Also, banks require financial statements of proprietorships that apply for loans.) One other piece of advice for single proprietors is: although you do not have to separate invested capital from retained earnings like corporations do, you should still keep these two accounts separate – not only for the purpose of tracking the business but for any future buyers of the business as well.

Partnership

A partnership is a business owned by two or more persons associated as partners. The partnership is created by a partnership agreement setting forth the terms of the partnership. Preferably, the agreement should be in writing, but it may be oral. Included in the agreement will be such things as the initial investment of each healthcare professional partner, the duties of each partner, the means of dividing earnings and profits between the partners each year and the settlement to be made upon the death or withdrawal of a partner. A partnership often evolves out of one or more sole proprietorships. For instance, Dr X and Dr Y, both medical doctors in practice as single proprietors, see the need to have another medical doctor serve their patients during vacations and days off. Also, there may be a need to combine their strong points (X is a good obstetrician and Y is a good gynecologist) to improve service to their patients. They may decide to combine their single proprietor-ships into a partnership. Partnerships, like single proprietorships, are commonly found in the service and retail fields. Partnerships avoid the double taxation feature that corporations are subject to. Partnerships also differ from corporations with respect to liability. A partnership's owners fall into two categories.

(1)   General partners – subject to unlimited liability. If a business cannot pay its debts, its creditors can reach into the general partner's personal assets. General partners have the authority and responsibility to manage the business. They are roughly equivalent to the president and high-level managers of a business corporation. The general partners usually divide authority and responsibility among themselves, and often they elect one member of their group as the senior or managing general part-ner or elect a small executive committee to make major deci-sions

(2)   Limited partners – subject to limited liability. Limited partners have ownership rights to the business's profits, but they do not participate in the management of the business.

If a partner leaves the healthcare group or dies, the partnership is technically dissolved, although the formation of a new partnership may be transparent to outsiders. As far as outsiders can tell, the business continues as before. Generally, a partner cannot sell his or her interest to an outsider without the consent of all the partners. You cannot just buy your way into a partnership. In contrast, you can purchase shares of stock and thereby become an owner of a corporation and you do not need the approval of the other owners of the corporation or the board of directors of the corporation.

Corporations

A corporation is a business that may be owned by a few persons or by thousands of persons and is incorporated under the laws of one of the 50 states. It is often managed by persons other than the owners, although major owners, i.e. founding members of the healthcare corporation, sometimes serve as officers (managers) of the corporation. Ownership in a corporation is divided into units known as shares of stock. Thus, owners are called stockholders or shareholders. Ownership interest is easily transferred by selling one's shares of stock to another. Organized exchanges (such as the New York Stock Exchange) exist for this purpose. The law views a corporation as a 'person'. That means that a corporation, unlike the single proprietorship or partnership, is considered to be its own entity, separate from its owners. The owners are not personally responsible for the debts of the corporation. So if a corporation does not pay its debts, its creditors can seize only the corporation's assets, not the assets of the corporation's owners. This concept is known as limited liability. The distinguishing features of a corporation are the one or more types of stock shares it issues and the type of taxation to which it is subject. In return for their investment in the business, a corporation's owners receive shares of stock. A share of stock is one unit of ownership and how much a share is worth with respect to the value of the whole business depends on the total number of shares that the business issues. The corporate form is more likely to appear where huge amounts of capital are needed to start the business, where a wide range of talents is needed to manage a business practice and where the owners desire to limit their personal liability.

Shares of stock come in various classes, which define the rights of the stockholders. For example, a business may offer Class A and Class B shares, where Class A stockholders are given the right to vote in elections for the board of directors and Class B stockholders do not get the right to vote. A corporation may have one class or many classes of stock and state laws are very generous regarding the different classes of stock that can be issued.

Income taxes and legal structure

In deciding which type of ownership structure is best for securing financing capital and managing their business as well as the income tax aspects of the business entity selected. But before discussing taxation aspects, one should be introduced to another business form not discussed above – the limited liability company (LLC).

The LLC is a relatively new type of business entity. In fact, not all states recognize LLCs as valid types of business entity. A LLC is like a corporation regarding limited liability, and it is similar to a partnership regarding the ability to divide profits among its owners. The best way to think of a LLC is as a partnership with limited liability. The Internal Revenue Service even treats a LLC like a partnership for federal income tax purposes. Which means that a LLC is not subject to the potential of double taxation like a traditional corporation. The primary advantage to a LLC is flexibility. The company has the ability to determine how profits and management authority are divided among owners and operators. The key to this is the operating agreement, which is drawn up and clearly states ownership, profit division and management responsibility. For example, a new LLC permits the founders of the business to put up only 10–20% of the operating capital to start the business and still be able to keep all the management authority in their hands.

LLCs have more flexibility than traditional corporations, but more flexibility can be a bad thing too. The owners must enter into a very detailed agreement called an 'operating agreement' that specifically spells out division of profits, division of management authority, rights to withdraw capital and their responsibilities to contribute new capital as needed. Operating agreements can get very complicated and difficult to understand and like any legal document need an attorney to establish them and then untangle them.

Doctors or other healthcare professionals may choose to become professional corporations, which are a special type of legal structure that states offer to professionals who would otherwise have to operate under the limited liability partnership laws. Some states also permit limited liability partnerships, or LLPs, for qualified professionals in which all the partners have limited liability. These types of legal entities were created mainly as a direct result of large damage awards and lawsuits against professionals. Today, almost all healthcare professional associations are organized as professional corporations or limited liability partnerships. They function much like partnerships but without the unlimited liability.

The regular type of corporation is called a 'C' corporation in tax law, that is, unless the entity qualifies as an 'S' or small business corporation as discussed later. 'C' corporations pay income tax on their annual earnings and profits. The shareholders are then taxed a second time on the same earnings and profits when the corporation pays them cash dividends. This makes 'C' corporations subject to double taxation.

Suppose you are the owner of a 'C' corporation with the following income for the year:

Gross receipts or gross income	$ 100 000.00
Expenses of corporation	$ 50 000.00
Net income	$ 50 000.00
Income tax on net income (15% of net)	**$ 7 500.00**
Net income available to shareholders	**$42 000.00**

The only way the shareholders can share in the earnings and profits of the corporation is payment of income after expenses and income taxes have been paid. These payments are called dividends and are also taxable to the shareholder as well. If a shareholder of the above corporation is in the 31% individual income tax bracket the dividends he or she receives will first be subject to 15% tax at the corporate level and then 31% tax at the shareholder level or a combined effective tax rate of 41.35%. If a corporation is closely held and the owners participate in management of the corporation there are other means available to have access to corporate earnings such as salary or rents paid to the shareholder owner. These payments are deductible by the corporation and only taxable at the shareholder level. The primary reason for choosing a 'C' corporation structure for a business entity is the flexibility and limited liability. There are other factors to consider such as deductibility of shareholder benefits such as pension plan contributions and payment of health and insurance benefits on behalf of shareholder managers. Congress saw the need for some relief to the provisions of corporate double taxation many years ago and created a hybrid corporation known as the 'S' or small business corporation. 'S' corporations are basic corporations that meet the following criteria, can file IRS Form 2553 and can elect to be treated as an 'S' corporation:

(1)   The corporation has only one class of stock;

(2)   The corporation has fewer than 35 shareholders;

(3)   It has the approval from the majority of shareholders to elect 'S' status.

In general an 'S' corporation does not pay income tax. Instead, the corporation's income and expenses are divided among the shareholders and passed through directly to the shareholders, who then must report income and expenses of the corporation on their individual returns and pay income taxes based on their share of the earnings and profits of the corporation. The 'S' corporation must file an annual return on Form 1120S and the tax year of an 'S' corporation must be a calendar year and provides each shareholder with an accounting for the year. Each shareholder then separately accounts for his or her *pro rata* share of corporate items of income, deduction, loss and credit on his or her income taxes. Any distributions of cash or property from the corporation to a shareholder that are from earnings and profits are not taxable to the shareholder because he or she has reported those earnings previously on his or her individual income tax returns. Owner managers of 'S' corporations beware – you may not be able to participate in company retirement plans and company-provided benefits such as health insurance.

Partnerships and limited liability companies are equivalent, from an income tax point of view, and are taxed much the same as the 'S' corporation discussed above. Partners in a partnership or shareholders in a LLC include their *pro rata* share of the business entity's taxable income items just like an 'S' corporation. Shareholders or partners include their share of the entity's taxable income in the computation of their personal income tax return for the year.

Financial statements of business enterprises

Although a modern business firm has many objectives or goals, the two primary objectives of every business firm, including healthcare corporations, are profitability and solvency. Unless a practice can produce satisfactory earnings and pay its debt obligations timely, all other objectives will never be realized simply because the corporation or practice will not survive. The financial statements that reflect a practice's solvency (the balance sheet), its profitability (the earnings or income statement) and its changes in retained earnings (the retained earnings statement) are illustrated and discussed below. A fourth statement that will be briefly discussed is the statement of cash flows.

The balance sheet

The balance sheet is often called the statement of financial position and it summarizes the assets owned by the business on one side and sources of those assets, liabilities and owners' equity, on the other side. It presents measures of the assets, liabilities and shareholders' equity in the business enterprise at a specific moment in time, usually the last day of the year or month or the end of the accounting cycle. Assets are things of value, they constitute the resources of the firm. Examples are cash on deposit at banks, accounts receivable or money owed to the business by customers, physical equipment used in business and buildings, or real estate owned by the business, and inventory held for sale by the business to customers. Assets have value to the firm because of the uses to which they can be put or the things that can be acquired by exchanging them. In the illustration below the assets of Nolan Medical, Inc., which performs delivery services, amount to $35 670. They consist of current assets of cash and accounts receivable and plant, property and equipment. Current assets consist of cash and other short-lived assets that are reasonably expected to be converted into cash or to be used up in the operations of the business within a short period, usually 1 year. Plant, property and equipment refer to relatively long-lived assets that are to be used in the production or sale of other assets or services rather than being sold.

Liabilities are debts owed by the firm. Typically, they must be paid at certain known moments in time. Current liabilities are those due within a relatively short period of time, usually 1 year. The liabilities of Nolan Medical, Inc. are both relatively short-lived and current liabilities. They consist of accounts payable (amounts owed to suppliers or vendors) and notes payable (written promises to pay a bank or other financial institution). Nolan Medical, Inc. is a corporation and therefore it is customary to refer to the owner's (physician's) interest in the corporation as shareholders' or stockholders' equity. Shareholders' equity arises from two sources: money invested by the owners and profits earned and retained by the business.

Always remember the following:

TOTAL ASSETS = LIABILITIES + SHAREHOLDERS' EQUITY

The income or earnings statement

The purpose of the earnings statement is to report upon the profitability of a business organization for a stated period of time. In accounting,

Nolan Medical, Inc.
Balance Sheet
December 31, 2001

ASSETS

Current assets

Cash	$ 12 470.00	
Accounts receivable	$ 700.00	
Total current assets		**$ 13 170.00**

Property, plant & equipment

Medical & surgical equipment	$ 20 000.00	
Office equipment	$ 2 500.00	
Total property, plant & equipment		**$ 22 500.00**
TOTAL ASSETS		**$ 35 670.00**

LIABILITIES AND SHAREHOLDERS' EQUITY

Current liabilities

Accounts payable	$ 600.00	
Notes payable	$ 3 000.00	
Total current liabilities		**$ 3 600.00**

Shareholders' equity

Capital stock	$ 30 000.00	
Retained earnings	$ 2 070.00	
Total shareholders' equity		**$ 32 070.00**
TOTAL LIABILITIES AND SHAREHOLDERS' EQUITY		**$ 35 670.00**

Nolan Medical, Inc.
Earnings statement
For the year ended December 31, 2001

INCOME

Service revenues	$5700.00

TOTAL INCOME $5700.00

EXPENSES

Salaries paid	$2500.00
Automobile expenses	$ 400.00
Rent	$ 300.00
Marketing	$ 200.00
Utilities	$ 100.00
Interest expense	$ 30.00

TOTAL EXPENSES $3630.00

NET EARNINGS $2070.00

profitability is measured by comparing the revenues generated in a given period with the expenses incurred to produce those revenues. Revenues are defined as the inflow of assets from the sale of products or the rendering of services to patients. Expenses are the sacrifices made or the costs incurred to produce revenues. They are measured by the assets surrendered or consumed in serving patients (customers). If revenues exceed expenses, net earnings result. If the reverse is true, the medical practice is said to be operating at a loss. The illustration above is of the earnings statement of Nolan Medical, Inc. The income statement, gets more attention from business managers and investors – not that they ignore the other two financial statements, but many feel the income statement tells more about the direction a business enterprise (practice) is moving toward than any other financial statement.

The statement of retained earnings

The purpose of the statement of retained earnings is to explain the changes in retained earnings that occurred between two balance

---

Nolan Medical, Inc.
Statement of retained earnings
For the year ended December 31, 2001

Beginning balance – retained earnings January 1, 2001	$ -0-
Add:	
Net earnings for 2001:	$2070.00
Retained earnings – December 31, 2001	**$2070.00**

---

sheet dates. Usually, these changes consist of the addition of net earnings and the deduction of the dividends paid. Dividends remember are the means by which a corporation rewards its shareholders for providing it with capital.

The effects of cash dividend transactions are to reduce cash and retained earnings by the amount paid out. In effect, the earnings are no longer retained but have been passed on to the stockholders. And this, of course, is one of the primary reasons why stockholders organize corporations. The statement of retained earnings for Nolan Medical, Inc. for the year 2001 is quite simple. Since the company was organized at the beginning of the year, there would be no beginning balance for retained earnings. The net earnings of $2070.00 from the earnings statement are added and since no dividends were paid this is the ending balance.

The statement of cash flows

This very important financial statement presents a summary of the sources and uses of cash in a business during a business cycle (usually 1 year). Smart business managers hardly get the word profit out of their mouths without mentioning cash flow. In order for a business to be successful they must manage both profit and cash flow. For financial reporting, cash flows are divided into three basic categories:

(1)   Operating activities or cash flows from profit-making activities;

(2)   Investing activities or cash flows from interest or investments earned;

(3)   Financing activities which are cash inflows or outflows from financing activities for the period.

Most of the information reported in these financial statements is found originally in the transactions entered into by the entity. These transactions are analyzed and their effects recorded as an increase or decrease in assets, liabilities, stockholders' equity, revenues and expenses – the five basic elements of accounting. The above formula can be expanded to:

ASSETS = LIABILITIES + EQUITY + REVENUES – EXPENSES

Historical perspective of accounting

Accounting, like other social science disciplines and activities, is a product of its environment. The environment of accounting consists of social, economic, political and legal conditions that change from time to time. As a result, accounting objectives and practices are not the same today as they were in the past and, given the recent 'collapse' of several large corporations in the United States, accounting principles and practices will not be the same in the future.

The users of financial accounting information have coinciding and conflicting needs for accounting information of various types. To meet these needs, and to satisfy the fiduciary reporting responsibility of a company and its management, accountants prepare a single set of general purpose financial statements. Financial statements are expected to present fairly, clearly and completely the economic facts of the existence and operations of the enterprise. In preparing financial statements accountants (like those involved in the communication process) are confronted with potential dangers of bias, misinterpretation, inexactness and ambiguity. In order to minimize these dangers and to render financial statements that can be reasonably compared between companies and between accounting periods, the accounting profession in the United States has developed a body of theory that is generally accepted and universally practiced. Without this body of theory, each accountant and each enterprise could develop their own set of accounting practices and accounting theory. The accounting profession, therefore, has attempted to establish a body of theory and practice that acts as a general guide. Its efforts have resulted in the adoption of a common set of accounting standards and procedures called 'generally accepted accounting principles' or GAAP. Although these principles have provoked both debate and criticism, most accountants and members of the financial community recognize them as the theories, methods and practices that, over time, have proved to be the most useful.

In the modern financial era, self-regulation by the accounting profession can be traced to just after the Securities and Exchange Commission (SFC) was established by the Securities Act of 1933 and the Securities Exchange Act of 1934. These new laws were passed by Congress in response to the vast sums lost by investors in the stock market crash of 1929 and the subsequent financial depression.

At the outset, there were serious discussions in Washington about whether the federal government should establish standards for preparing and auditing financial statements of publicly held companies. The SEC was given statutory authority to set accounting standards and to oversee the activities of auditors. The role of establishing auditing standards was left to the accounting profession. A number of organizations have been instrumental in the formation of accounting theory and standards in the United States. The major organizations are as follows:

(1) The American Institute of Certified Public Accountants (AICPA) – this is the national organization of practicing Certified Public Accountants (CPAs).

(2) The Financial Accounting Standards Board (FASB) – established in 1971 because its predecessor, the Accounting Principles Board, came under fire and because it failed to act promptly to correct alleged accounting abuses. Because of these problems with the APB, the leaders of the accounting professions, anxious to avoid government rule-making, dissolved the APB and established the FASB. There was widespread support for creating the unprecedented private independent board. The FASB is charged with the creation of accounting standards used throughout the industry.

(3) The Securities and Exchange Commission (SEC) – the Great Depression of the 1930s resulted in widespread collapse of businesses and the securities markets in the United States and was the impetus for government intervention and regulation of business. This intervention involved a great deal of concern with financial statements and financial reporting. A direct result was the creation of the SEC as an independent regulatory agency of the United States government to administer the Securities Acts of 1933 and the Securities Exchange Act of 1934, and several other securities acts. Companies that issue securities to the public or are listed on stock exchanges are required to file annual audited financial statements with the SEC. Congress has given the SEC broad powers to prescribe, in what detail it

desires, the accounting practices and standards to be used by entities that fall under its jurisdiction.

(4)   American Accounting Association (AAA) – the AAA is an organization of college accounting professors and practicing accountants that seeks to influence the development of accounting theory and practices by sponsoring accounting research.

(5)   The Internal Revenue Service (IRS) – this is one of the strongest influences on accounting practices. In an effort to lessen the impact of taxes and to avoid keeping two sets of books, many businesses frequently adopt 'acceptable' accounting practices that minimize taxable income. Tax laws and 'tax effects' are a pervasive influence in business decision-making and on the section of accounting methods.

For the past 60 years, the accounting profession's system of self-regulation has helped create the most respected financial markets in the world. This year it will result in almost 17 000 public company audits that will be completed without restatement or any allegations of impropriety. At the same time, the profession's self-regulatory framework is now about 25 years old. Although it has been continually enhanced and improved since its inception, the profession recognizes that it needs to be overhauled and modernized.

The SEC is now in the process of making its own proposals to create a new overseeing body made up of a majority of public members and operating outside the AICPA. At the same time, the AICPA, along with its membership, is forging ahead on implementing improved audit standards for detecting fraud and new measures for deterring fraud, such as expanded internal control procedures for management, boards and audit committees. Reforms also need to be made in the financial reporting model, the analyst community, boards of directors and audit committees, and in the corporate culture of companies.

Summary

Economic decisions in every society must be based upon the information available at the time the decision is made. For example, the decision of a bank to make a loan to a business is based upon previous financial relationships with that practice, the financial condition of the 'business' as reflected by its financial statements, and other factors. If decisions are to be consistent with the intentions of the decision-makers, the information used in the decision process must be reliable. Unreliable information may cause inefficient use of resources to the detriment of society and to the decision-makers themselves. In the lending decision example, assume the bank makes a decision to make a loan based on unreliable information and the borrower company is ultimately unable to repay, and as a result the bank loses its principal and interest? Without reliable financial information what would happen to the ability of society to place trust in financial information? It is our objective to assist you in making informed decisions regarding selection of business form and the need for adequate financial information in your practice.

Fundamentals of Finance in a Practice

16

Robert Bartolacci

We begin with the topics of finance, and synthesize these concepts into a closing discussion of practice sales and mergers. The intention is to provide the healthcare professional with a common-sense understanding of the financial fundamentals necessary to increase wealth. Following the introduction, the importance of cash, cost of money and future financial expectations will be introduced to form the considerations of practice investing and divesting.

Finance and financial management are not to be confused or aggregated with the practice of accounting. Although the scope of accounting and the role of the accountant sometimes suggest the area or ability to practice finance, there is a great divide between the two practices. The goals of accounting relate to proper financial reporting, tax interpretation and calculation, auditing and oversight, and related advisory services. The scope of finance is in the financial markets, investments and management finance. The goal of financial management is to increase the owner's wealth. Note that the goals and scope of accounting versus those of finance are vastly different. To the practicing financial manager, the differences are similar to (and equally insulting as) labeling physicians and other healthcare professionals as one and the same. Consider this the next time your accountant offers to provide you with financial management services.

With the goal of financial management broadly defined and undisputedly desirable, a practice's task should be to apply the proven fundamentals required to attain that goal. Increasing wealth extends beyond reducing costs or increasing profits; it takes a more holistic and longer-term approach to enrichment. Accordingly, a paradigm shift is usually required to operate outside the familiar model: to change from management by profit and loss statement exclusively, to management with the goal of increasing wealth.

This suggested paradigm shift is certainly not meant to imply that managing the profit and loss statement is to be abandoned, but, rather, the focus should be changed away from 'profitability of the current fiscal year' only. The new focus needs to be on increasing the owner's wealth through improved cash flow provided and used in operations, long-term asset management and short-term asset management. Let us put this proposition into physiological terms (because medical practitioners love to 'speak medicine' with business people!).

A physician on sabbatical decides to become the first person to circle the globe in a year or less, by walking and swimming only. In an effort to keep the required pace and to maximize hours, the ambitious doc reduces sleeping and eating time. Miraculously, doc crosses the finishing line in 364 days. Ironically, the physician drops dead from exhaustion and malnutrition several steps later. As life-giving as a single windfall year seems to a practice, the lack of financial support and preparations for business (and life) after the fiscal year ends can be exponentially more devastating. Let us begin with the common-sense academics of finance.

The essence of finance

Finance, along with all its principles, is not a difficult subject matter. In fact, this pales in comparison with the study of medicine, pharmacy or law. Unlike these more difficult academic pursuits, finance relies on just a few basic and core premises. The most essential, yet basic, premise is the simple concept of rent, i.e. paying for the use of something, such as office space, an apartment or even money.

With all due respect to the wizards of Wall Street, the practice of finance can become quite complex. However, the same fundamentals are always clearly evident in every financial transaction. Four essential fundamentals are:

(1)   Rent;

(2)   Risk and return;

(3)   Time value of money;

(4)   Expectations of the future.

Every financial decision that a practice manager encounters is directly related to one of the four essentials. For example, the decision to promote an associate to a higher position may seem like a fairly straightforward business decision. However, there are numerous finance implications to that decision. Let us examine the fundamentals at work. The manager must decide whether to pay an increased salary to the associate now (rent) for some expected future benefit (return), i.e. increased total revenue for the practice. There is risk in assuming that the expected incremental revenue brought in by the associate (to be received some time in the future) will be worth more than the incremental raise that the manager must pay now (time value of money). This decision is further complicated by the manager's alternative options. In lieu of giving the associate an $X raise, the manager can alternatively not promote the associate, invest the $X in a federal bond and earn interest. However, the interest received is probably less than the expected return from the associate's potential future revenue. Nevertheless, the manager would be guaranteed the interest, and correspondingly a known return from investing in government bonds – there are no guarantees when promoting an associate. Promoting the associate can provide a larger return, but comes with considerable risk. Investing in a federal bond provides less return, but no risk (risk and return). Do you get the point? It is almost certain that every reader can identify at least one current financial decision that is being considered. Your first homework assignment is to find the fundamentals at work in your practice and the available alternatives.

Cash: the lifeblood of every practice

Although cash is not one of the four identified financial fundamentals, it is in reality completely essential. Borrowing concepts again from physiology, cash is the lifeblood of every practice. Quite frankly, it is the lifeblood of every financial being – for profit, non-profit and so on. Everyone is aware of the importance of blood to a body. But because it works in an unseen fashion, we just assume (and pray to God) that it is healthy and functioning well. Similarly, every financial entity is aware that cash is required to continue as a going concern. However, as in the example of the human body, most managers, physicians or other leaders in a practice will assume that it is flowing into the business and is healthy and strong. This is a bad assumption!

Let us review an analogy. It is unlikely that a physician would be more concerned about an athlete's performance than the athlete's bleeding gunshot wound – even if the athlete could still win the event despite possibly bleeding to death. Yet, many practices are more concerned about profitability (or winning the event) than they are about bleeding cash out of the business. The underlying implication is that if the business is profitable, cash flow must be well. Again, this is a bad assumption!

There is no intention to insult the intelligence of the reader, but the following text describes some of the benefits of cash. Cash is a practice's most liquid asset. That is, it takes no time to be converted to an acceptable medium or currency, and is readily traded with no loss in value. Perhaps the most illiquid asset is real estate. It does take time to convert (has to be sold, closed on, etc.) to an acceptable medium or currency, i.e. cash, and is not always readily traded with no loss in value. For instance, you put your summer home up for sale, hoping to take the $1 million of equity and invest it in a new medical practice that you have already agreed to purchase and close on in 60 days. The purchase of the new practice is contingent upon the down-payment that is only available to you through the sale of your summer home. After 30 days, to ensure a quick sale, you lower the price by 50% and sell the home the next day. It will now take 30 days for you to receive a check from the buyer's bank, just in time for you to close on your new practice.

This example describes well the two problems of non-liquid assets. The first problem is the time required to convert non-liquid assets to cash. If you had the $1 million in cash rather than invested in your summer home, you would have easily been able to produce the desired down-payment as needed. The obvious aside, the second problem relates to the ability to convert with little or no loss in value. In this example, quick conversion would only occur when there was a loss in value.

Although the medical field has not been able to find a cure for the common cold, finance has found a cure for the common bankruptcy – cash. Bankruptcies would not occur if financial entities had enough cash to pay their creditors. Creditors are not primarily interested in a firm's accounts receivable, property, equipment, revenues or bottom lines. Creditors really want just cash. While some non-cash assets are required and exist in the operation of almost every financial entity (for example, accounts receivable in a medical practice), neither the operations nor assets are much consolation to firms in bankruptcy. Accordingly, practices must be diligent to ensure that there is sufficient cash, while maintaining the firm's non-cash assets.

Along with being the remedy for bankruptcy, sufficient cash provides ready access to low-hassle financing for funding new opportunities. As described in the example above, the inability quickly to convert assets into cash can present what economists call opportunity costs. Opportunity costs are the benefits of option A foregone when option B is chosen. In the example above, your summer home represents option B, while investing in the new practice represents option A. Let us assume that option B provides you with no financial benefit (i.e. rent) and that option A would provide you with $250 000 per year in additional income. An inability to sell the summer home and, consequently, not secure financing for the new practice would present an opportunity cost of $250 000 per year. While not tangible, these costs are quantifiable, and were directly attributable to a lack of cash.

The cost of money

Rent

There is a phrase made popular by a song that states 'ain't nothin' goin' on but the rent'. Although this phrase most certainly was not making reference to financial fundamentals, it does make a relevant point. Every asset employed at a practice, whether liquid or non-liquid, costs the practice rent. An obvious example of this is a leased photocopier or vehicle. The rent is clearly the monthly lease payment charged to the practice. Cash received from a bank loan represents another clear example of rent. Every dollar of interest paid on the outstanding principal of the loan is rent. Some less obvious realities of assets that cost the practice rent are: receivables, securities, equipment, buildings and every other asset in the practice. Let us examine this. Because of the concept of opportunity costs, every asset has a cost (the cost of not choosing the alternative). For every dollar in the practice's accounts receivable, one reasonable alternative usage would be investment in federal bonds. The opportunity cost is the interest income foregone by having the money tied up in receivables rather than bonds.

Opportunity costs aside, the rent on all assets can be determined by their method of acquisition. For example, rent on cash acquired from a bank loan can be determined by the interest charges. The rent on the practice's office building acquired by the owner's start-up money (or equity) can be determined by the return that the owners require on their investment in the building.

Accordingly, assets that sit idle waste money. Idle assets waste the cost of the interest or the owner's required return. Assets not producing returns that exceed the cost of interest or the owner's required return also waste money. The practice needs to consider ways productively to use every asset entrusted to the operation – otherwise the asset should be sold and the money returned to the financing entity (bank or owner), or reinvested elsewhere.

The rent of assets is not always clear to practice managers since there can seemingly be different rents for different assets. Financial managers term the aggregated rent of a firm's assets its cost of capital – or cost of raising money. Your financial management advisor (notice I did not say accountant!) can calculate the cost of capital for your firm. Knowing a practice's cost of capital presents the practice manager with a rent-benchmark – a percentage rate that represents a weighted-average of what it costs to borrow, or raise money from owners (equity investors).

Risk and return

A practice's cost of capital is not a static indicator of a firm's asset rent. However, it does provide a relatively stable benchmark that is based on the perceived risk associated with the practice's assets. Let us examine this statement.

Banks invest their capital by lending to consumers. The interest paid on the loans represents a return on the capital invested by the bank. Banks, like individual investors, would like the highest possible return for their investment. Fortunately for the consumers, the effects of government regulation and competition in the banking industry prevent banks from making huge returns by charging exorbitant rates. Notice, however, that banks charge less of an interest rate for mortgage loans than for credit cards. The primary reason that mortgage rates are lower is that the lent funds go to purchase property, which is used as collateral until the debt is extinguished. Banks take no collateral with assets purchased on credit cards (imagine a bank trying to take collateral on dinner at a fancy restaurant!). The bank has far less recourse to collect on defaulted credit card debt than on defaulted mortgage debt. Accordingly, there is significantly more risk of default (non-payment) on credit cards than there is on mortgages. Consequently, banks will charge interest rates according to the risk of the asset. That is, their required return is based on risk. The higher the risk, the higher the return required.

Owners should be no different in their risk–return considerations. Their required return for investing in assets should be commensurate with the associated risk. Investors would require less return on investments in low-risk federal bonds than they would on investing in the office building of an unproven-start-up medical practice. The concepts of rent, and risk and return, need to be considered in every financial decision if the goal of increasing wealth is to be reached. For instance, assume that a physician has sufficient personal funds to invest in the purchase of new office space. The familiar argument of 'why borrow money when I have enough to buy?' will surely arise. In this example, the physician agrees that a required return for investing in the practice is 10%, maybe even a little higher since the investment is for real estate and not medical equipment. The bank is willing to provide a mortgage at 8.5% interest. Assume that the practice, and more specifically the new office space, generates a 10% return. Had the physician invested the money from personal savings, the risk of the investment would have been adequately rewarded. Had the physician borrowed the money from the bank, the 10% return would exceed the 8.5% cost of debt by 1.5%.

Even without considering the further tax benefits of using debt capital over equity capital, the physician is 1.5% wealthier from using the bank's money rather than personal funds. Let us take this example a few steps further. Assume that the conservative physician had the personal funds invested in federal bonds that yield 7%. The physician's actual yield is the 7% from the bonds, plus the additional 1.5% return provided from the use of debt, or 8.5% total return. Now the skeptical reader is probably remarking that this is a mistake since the 10% return afforded by the investment in office space is higher than the 7% from the bonds, and higher than the 8.5% total return. That is true. However, let us assume that rather than providing a 10% return, the office space project fails miserably. This is completely possible, that is why it is called *risk*. If the physician funded the project with personal funds, business wealth and personal wealth are lost – a tragedy. If however the physician opted for the mortgage financing, wealth is preserved. In the face of the project failure, the bank would foreclose on the property and regain the collateral – which is fair. The physician however, continues to earn the 7% from the federal bonds. The bank is certainly not pleased; however, that was the risk that they accepted at 8.5% interest. Not only is the physician financially unharmed by the project failure, no further uncompensated risk had to be accepted to continue the increase of personal wealth.

Time value of money

The concept of time value of money is contingent upon the concept of rent. Time value of money assumes that for every dollar lent, that dollar will be returned plus some additional amount of rent earned. Likewise, every dollar borrowed must be returned plus some amount of rent owed. Assume that the local bank is charging 8% annual interest on money borrowed. Then, for every $1 borrowed today, the bank will require $1.08 to be paid back in 1 year from now. To the bank, the future value of that $1 lent is $1.08. The $0.08 is the rent or premium paid to use the money. Since we can look forward in time to see how much $1 will be worth in 1 year, we can also look backwards in time. Assume that the local bank is paying 5% annual interest on money deposited into a savings account. If you opened a savings account 1 year ago, and there is presently $1.05 in that account, you must have deposited $1, 1 year ago. We know that to be true because the bank owes you a premium or rent on that money of $0.05 per year. Similarly, if someone promises to pay you $1.05 (which assumes 5% annual interest) in 1 year from now, there will be a 5% premium paid during the year. If we did not want to wait the 1 year to collect the premium or rent, the other person could just pay you $1 today. You could invest the $1 yourself in the bank and still have $1.05 at the end of the year (and not have to worry about default or bad debt).

The process of evaluating what the amount is today, by calculating the value of the premium or rent, is called discounting. The discounted amount, evaluated to determine worth today, is termed the present value. Present value is a terribly important concept in finance. For every financial situation that promises you some future reward, there is a present value. Knowing the present value helps you to evaluate whether what you are giving up today (services or investment) is worth what you will receive in the future. It removes the benefit of the premium or rent – which you can earn on your own if you had the cash now. The formula for discounting is:

$$\frac{\text{Future value}}{(1 + \text{Discount rate})^t}$$

where the discount rate is the cost of capital or required return on the asset (whichever is known), and t is the time (usually number of years) being discounted. Using the example above:

$$\frac{\$1.05}{(1 + 0.05)^1} = \$1.00$$

A common example of present value and discounting is state lottery payouts. Most state lotteries will give the winner an option, to receive $X a year for so many years, or to receive a one-time payment of $Y. The one-time payment is the present value of the $X annual payments. Alternatively, by choosing the annual payments, the winner is actually receiving part of the winnings every year, plus some rent or premium for the state's continued use of the money.

Another example commonly seen is the valuation of salary contracts for professional athletes. Suppose you decide to quit your practice and join a professional basketball league. The newspapers are quick to print the '$5 million 5-year contract for ex-physician' article in the sports page. Essentially, these deals provide the athlete with $1 million dollars every year for 5 years. Based on the discounting tool described above, the present value of the payments is necessarily worth less than $5 million today (Figure 1). In fact, the contract is really worth a little over $4.3 million today when discounted by 8% (assuming that the $4.3 million was invested at 8%). Not that $4.3 million is something to take lightly, but it is a misrepresentation of the financial situation.

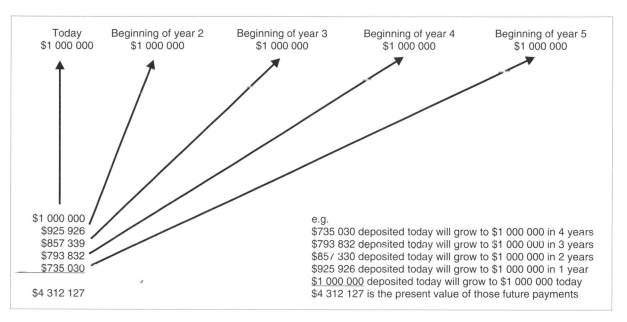

Figure 1 Valuation of salary contract

The time value of money concept is absolutely invaluable for any financial decision where the underlying benefit or obligations extend for any period of time.

Expected future cash flow

Now that the concept of discounting has been described, the single most common unknown element in finance is 'the value of the expected future cash flow'. Anyone attempting to sell you something either implicitly or explicitly describes the expected future benefit of the service or product. One example is a medical practice agreeing to market services through the use of a brochure: what is the expected future benefit? Even purchasing a used car can have the new owner wondering 'what is it going to cost me in repairs to keep this thing on the road?' From the previous section of this chapter, we saw that the discounting tool allows the financial manager to determine today's value of expected future receipts or payments. Unfortunately, the difficult task is estimating the future value of an expected benefit or obligation to pay. If the future expected benefit or obligation is incorrect, then discounting those amounts will provide an incorrect present value.

Selling or merging practices

Now that the foundations have been explained and hopefully understood, we can apply these concepts to buying, selling or merging physician practices. But, before we conclude, it seems most appropriate to define the terms clearly. Selling a practice, or a divestiture, is the sale of a portion or all of the practice to an outside party in exchange for cash or other assets given as consideration by the acquiring party. Merging, on the other hand, is a marriage between two or more entities (practices). Most practices (for legal and managerial reasons) will combine as horizontal mergers. A horizontal merger is a marriage of entities in the same line of business, for example, two pediatric practices. A vertical merger is one between two entities along the same process line, but at different stages or of different focus. Typical vertical mergers involve companies that merge with a supplier, or a distributor of products, i.e. merging with an entity that helps to complete the process cycle. An example of this would be a practice merging with a radiology lab, or an insurance company – the same healthcare industry but at different stages. Conglomerate mergers are between entities in completely unrelated industries, such as a practice merging with an autobody shop. Again, legal and managerial reasons preclude this from being prudent for a healthcare practice.

To define selling or merging a practice more specifically, we need to define further the types of sales or mergers. There are several ways to sell a business. The owners can sell all or part of the entity's assets. A sale of assets leaves the corporate shell intact. Compare this with a sale of a corporation's stock, which transfers ownership of the entity, but not the assets. The assets still remain the property of the acquired entity. The acquired company is treated as a separate company with new owners. For example, if you purchased shares of stock in IBM, you would be considered an owner of the company, but IBM is considered the owner of the assets.

There are significant tax implications and guidelines that can work towards your increasing of owner's wealth. For instance, the ability to sell the practice in accordance with the Internal Revenue Service's 'B' or 'C' reorganization regulations can allow you to defer the tax on gains from the sale. This discussion on the types of sales is not all-inclusive (it excludes instalment sale, for example). You should consult your tax attorney on which sale type is most appropriate for your practice when considering a sale.

There is more, however, to describe about mergers or consolidations. In a merger, two or more entities combine and leave one of the combining companies as the remaining entity. Under a consolidation, two or more entities combine and form a new and separate economic entity – all of the combining entities would cease to exist. For example:

Merger: $a + b + c = \mathbf{a}$

Consolidation: $a + b + c = \mathbf{d}$

Now that the terms are defined, the real issue to address is 'why?' Why is the practice selling or looking to merge? More specifically, 'what' is the sale or merger trying to accomplish? What is the desired goal or outcome? Academically, the answer to all these questions is 'to increase the owner's wealth'. But the questions continue. Why should someone pay a seller's asking price – what is the essence of the valuation? How will the merger increase the owner's wealth – what is the essence of the improvement that would cause an increase in the owner's wealth? The remainder of this chapter addresses these questions. But let us take a look at some reasons why an owner might consider the sale or merger of all or part of a practice:

- Better alternative uses for the dollars invested: an owner may have better investment opportunities that will increase wealth

- Diversification: for the physician/owner, having a significant amount of personal wealth invested in the practice that he/she is also employed in is like keeping all of your eggs in one basket. The owner may choose to diversify by selling the practice (or re-capitalizing with more debt rather than personal equity), investing the personal capital elsewhere, thereby diversifying the total portfolio of investments. As such, in the event that the physician or practice would no longer be a viable cash producer, personal wealth would not necessarily be destroyed

- If the practice is experiencing operating losses due to limited markets or growth, poor management, marginal profits and so on, depending upon the circumstances, a merger or sale can often be a financial remedy for a practice that experiences continued operating losses

- If the practice is too small to leverage operating expenses but too large to be managed with a small staff, a sale would allow the owner to remove capital while a merger could produce synergies

- If funds are needed to finance other opportunities, a partial or complete sale, or a practice merger can help

- Managed care: if the effects of managed care (or business in general) create an environment where it is better to be an employee rather than an owner, then a sale or merger can return invested capital

- Product or service fit/change in strategies: if the practice is vertically integrated and/or owns assets that are no longer providing a sufficient return, then those assets may be more valuable (and worth a premium) to another owner

What is the essence of the valuation? What does the 'for sale' practice have that someone would pay for? Is it a patient list or book of business? Are there hard assets (land, buildings, equipment) that are worth being purchased? Are there future prospects? What would you be willing to pay for if you were a potential acquirer? Both buyers and sellers need to consider that there are several basic ways to value a business (and even several more complicated ways). The two most agreed-upon foundations for valuations are based on assets and cash flow. Let us first discuss asset-based valuations.

Businesses that are asset-intensive (for example, heavily invested in inventory or fixed assets) can be valued by examining the market value of the assets to be transferred. The essential idea is to identify the 'street value' of the assets if each were sold separately or, alternatively, together as a cohesive package. This type of valuation typically makes no provision for asset operation or even operational benefit to the acquirer. Asset-based valuation should not be the foundation for valuing medical practices, which are almost by definition labor-intensive (heavily invested in human resources). While medical practices will most likely have fixed assets, it is not the primary basis for increasing owner wealth. The fiscal intention of medical practices is to increase owner wealth through human resources (practitioners) and ancillary assets that generate cash flow. Therefore, the more appropriate valuation method is based on cash flows.

Cash flow-based valuation is by far the most commonly accepted and used valuation method in the finance community. This method views the business or practice as a cash-producing machine (cash flow after taxes). Valuation is based on the machine's ability to produce future cash flows, rather than the assets used in operations. If you were a potential acquirer, the prospects of purchasing a machine that produces cash versus purchasing assets that will require incremental costs to operate should interest you. The process of cash flow valuation requires an examination of the after-tax cash that an entity has produced, and estimates of expected future cash flows.

The cash flow valuation model actually relies on all four finance fundamentals: rent, risk and return, time value of money and expectations of the future. Let us examine how. The potential acquirer of a practice will have to fund the purchase somehow. As already discussed, that financing will come from personal funds, borrowed funds or some other equity owners. In any case, the funds all come with a cost – rent or cost of capital. As mentioned in the previous paragraph, the valuation requires that expectations of future cash flows be projected. Those expected future cash flows must be discounted (using the cost of capital) to determine the present value. If the acquirer perceives any risk in the machine's ability to generate the future cash flows, then a higher return would be required. One way of factoring in a higher return is to increase the value of the discount rate. This is known as adjusting the cost of capital. By adjusting the cost of capital, the future cash flows are discounted at a greater rate, thus producing a smaller present value.

Let us use another example to explain this valuation process. Assume that you are evaluating the purchase of a practice currently for sale for $10 million. The business broker promoting the sale believes that this is a fair price since pre-tax profit is $2 million per year – a 5-year payback rationale. Your intention is to grow your current practice and retire in wealth in 5 years. Your financial manager determines that, although the acquisition target earns $2 million in pre-tax profit, actual after-tax cash flow is $800 000 per year. You and the financial manager create an expectation of future earnings based on the practice's historical financial, economic and market data. That expectation needs to be based on a realistic financial projection of anticipated cash flows as tempered by: incremental cost savings or new expenses, improved revenue streams, weakened or improved financing (i.e. receivables collections, etc.) and all other relevant factors that have a monetary effect.

To continue the example, the practice should derive some incremental improvements that would improve annual after-tax cash flow to $1 million for the 5 years of your ownership. Moreover, you believe that the practice can be sold for five times cash flow ($5 million) at the end of 5 years. Funding for the project would cost 8%. The practice would be valued using the discounted cash flow method as shown in Figure 2.

Each of the expected future cash flows are discounted at the 8% cost of capital, including the expected $5 million sales value at the end of year 5. Based on this valuation, the practice is worth $7.395 million, rather than the $10 million asking price. The implication is that if anything over $7.395 were paid, the acquirer would receive less than an 8% return on the dollars invested. Furthermore, a critical assumption is that the risk associated with the acquisition is comparable to the risk expected for other investments yielding an 8% return, i.e. government

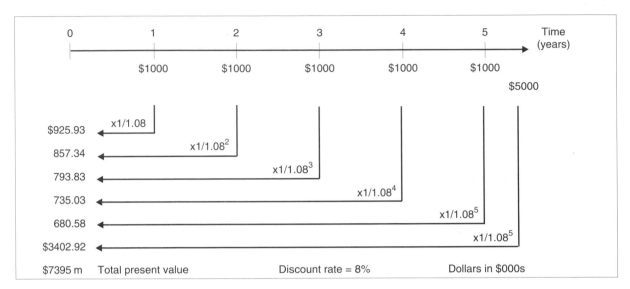

Figure 2 Valuation using discounted cash flow method

bonds. If the risk for this project is greater than our 8% government bond example, then it is prudent to raise the required return to match the risk you expect to bear. Assume that you believe that the risk associated with this acquisition is no greater than your investment in the high-tech stock 'AskDr.Bartolacci.com'. The stock is currently yielding 12%, and as such you would be satisfied with a 12% return for assuming the risk associated with the acquisition. Therefore, the acquisition has to be re-evaluated using a 12% adjusted cost of capital or discount rate (Figure 3).

Because the valuation is based on a higher required return or discount rate, the mathematics produce a lower total present value. Note that the new valuation displays a recommended purchase of $6442 million, which is $953 000 less than the valuation that required an 8% return. The long and short of this analysis is that more risk deserves more return. In this case, more return is exhibited as a lower (or discounted!) purchase price.

Physicians selling a practice should use this methodology to determine a price range. The range (the low end using conservative estimates of future cash flows, and the high end using aggressive estimates of future cash flows) provides a basis for negotiation. By applying the discounted cash flow methodology to the most realistic expectations, the physician can determine 'economic break-even'. At economic break-even, the physician's financial position would neither be strengthened nor weakened by the sale of the practice. Any amount under economic break-even would cause the owner to lose wealth, and any amount over would cause the owner to increase wealth.

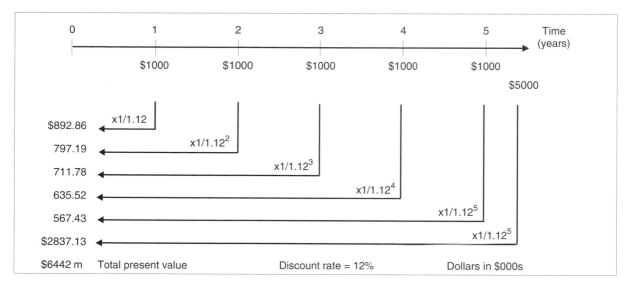

Figure 3 Re-evaluation using discounted cash flow method

What is the essence of the expected improvement from merging practices? What changes create value through a merger? The following is a list of some possibilities:

(1) Synergies: the value of the whole (new combined firm) is greater than the sum of the parts (previously separate entities);

(2) Revenue improvements;

(3) Lower costs: elimination of redundant positions, rents or other expenses;

(4) New financing capabilities: pooling of cash or other monetary assets to improve liquidity, refinancing at the more favorable rates of one of the previously merged entities, etc.;

(5) Volume purchasing opportunities: increased size (economies of scale) that allows for volume purchase discounts;

(6) Exploiting untapped or missed opportunities that were previously overlooked or not possible by the previously merged firms;

(7) New technologies, assets or skill sets;

(8) Process or management improvements;

(9) Greater market share or access to a broader patient base;

(10) Tax benefits: using the tax advantage of one or more of the entities to lower the benefit of the whole firm.

This list is certainly not exhaustive, nor does it address the instant value added when one firm is able to purchase another well below market value. It is, however, meant to get the reader thinking about the benefits of merging two or more practices together. This chapter's text would not be complete unless it also spelled out the downsides or potentials to reduce the owner's wealth. The most significant of the dangers in forming mergers is overpayment. The acquiring company can exchange its stock for the stock of the company (or companies) that it wants to fold into a single operation, or it can pay cash, or provide consideration through a combination of both cash and stock. Because the merger will essentially resemble an acquisition, the same issues and concerns of an acquisition will apply to a merger. The fundamentals of a merger's valuation, like that of an acquisition, will also be rooted in the discounted cash flow methodology.

Recent financial analysis and research have provided results that indicate the prevalence of merger and acquisition failures, with overpayment as the common reason cited. The firms being bought have consequently been shown to exhibit correspondingly high returns to the owners. Other factors that present dangers to a merger include:

(1)   Incorrect expectations and projections of future cash flows: if the cash flows used in the discounted cash flow valuation are incorrect, then the calculated present value (purchase price) will be incorrect:
  (a)   Overaggressive or unrealistic synergy or cost-saving assumptions;
  (b)   Overoptimistic expectations of revenues;

(2)   Costly or incomplete integration of the firms;

(3)   Cultural differences:
  (a)   Loss of key personnel;
  (b)   Loss of management direction, strategy or guidance;

(4)   Expensive 'surprises' or unexpected costs;

(5)   Overvaluation of the assets, or skills of the human resources.

The expected benefits of a merger seem to be easier to identify, and are certainly more enticing since they appear to mitigate whatever post-merger risk is lurking. The essence of improvements from a merger relates to the incremental benefits net of any risks associated with the post-merger firm. Both the incremental benefits and risks have to be quantified as present or future financial expectations. The discounted cash flow valuation should be used to determine whether the present value of the benefits would provide a sufficient return to the investor. If the calculated present value is greater than the amount required to purchase the target firm(s), then the deal will increase shareholder wealth (if all inherent assumptions are correct). If the calculated present value is less than the amount required for the merger, then the incremental expected benefits will not provide the investor with a return that is at least as high as the cost of capital used to fund the project. The merger should not be undertaken at that price.

Conclusion

It is hoped that the basic fundamentals described here will create a philosophical metamorphosis in the way that the reader approaches the practice operations, and its sale or merger. Increasing the owner's wealth is based on the concept that every asset (including a practice) has a cost that extends long after the purchase price has been paid. Every asset's cost needs to be continually compared with its alternative use so that incremental changes will add value. Aggregation of the incremental value-adding changes is the path to increased owner wealth. The idea of 'continuous improvement' extends far beyond the profit and loss statement and the constant ratcheting down of expenses. Finance is not the practice of downsizing and cost reductions. Finance in a practice creates growth – ultimately for the practice owners (sometimes through a sale or merger). But be cautious: growth does not necessarily mean pouring good money after bad. Always examine the opportunity cost and evaluate those alternatives against the cost of the assets currently employed or required.

Financial Planning

17

Bates H. Whiteside and Thomas E. Nolan

Why financial planning?

Let's face it. Financial planning is not the activity of choice for most individuals. If each of us had our way, the various pieces of our financial lives would magically fall into place. All of our financial needs would be met effortlessly without our having to devote even a minute of time planning.

Unfortunately, life does not work that way. Making sense of your finances requires more time and effort than ever in today's constantly changing economic environment. You are likely to have many different, and sometimes conflicting, financial goals. Deciding how to meet those goals requires careful planning. Higher earning levels, increased wealth, shifting tax laws, and the sheer number of financial products available in the marketplace today also contribute to the need for financial planning.

Financial planning involves several steps. Each one is important, and all must be coordinated if your financial plan is to succeed. The four main steps to the process are:

(1) Knowing where you are today (Evaluating your current situation);

(2) Deciding where you want to be sometime in the future (Setting your goals);

(3) Setting out a plan to get there and putting it into effect (Putting your plan together);

(4) Reviewing the plan regularly to see that it continues to meet your goals (Monitoring your plan).

We will look at these financial planning steps and explain how to go about setting your plan. Included are a number of worksheets that can help one along the way. We will also discuss some specific strategies you may find worthwhile.

This segment of the *MBA Handbook for Healthcare Professionals* is not intended to take the place of professional advice. You will want to consult with a professional before using any of the planning tools or strategies we will discuss here.

Evaluating your current situation

Knowing where you stand today in terms of your finances is the first step in developing any financial plan. The accompanying worksheet (Figure 1) is designed to give you a 'snapshot' of your current financial

---

How much are you worth?

	Current Value ($)
Assets	
Personal bank accounts (checking, savings, money market deposit accounts)	_____
Certificates of deposit	_____
Other income investments (bonds, bond mutual funds, money market mutual funds)	_____
Stocks and stock mutual funds	_____
Real estate investments	_____
Business interests (proprietorships, partnerships, company stock)	_____
Retirement plan investments	_____
Individual retirement accounts (IRAs)	_____
401(k) or 403(b) plans	_____
Keogh plan	_____
Simplified employment pension (SEP)	_____
Profit sharing plan	_____
Pension plan	_____
Market value of home(s)	_____
Cash value of life insurance	_____
Personal property (jewelry, collectibles, cars, furniture)*	_____
Miscellaneous (trust interests, inheritances)	_____
Total Assets	_____
Liabilities	
Mortgages	_____
Car loans	_____
Credit cards	_____
Student loans	_____
Other loans	_____
Outstanding bills and obligations	_____
Total Liabilities	_____
NET WORTH (subtract Liabilities from Assets):	
Assets	_____
Liabilities	
Your Net Worth	_____

*While items such as jewelry and collectibles may have a high retail value, their true net worth is closer to wholesale value

---

Figure 1 Worksheet for evaluating current financial situation

situation. It will help you determine your net worth (your assets minus your liabilities) and what resources you can apply to meet your goals.

Net worth is the main measurement of wealth. If your net worth is small (say, due to your having large debts outstanding), you will want to concentrate on increasing it. The most straightforward ways to increase your net worth are to increase your assets (by investing current assets and accumulating more) or to reduce your debts.

The other number to look at in evaluating your current situation is your net income (your gross income minus your expenses). Try using the Monthly Budget Worksheet (Figure 2) to track your expenses for a few months or use Quicken or other commercially available software. It will tell you where your current income comes from and where it goes. This information can help you better budget your spending and determine how much you can set aside for meeting needs and goals.

Budgeting and debt management

Many people find they are spending more than they bring in. It is difficult to increase your net worth (and meet your financial goals) if you are constantly falling behind on the income front. After reviewing the information you entered on the Monthly Budget Worksheet, you might have to ask some hard questions.

For example, are you spending more on entertainment or other non-essential expenses, than your income supports? Or are you spending more than you have to for necessities such as housing, an automobile, clothing or other similar items? The answers will probably point you to one or more possible solutions, such as cutting back on the non-essentials or finding less expensive alternatives. Then, you can put the money you save to work toward meeting your goals.

Most causes of overspending can be addressed through the use of a budget. Simply going through the process of putting together an annual budget can help you prioritize expenses and uncover areas where you may be able to free up more money to use for savings and investments.

Many people find that they can develop the discipline needed to put money aside on a regular basis by budgeting for savings and investments the same way they do for other expenses. A good way to make sure your budgeted amount actually does go into savings and investments is to set up an automatic savings/investing plan with a bank or a mutual fund company.

Monthly Budget Worksheet

Monthly Expenditures

Food	$_____
Rent or mortgage payment	$_____
Child care	$_____
Utilities	$_____
Household maintenance	$_____
Saving/investing	$_____
Retirement savings plan contribution	$_____
Auto loan payment	$_____
Auto maintenance	$_____
Transportation (gas, fares)	$_____
Income and Social Security taxes	$_____
Property taxes	$_____
Clothing	$_____
Insurance	$_____
Credit card payments	$_____
Contributions	$_____
Entertainment	$_____
Dues	$_____
Other	+_____
Total Monthly Expenditures	$_____

Monthly Receipts

Wages or salary	$_____
Interest (CDs, savings account, etc.)	$_____
Dividends (mutual funds, stocks, etc.)	$_____
Other	+_____
Total Monthly Receipts	$_____

Net Cash Flow

Total Monthly Receipts	$_____
Total Monthly Expenditures	−_____
Monthly Net Cash Flow*	$_____

*A positive net monthly cash flow means you have additional money available for saving and investing. If the figure is negative, you need to find ways to trim your monthly expenses, or you will not be able to achieve your financial goals

Figure 2   Monthly budget worksheet

Trimming your budget

Cutting your expenses will take some effort. You may have to delay some purchases and find ways to spend less on the things you need to buy. Compare your monthly expenses to the average shown in Figure 3. By cutting costs, you should be able to afford to contribute more to your savings and investments. Similarly, if large debt payments are making it difficult to save, you need to look at ways you can reduce this burden so that you can move ahead toward your financial goal. Some money-saving ideas are discussed below.

EXPENSE	AMOUNT PAID	% OF INCOME
Housing	$1650	36%
Transportation	$880	19.2%
Entertainment	$353	7.7%
Groceries	$316	6.9%
Eating out	$289	6.3%
Clothing	$275	6%
Healthcare	$202	4.4%
Charitable gifts, alimony & child support payments	$202	4.4%
Education	$87	1.9%
Other	$329	7.2%

Figure 3   Average monthly expenses (assuming an after-tax annual income of $55 000). From US Department of Labor and NPI

Reduce housing costs

One good avenue to explore is the possibility of refinancing your mortgage. The rule of thumb is to consider refinancing your home when mortgage rates drop two percentage points or more below the current rate. But people who plan to remain in their home for a while can come out ahead with a rate reduction of as little as one percentage point. (See *When Refinancing Can Make Sense* later in this chapter.)

Very good and sophisticated calculators can be found on the Internet at sites such as www.smartmoney.com or www.cnnfn.com and other financial web-sites.

Consolidate debt

Refinancing is not the only way you can use your home for additional investment funds. If you have high credit card balances, you may want to consider using a home equity loan to pay them off. With high credit card rates, consolidating your debt with a home equity loan could reduce the interest rate you are paying and cut your monthly payments considerably. As an added bonus, the interest you pay on your home equity loan may be tax deductible for federal income tax purposes, which would increase your savings further.

Buy smart

How and when you shop can make a discernible difference in your spending. Different items generally go on sale at different times during the year (Figure 4).

January	Coats, furs, diamonds, lingerie, cosmetics, luggage, TVs
February	Furniture, hosiery, furs
March	China, glass, silver, washers & dryers
April	A/C units, diamonds, sleepwear
May	Luggage, housewares, home furnishings
June	Sleepwear, lingerie, furniture
July	Swimwear, gardening supplies
August	Garden furniture
September	Store-wide sales
October	Coats
November	Coats, furniture
December	After Christmas, store-wide clearance sales

Figure 4   What's on sale when. From National Retail Merchants Association

Review insurance costs

Insurance costs can be a major expense. Take a look at your policies and consider these cost-cutting measures: raising the deductible on your homeowner's or automobile insurance from $250 to $500 could cut your premiums by more than 10%. Consolidating your home and auto policies with the same insurance company may save another 5–15% off your premiums without sacrificing coverage.

Setting your goals

No matter what your age or financial status, you have financial goals. Your goals are the things you want to make the future brighter for you and your family. It is easy to come up with some general goals for ourselves – 'to be successful', 'to be financially secure', 'to live the good life', and so on. But the easiest goals to work toward are those that are more specific. They may include, among others:

- An emergency fund

- A comfortable retirement

- College education for your children

- Capital to start a business

One key element of financial planning, therefore, is to define your goals clearly, and then prioritize them. With specific goals, you can estimate the time frame in which each goal must be realized. Some goals are long term. Others are short term, ones you will want to achieve in 5 years or less – money for a new car, a down payment on a home, or next year's vacation money, for instance.

Having specific goals also helps you determine the amount of money that you will need to meet each goal. Then, you can plan for how you will obtain the necessary funds within your desired time frame. Our Goal Worksheet (Figure 5) together with Tables 1 and 2 should help. A difficult problem for many people is that they have multiple goals. For example, you might want to save for retirement at the same time as you want to finance your children's college education. You might feel that you have only so much money to go around and that one or other of the goals may have to be abandoned.

Once you prioritize your goals, however, you can look for ways to make each of your major goals achievable. Yes, some trade-offs may be necessary. But getting the most you can from the resources available to you is only possible if your goals are spelled out in as much detail as possible.

Goal Worksheet

	Example	Yours
1. Goal	Down payment for home	_____
2. Years until money is needed	3	_____
3. Total amount needed for goal in today's dollars	$20 000	
4. Inflation factor (from Table 1; our example assumes 4% average annual inflation)	× 1.13	_____
5. Projected future value of amount needed	$22 600	_____
6. Amount already saved toward goal	$7 000	_____
7. Return factor (from Table 1; example assumes 7% return)	× 1.23	_____
8. Projected future value of amount saved	$8 610	
9. Additional money needed to reach goal (subtract #8 from #5)	$13 990	_____
10. Annual savings factor (from Table 2; example assumes 7% return)	× 0.301	_____
11. Annual savings needed	$4 211	_____
	÷ 12 months	÷ 12 months
12. Monthly investment needed to reach goal	$351	_____

Figure 5 Goal worksheet

Table 1 Inflation/return factors*. Source: NPI

Assumed rate**	1	2	3	4	5	10	15	20	25	30	40
3%	1.03	1.06	1.09	1.13	1.16	1.35	1.57	1.82	2.12	2.46	3.32
4%	1.04	1.08	1.13	1.17	1.22	1.49	1.82	2.22	2.71	3.31	4.94
5%	1.05	1.10	1.16	1.22	1.28	1.65	2.11	2.71	3.48	4.47	7.36
6%	1.06	1.13	1.20	1.27	1.35	1.82	2.45	3.31	4.46	6.02	10.96
7%	1.07	1.15	1.23	1.32	1.42	2.01	2.85	4.04	5.73	8.12	16.31
8%	1.08	1.17	1.27	1.38	1.49	2.22	3.31	4.93	7.34	10.94	24.27
9%	1.09	1.20	1.31	1.43	1.57	2.45	3.84	6.01	9.41	14.73	36.11
10%	1.10	1.22	1.35	1.49	1.65	2.71	4.45	7.33	12.06	19.84	53.70
11%	1.12	1.24	1.39	1.55	1.73	2.99	5.17	8.94	15.45	26.71	79.83

*Returns do not represent the actual results of any particular investment. The factors assume monthly compounding. If inflation is higher or your returns are lower, you will need to invest more to reach your goal

**For inflation, the rate is the average annual inflation rate you expect to apply; for return, the rate is the average annual investment return you expect

Table 2 Annual savings factor*. Source: NPI

Assumed average annual return	1	2	3	4	5	10	15	20	25	30	40
4%	0.982	0.481	0.314	0.231	0.181	0.081	0.049	0.033	0.023	0.017	0.010
5%	0.977	0.476	0.310	0.226	0.176	0.077	0.045	0.029	0.020	0.014	0.008
6%	0.973	0.472	0.305	0.222	0.172	0.073	0.041	0.026	0.017	0.012	0.006
7%	0.968	0.467	0.301	0.217	0.168	0.069	0.038	0.023	0.015	0.010	0.005
8%	0.964	0.463	0.296	0.213	0.163	0.066	0.035	0.020	0.013	0.008	0.003
9%	0.959	0.458	0.292	0.209	0.159	0.062	0.032	0.018	0.011	0.007	0.003
10%	0.955	0.454	0.287	0.204	0.155	0.059	0.029	0.016	0.009	0.005	0.002
11%	0.951	0.449	0.283	0.200	0.151	0.055	0.026	0.014	0.008	0.004	0.001

*Returns do not represent the actual results of any particular investment. The factors assume monthly compounding. If inflation is higher or your returns are lower, you will need to invest more to reach your goal

Putting your plan together

Now that you have collected your financial information and set your goals, the next step in developing your plan is to analyze your information and develop and implement your overall plan. You will need to take into account any planning strategies you already have in place. For example, if you have existing investments, one or more retirement plans, a Will, life insurance policies, and other financial documents, these must be examined and, if needed, revised in light of any new plan you establish.

Your financial plan will consider all aspects of your financial life. It should include an annual budget or spending plan. If your outstanding debt is significant in relation to your assets, a debt reduction plan may be an important part of your overall financial plan. In addition, your plan should cover each of the following areas to the extent needed to reach your goals:

- Life insurance and disability planning

- Investment planning

- Education funding (if applicable)

- Retirement planning

- Estate planning

Life insurance and disability planning

What would happen to your goals and your family's financial security if you were to die or were disabled and no longer able to work? With adequate insurance planning, major lifestyle changes due to a lack of income should not be necessary.

Life insurance

With life insurance planning, the first question is always, 'How much is enough?' Whether you need life insurance at all and, if you do, the best amount of insurance coverage to have depends on your particular circumstances. Many people start thinking about life insurance when they marry and have children. But, even if you are not married, you may have someone else, such as a parent or sibling, who depends on you for financial support. The longer your dependents will need support the greater your need for coverage.

The worksheet shown in Figure 6 will help you figure out how much additional coverage you need, if any. Start by establishing the income your spouse and/or dependents will continue to receive after your death. Then, estimate their annual expenses. Any shortfall between the expenses and expected income is the amount of income your insurance needs will need to provide. One method financial planners use to calculate the amount of life insurance coverage is to figure $100 000 of coverage for each $5000 of additional income needed. For a more accurate estimate of your life insurance needs contact a qualified financial planner.

Insurance Worksheet		
Household income without your earnings	**Life**	**Disability**
Spouse's (dependent's) earnings	$_____	$_____
Social Security benefits	$_____	$_____
Retirement plan benefits	$_____	$_____
Investment portfolio income	$_____	$_____
Income from investing the proceeds of any existing life insurance policies on your life	$_____	$ NA
Income from any current disability coverage you have	$ NA	$_____
Total annual income	$_____	$_____
Annual expenses	– $_____	– $_____
Additional annual income needed from life and/or disability insurance	$_____	$_____
	÷ $5 000	
	× $100 000	
Additional life insurance needed*	$_____	

*Note that this calculation does not consider that your family could also spend down the insurance proceeds over time, a factor which would lower your coverage needs

Figure 6 Insurance worksheet

If you discover you need additional coverage and you are still relatively young, term life insurance is generally the least expensive way to go because it provides 'pure coverage': you build no cash value in the policy. The cost of term insurance goes up as you get older, but the amount of coverage you will need should diminish as you get older. Term insurance provides protection for a specific number of years, with the death benefit paid to your beneficiaries if you die during the policy term. When the term ends, so does your coverage, unless you renew the policy. Cash value life insurance, such as whole life, universal life, and variable life policies, provides protection over your entire life. For younger people, cash value insurance is more expensive than term insurance. But the premiums are generally fixed, and as the years go on can become less expensive. Cash values and interest accumulate in the policy tax deferred, and you can borrow from the cash value. However, it must be remembered that cash value policies do not reflect inflation rates or protect against loss of purchasing power in high inflation environments. A $50 000 policy bought in 1978 would have seemed like a great deal of money, while in 2002, its true value has diminished because of the rapid inflation that occurred in the late 1970s and early 1980s.

Disability insurance

Like life insurance planning, disability insurance planning is based on your particular needs, circumstances and resources. Completing the disability worksheet should help you determine if you need additional coverage to protect your family should you become temporarily or permanently disabled. In addition, you may want to include long-term care insurance in your financial plan to help preserve your assets for your family in the event you suffer a prolonged illness.

Long-term care insurance is a relatively new coverage concept that is still emerging as an insurance entity. Individuals should begin to consider long-term insurance between ages 55 and 60. As with most insurance, the earlier one begins paying, the less expensive the policies are. After age 70–75 many of these policies become overly expensive.

Disability and long-term care insurance are not the only aspects of disability planning. You need to think about who will manage your assets if you become incapacitated and can no longer handle this responsibility yourself. A power of attorney may be a good solution. With a power of attorney, you choose someone to make financial decisions for you if you are unable to do so yourself.

Healthcare provision

Consider creating a Living Will and/or a durable power of attorney for healthcare to help ensure your wishes concerning the care you receive are carried out if you are unable to make healthcare decisions yourself. A Living Will is generally used to express the desire not to receive extraordinary medical treatment. You determine the kind of medical care you want under the circumstances you describe. You should express your wishes in as much detail as possible.

A durable power of attorney for healthcare – sometimes called a healthcare proxy – designates someone else to make decisions for you. The scope of a durable power of attorney generally goes beyond that of a Living Will. A durable power of attorney can address nearly any healthcare decision. Your attorney can advise you concerning applicable law and draft the relevant documents for you.

Investment planning

Good investment planning can turn your goals from dreams into realities. This planning involves more than trying to pick the 'right' investments. How you allocate your money among different types of investments can have a greater effect on investment success than the individual investments you choose. So, your first step in investing toward your goals is to work out an asset allocation for your investments.

Asset allocation

Very simply, asset allocation is the process of deciding what percentage of your money to put in the different investment classes: stocks, bonds, money market and other investments, such as real estate. Your asset allocation will depend on your investment time frame, your savings goal, and how much risk you are willing to take to achieve that goal.

Diversification

After you decide on an asset allocation, the next step is to diversify your money within the different investment classes. By putting your money in numerous different investments, you 'spread the risk'. To illustrate, rather than invest in one stock, you might invest in a variety of stocks. That way, if one stock performs poorly, it represents a smaller portion of your overall stock portfolio.

Before you can set an asset allocation and diversify your investments, however, you need to know more about the choices available to you. In the next section, a brief overview of the basic investment choices is provided.

Stocks

Investing in stocks gives you an ownership interest in the corporation issuing the stock. If the corporation does well, your investment should do well. If not, you could lose some (or all) of your money. The advantages of investing in stocks include the potential for higher returns over time that have, historically, outpaced inflation. A balanced portfolio generally reduces the risk of loss over the long haul. The problem with other investments is the loss of purchasing power because of inflation.

Bonds

Bonds and other fixed income investments pay a set income over a set term. At the end of the term, the amount you have invested is returned to you. Fixed income investments offer a steady income stream and, historically, less volatile price fluctuations than stock investments. But fixed income investments are not without risk. Sometimes a bond issuer, for example, can run into financial difficulties, default on its bonds, and not be able to return the face amount of the bonds to investors.

Also, bond prices move up and down, largely in reaction to investment rate swings. Thus, investors in individual bonds who do not plan on holding them until maturity face the possibility of risk of losing principal.

Money market investments

Like fixed income investments, money market investments pay a defined income over a set term. (The income may be fixed or variable.) The advantage of money market investments is that many of them are backed by the US government or insured by the Federal Deposit Insurance Corporation (FDIC), so return on your principal is practically guaranteed. This makes money market investments an attractive choice for investors with short-term goals. But be aware that a money market fund is neither insured nor guaranteed by the US government, and there can be no assurance that money market funds will be able to maintain a stable net asset value of $1.00 per share. The major disadvantage of this investment class is that the investment, historically, has not produced returns much greater than the inflation rate.

Mutual funds

Mutual funds are one of the most popular ways to invest. With a mutual fund, your money is pooled with that of other investors to purchase a variety of securities. The fund is professionally managed as a single investment account. Mutual funds offer you automatic diversification because each fund invests in numerous different securities. When you buy shares in a stock mutual fund, for example, you are actually buying an investment in the stocks of many different companies. If one company or industry has a problem, the fund will be less likely to suffer a major loss because it is diversified.

You can choose from thousands of stock, bond, balanced (stock and bonds), and money market mutual funds. Each fund is managed to meet a particular investment objective, such as growth, income or asset preservation. The mutual fund's prospectus will explain the fund's investment objective and tell you what types of securities the fund can hold.

Investment return

When choosing investments, potential return is a key consideration. The higher your return, the faster your investments will grow and the sooner you will reach your goal. But be aware that the annual percentage returns and yields you see published in the advertisements, prospectuses and articles do not take into account taxes and inflation, and are two key factors you need to consider in your investment planning.

You can use the Figure 7 worksheet to calculate the real rate of return of any investment you are considering. In some cases, you may

Example – Your investment:

1.	Annual return*	12%	_____
2.	Combined state and federal tax rates	35%	_____
3.	(1 times 2) Return lost to taxes	4.2%	_____
4.	Annual return	12%	_____
5.	Minus return lost to taxes (line 3)	4.2%	_____
6.	After-tax return*	7.8%	_____
7.	Minus current inflation rate	–3%	_____
8.	Real after-tax return	4.8%	_____

*When calculating your real rate of return for a tax-exempt investment, start with 'After-tax return' (line #6)

Figure 7 Worksheet for calculating real rates of return

find that a tax-exempt investment posting a lower rate of return will actually give you a higher real return than a similar taxable investment.

Risk

You also need to weigh an investment's risk. Generally, the more risk involved with an investment, the higher its potential return. Consequently, the more risk you are willing to take, the more potential your savings have to grow over the long term. Before choosing an investment, you should make sure you understand the investment, the risk it carries, and how that risk relates to your investment goal.

For instance, if you are investing for your 2-year-old child's college education, you can probably afford to assume more risk in your investing than someone whose child will begin college in 2 or 3 years. With more than 15 years before you will need your money, you should have time to make up any short-term losses your investments may experience. Of course, there can be no assurance that any losses will be made up in a 15-year time period.

As the investment pyramid above shows, short-term investments, such as money market funds, offer the least risk. Fixed income investments offer potentially higher returns with added risk. Stock investment offers the highest potential returns with the greatest amount of risk. A combination of money market, fixed income and stock investments can provide potentially higher returns than either money market or fixed income investments alone, with only slightly greater risk.

As you near your goal, your risk tolerance may drop and you may want to change your asset allocation. Protecting and preserving your savings might be important. You may be willing to give up the growth potential of most of your long-term investments in favor of the greater security offered by short-term investments.

Education planning

When should you start planning for a child's college education? Ideally, as soon as the child is born. The cost of 4 years at a private college or university currently averages about $79 000. The average 4-year cost for a public college is about $32 000. With college cost inflation now at an average of 5% – and it has been considerably higher in the past – a child born today could need at least $77 000 to attend a public college for 4 years and more than twice that amount, $190 000, for a 4-year stint at a private college.

Do not be alarmed if you have not started planning for your child's college education. No matter what the child's age, strategies are available to help you come up with the necessary funds.

Personal investing

For young children, start putting money away regularly now, investing in higher potential growth securities and mutual funds as you would other long-term goals, such as retirement. As your income increases, try to increase the amount you are investing. When a child reaches high school age, you will probably want to begin moving college investments into less risky investments.

At this point, if you own appreciated assets that you intend to use to meet college expenses, consider giving them to the child, and letting the child sell them. The advantage? Potentially more after-tax money to meet expenses. If you sell assets you will have to pay capital gains tax at your rate, now more likely to be ≥20%. A child in the 15% federal tax bracket will be taxed at just 10% on the same gain.

If you are eligible, you may want to consider using an Education IRA to help you save for your children's higher education. The Education IRA lets you contribute toward a child's future education expenses until the child turns 18. Your contributions and the account earnings generally can be withdrawn from the IRA tax free to pay qualifying education expenses of the child. Recently, educational IRAs have been renamed Coverdell IRA and allow for contributions from $500 a year to $2000 a year (phase-out of contributions begins with a joint income of $160 000 and is disallowed above $220 000). Educational IRAs are restricted in that the money can only be used toward tuition, books and other expenses directly related to education.

New ways to pay for education have been expanded in the last several years. Popularly referred to as 529 plans, after tax income they can be invested for children's education expenses. When the money is withdrawn for educational expenses, there is no tax on earnings. These plans are not currently available in all states (42 are now allowing the plans) and they use popular mutual fund companies as the primary investment vehicles. This is a rapidly expanding area and information should be obtained either from your state education office or from various Internet sources such as www.Vanguard.com, www.Fidelity.com, www.savingforcollege.com or www.tiaa-cref.org.

Prepaid tuition plans

Many states offer prepaid tuition plans. Generally, with a prepaid tuition plan, you make a series of payments or a lump sum payment to a state program and designate your child as the beneficiary of the program account. If the plan meets all the applicable tax law requirements, the earnings on your account accumulate tax free and can be used to pay for the college tuition or expenses of your child. Some individual colleges and universities offer prepayment programs, as well.

By paying in advance, you can lock in current tuition costs for your child's education years from now. A growing number of tuition plans even allow students to use the money saved in the prepaid plan at a different school. If your child chooses not to attend college, most programs refund some or all of your account balance. Be sure to check the refund terms of any tuition program you are considering before making a decision.

Loans

What if you have not been investing regularly for your child's education or your investment plan is falling short? You may need to borrow. A variety of government subsidized and unsubsidized education loans are available to students and parents. Interest paid on qualifying student loans is tax deductible within certain income limits and the amount of interest that is deductible is capped each year. Another strategy used by many parents is a home equity loan. With a home equity loan, the interest you pay on the loan also may be tax deductible.

You might also consider a loan from your employer-sponsored retirement savings plan. Or you may be able to take penalty-free withdrawals from your individual retirement account to pay for qualified higher education expenses incurred by you, your spouse, your children, or your grandchildren. Be aware, however, that you may have to pay federal income tax on some or all of the money withdrawn from your IRA. And use caution when borrowing or withdrawing money from any retirement account. You do not want to short-change your retirement.

Tax credits

If you already have children in college, see if you can make use of the *Hope Scholarship* and the *Lifetime Learning Credits* on your federal income tax return. The Hope Scholarship Credit is available for a student's first 2 years of post-secondary education. Students must be enrolled at least halftime to qualify. The Lifetime Learning Credit can be used for courses to acquire or improve job skills, as well as for undergraduate level courses at an eligible educational institution.

Retirement planning

Are you old enough to remember the good old days when a worker stayed with one employer and retired with a 'nice pension' plus Social Security? Those days seem to be gone, maybe for good. Today, you need to take charge and plan for your own retirement security. Relying on Social Security for the bulk of your retirement income is an iffy proposition at best. Also, many companies today do not have traditional pension plans.

How much income should you plan on needing when you retire? A financial planning rule of thumb is to figure on needing 70–80% of your

Estimated Retirement Income Worksheet

	Example	Yours
Current annual income	$30 000	$_____
Percentage of pre-retirement income needed for retirement	× 80%	× _____ %
	$24 000	$_____
Minus social security (average annual payment)	−$9 180	$_____
	$14 820	$_____
Inflation factor (from below; example assumes 25 years until retirement)	× 2.67	× _____
	$39 569	$_____
Minus projected Income from pensions	−$5 000	$_____
Estimate of retirement income needed (in addition to social security, pensions, etc.)	$34 569	$_____
Savings necessary to produce needed income (multiply needed income by 15; assumes 4% inflation, 7% investment return, a retirement of 20 years, and full depletion of retirement savings by the end of that period)	$518 535	$_____
Value of current assets (savings, investments, etc.)	$70 000	$_____
Growth factor (from below; assumes 25 years until retirement)	× 5.43	× _____
Estimated future value of current assets	$380 100	$_____
Total amount you need to save (subtract the future value of assets from savings necessary to produce needed income; $518 535 − $380 100)	$138 435	$_____
Annual amount you need to save (divide total amount by the savings factor below: example $138 435 ÷ 63.25)	$2 189	$_____

Figure 8 Worksheet for estimating retirement income

pre-retirement income. That income is the income you will be earning at the time you retire, not the amount you are earning now.

In doing your projections, be sure to consider the dramatic effect inflation can have on earnings and expenses. Even at the relatively low 3% annual inflation we have been seeing in recent years, someone earning $30 000 today may be earning $40 000 in 10 years, $54 000 in 20 years, and $73 000 at retirement in 30 years if he or she receives nothing more than cost of living raises.

You can use the worksheet in Figure 8 to estimate what you need to plan for meeting those needs. The most advantageous way to invest for retirement is to take advantage of various opportunities to defer or avoid federal income tax on retirement investment earnings.

401(k) and 403(b) plans

Participating in an employer-sponsored 401(k) or 403(b) tax-deferred retirement plan is a smart way to build savings for retirement. You contribute part of your pay to a plan account set up just for you. You do not pay taxes on the amount you contribute or on the investment earnings in your plan account until you withdraw funds from the plan, usually at retirement. If your employer matches any of your contributions, this is an added benefit.

401(k) and 403(b) plans underwent significant modifications by Congress in 2001. Because of the elimination of defined benefit programs by most employers, most individuals will be reliant on these plans for their retirement needs. Recently, the Federal government has noted that the levels of contributions need to be increased if retirements are to be adequately funded. Additionally, with a recent focus on the lack of retirement planning by baby boomers, higher limits are now allowed for individuals aged 50 or older. This applies to Roth IRAs, traditional IRAs and 401(k) and 403(b) plans. Keough plans have increased the maximum annual contributions to $40 000. A graduated phase-in period began in 2002 and will finish by 2006. An individual IRA will increase to $5000 per individual per year by 2006. Individual 401(k) and 403(b) plans will increase to $20 000 for individuals over the age of 50. Popular web-sites and financial planners will help in defining what maximum levels are allowed.

Traditional individual retirement accounts

Anyone who is employed or self-employed can open an individual retirement account (IRA) and can currently contribute up to $2000 per year (or their earned income, if less). Married couples can contribute up to a total of $4000, even if one spouse is not employed outside the home. Depending on your individual circumstances, you may be able to deduct part or all of your IRA contributions on your federal income tax return.

All investment earnings in your IRA compound on a tax-deferred basis. You pay tax on your earnings and any deductible contributions when you withdraw the money from your account. Any withdrawals you make before age 59½ may be subject to a 10% early withdrawal penalty in addition to income tax.

Roth IRAs

Roth IRAs are a variation of the traditional IRA that offers an opportunity for tax-free, rather than tax-deferred, investment earnings. If you qualify, currently you can contribute up to $2000 a year to a Roth IRA. Contributions are not deductible, but you generally have access to them at any time. After you have had a Roth IRA for at least 5 tax years, you can withdraw investment earnings tax free if:

(1)   You are at least age 59½;

(2)   You make the withdrawal in a year you pay qualified first-time home buying expenses up to $10 000 (lifetime cap);

(3)   You become disabled.

After the 5-year waiting period has been met, distributions from the account to your beneficiaries or estate at or after your death also avoid income tax. A traditional IRA can be converted to a Roth IRA if certain requirements are met. Other rules and an income-based phase-out apply.

Roth IRAs have income limits which disallow high-income individuals from using them. Most physicians earn more than is allowed for Roth IRAs ($150 000 for individuals, $160 000 for married couples, indexed for inflation). Therefore, early in a physician's career the use of Roth IRAs may be available, but with increasing earnings this saving option may be eliminated.

Annuities

Annuities are another tax-deferred way to save for retirement. While contributions to annuities are not tax deductible, the annual earnings on the annuity's investments are tax deferred. When you buy an annuity, you enter into a contract with a life insurance company. The company agrees to make payments to you and/or your beneficiary over your lifetime(s) or a set period, usually beginning at retirement. If you die before payouts begin, a death benefit is payable to your beneficiary.

As with most other tax-deferred savings plans, you will have to pay federal income tax on any earnings you withdraw from the annuity during retirement or before and withdrawals before age 59½ may be subject to the 10% early withdrawal penalty. Also, surrender charges may apply if funds are withdrawn before the contract's surrender period expires.

Self-employed plans

If you are self-employed, you have other alternatives for building a tax-deferred retirement fund such as a Keogh plan, a simplified employee pension (SEP) or a SIMPLE (Savings Incentive Match Plan for Employees). Contributions to these plans (within tax law limits) and any earnings on the plan investments are not taxed until distributed from the plan. Your plan also must cover any eligible employees you may have.

Estate planning

Estate planning starts with a Will. If you die without a Will you lose the privilege of choosing how your assets will be distributed. Instead, the state intestacy law will decide to whom your assets will be distributed and the amount each person will receive. You also give up the right to choose an executor (or personal representative) to settle your estate or a guardian for your children. A state court will choose an administrator and guardian for you. And, without a Will, you cannot take advantage of certain planning opportunities that can reduce estate taxes and protect your assets for your family.

Married people often think that a simple Will that leaves all of their assets to their spouses is an adequate estate plan. Usually, it is not. Such a Will can pave the way for a substantial federal estate tax bill at the death of the surviving spouse. In addition, a simple Will cannot address concerns you may have about how well your heirs will be able to manage your assets or what may happen to your practice after your death. So, in addition to a Will, you may want to include other planning strategies in your estate plan.

Estate planning has changed dramatically following congressional changes enacted in 2001. Various increases in unifying credit limits have changed and will change yearly until 2010, when all estate taxes may be eliminated. This particular legislation (the 'death tax') was highly contentious, and most planners think these laws will be changed in the future.

Testamentary trusts

A trust established in your Will can provide asset management for your family after your death. You also may be able to use a testamentary trust to reduce estate tax on your and your spouse's estates and to give your spouse income for life while ensuring your children will receive your assets at your spouse's subsequent death.

Life insurance trusts

Most people do, and should, own life insurance. In the business world, life insurance provides family members with the cash needed to pay estate taxes without having to sell part or all of the business. Earlier, you checked to make sure you have sufficient life insurance coverage on your life for family members to maintain their current lifestyle after you are gone. If you have a substantial amount of life insurance, you may want to create a life insurance trust to help beneficiaries manage the proceeds and potentially reduce estate taxes.

Charitable trusts

Gifts to qualified charities can provide income, gift and estate tax savings, as well as help to further the work of organizations you believe in. Using a charitable remainder trust or charitable lead trust to make lifetime gifts can give you a current income tax deduction in addition to remove assets from your taxable estate, thus reducing estate taxes.

Other lifetime gifts

A well-planned program of lifetime gifts to family and friends can save estate and gift taxes, preserve more of your assets for your family and other heirs, and ensure your property goes to the people you want to have it. Each year, you can give any number of people up to $ 10 000 each in assets ($20 000 if your spouse joins in the gift) without triggering any gift or estate tax consequences. This annual exclusion is currently being adjusted for inflation. Making gifts of appreciating property to family members now may significantly reduce the amount of assets subject to estate tax in the future.

Monitoring your plan

Financial planning is an ongoing process. At different stages of your life you will have different financial needs and goals. As you achieve one goal, another will take its place. Consequently, most financial planners advise you to review your financial plan annually – or more frequently if a major change occurs in your circumstances.

By looking at your plan each year, you can see where you stand, check the progress you have made toward your goals, and decide if you need to revise any of your current goals or set new ones.

Glossary

asset allocation	The process of dividing investor funds among several classes of assets to limit risk and increase opportunities.
bond	The debt instrument (or 'IOU') of a corporation or government entity that promises to pay you a specified rate of interest for a specified time period, with principal to be repaid when the bond matures.
charitable trust	A trust having a charitable organization as a beneficiary.
common stock	Securities that represent an ownership interest and give you voting rights in the issuing corporation.
diversification	Investing in different companies in various industries or in several different types of investment vehicles to spread risk.
durable power of attorney for healthcare	A legal document giving another person power to make healthcare decisions on your behalf.

estate tax	The tax paid by the administrator or executor of a person's estate out of the estate's assets.
financial planning	The development and implementation of total coordinated plans for the achievement of one's overall financial objectives.
gift tax	Tax on gifts generally paid by the person making the gift rather than the recipient.
gift tax annual exclusion	The provision in the tax law that exempts the first $10 000 in present-interest gifts a person gives to each recipient during a year from federal gift taxes.
inflation	The rate of change in the prices of consumer goods. Usually, inflation is measured by the Consumer Price Index for All Urban Consumers, which is computed monthly by the US Department of Labor.
investment return	The profit (or loss) you earn through investing.
life insurance trust	A trust that has the proceeds of a person's life insurance policy as its principal.
living Will	A document expressing your wishes as to the kind and extent of medical care you want under described circumstances.
money market fund	A mutual fund that invests in money market instruments.
mutual fund	An investment company that enables its shareholders to pool their funds for professional management as a single investment account.
net worth	The residual value of assets after liabilities have been subtracted.
power of attorney	A legal document giving another person authority to make financial decisions on your behalf.
principal	The capital sum you invest for retirement or other purposes, as distinguished from interest or profit.
risk	The chance that the value of an investment could decline in the marketplace.
trust	A legal relationship where property is transferred to and managed by another person or institution for the benefit of another person.
will	A legally executed document which explains how and to whom a person would like his or her property distributed after death.

Suggested reading

Sutherland P. *Physician's Financial Sourcebook*. Financial Sourcebook Publishing, Inc.

Web-sites

Yahoo.com, the financial section

Smartmoney.com – great retirement planning sheets

Vanguard.com and Fidelity.com – general good information on investing

Cnnfn.com – good general site and links to multiple planning sites

Quotesmith.com – the best insurance source around

Tiaa-cref.org – cheapest annuities and mutual funds in the business, good overall site

Glossary

Stephen K. Klasko

---

adjusted cost per admission	The typical cost for a single hospital stay for one patient. Typically adjusted by age, sex, institutional status, Medicaid, disability and possibly the presence of a specific disease state[1].
best care	Treatment that is judged most likely to benefit the patient upon considering the available scientific evidence (measuring the general efficacy, the particular effectiveness and the expected outcome) for various treatment options[2].
best practices	Practices, procedures, systems that result in unusually strong performance or that set a standard for performance[2].
binding arbitration	Settlement of a dispute by a third party (arbitrator), where the disputants agree to be bound by the arbitrator's decision before beginning the arbitration process[2].
capitation	A method of payment for health services in which a practitioner or hospital is prepaid a fixed, per capita amount to cover a specific period of time for each person served, regardless of the actual number or nature of services provided to each person[3].
care management	The comprehensive management of a member's health problems wherein the chronically ill or otherwise impaired individual may require long-term and/or costly care[4].
care panels	The group of patients for whose healthcare a single primary-care physician or group of physicians is responsible[2].
carve-out benefits	Services which are managed, financed and risked separately from other health services, primarily high-cost or specialty services such as mental health, vision, dental or substance-abuse programs[1].

case management	A managed-care technique in which a patient with a serious medical condition is assigned an individual who co-ordinates, manages and monitors continuous, cost-effective treatment, sometimes outside a hospital setting[2].
cash flow risk	The possibility of running out of cash on hand to meet current obligations.
claims data	Data collected by an insurance company in the process of assessing and paying for healthcare costs (claims) for their insureds[2].
clinical pathways (critical pathways)	A timed sequence of interventions in the patient's care plan to achieve desirable outcomes and reduce variations in healthcare procedures. They are designed to prevent unnecessary utilization of services, reduce costs, decrease length of stay and optimize cost savings. In managed care, clinical pathways also serve as predictors of achievable clinical outcomes[5].
collaborative bargaining	A form of negotiation in which a problem-solving approach is used creatively to find the 'best' solution in which the result is the best possible for all parties.
collection risk	The possibility that an amount of money owed will not be paid.
consumerism	In medicine, the movement to change the processes of the clinical environment so as to be more patient driven, leading the way to such entities as 'medical malls', 24-hour service, women's health centers and various combinations of traditional and alternative medicine.
continuous quality improvement (CQI)	A systems approach to identifying problems in healthcare delivery in a continuous fashion. Scientific methods are often employed to improve work processes, eliminate wastes, etc. in order to meet and exceed customer needs and expectations (see TQM)[1].
co-ordination of benefits	A process wherein, if an individual has two group-health plans, the amount payable is divided between the plans so that the combined coverage amounts to, but does not exceed, 100% of the charges[4].
co-ordination of care	A process whereby different providers delivering healthcare to a single individual are co-ordinated to avoid repetition and harmful interactions.

co-payment	A type of cost-sharing whereby insured or covered persons pay a specified flat amount per unit of service or unit of time, with the insurer paying the rest. The co-payment is incurred at the time the service is used. The amount paid does not vary with the cost of the service (generally included in managed-care plans)[3].
cost-effectiveness	The value of a product or service in relation to its cost.
covered lives	The group of people who receive benefits from a health plan. In a health maintenance organization these are also called members.
customer differentiation	A market coverage strategy in which a hospital or group of physicians decides to operate in several segments of the market by tailoring a specific strategy for each group of customers. Patients are usually better served because products offered are specifically designed to meet the needs of specific segments[2].
customer service	A term that has not traditionally been used in clinical practice, but now applies to innovative processes that do not necessarily increase the quality of care but allow patients easier access to services or information.
direct costs	Costs incurred as a result of providing a service that can be directly linked to the provision of that service. For example, materials used during that visit are a direct cost[2].
disease management programs	Programs designed to ensure that individuals with specific diseases receive a full range of appropriate diagnostic tests and treatments. Typically these programs result in lower healthcare costs because they substitute preventive care and early diagnosis for acute care[2].
distributive bargaining	Often called 'a zero sum game', distributive bargaining consists primarily of concession making (buying a used car) vs. collaborative bargaining, which involves a search for mutually profitable alternatives.
economic credentialing	Taking a physician's economic behavior into account (i.e. tests ordered, hospital bed days, outcomes) in deciding upon medical staff appointment or re-appointment[4].
economies of scale	The lowering of average costs per service or item as a result of delivering a larger volume of those goods or services.
exclusive provider organization (EPO)	A type of managed-care plan in which the member must remain within the provider network to receive benefits.

experience rating	A method of setting premium rates based on the actual healthcare costs of a group or groups primarily used by managed-care organizations and insurance companies[1].
fee for service	Traditional method of paying for medical services whereby a practitioner bills for each encounter or service rendered. Also known as indemnity insurance. This system contrasts with salary, capitated or prepayment systems, in which the payment is not changed with the number of services actually used[3].
foundation model	A healthcare system which contracts with a medical group for professional services and manages all non-physician staff and facilities[1].
gate-keeper	The primary-care physician who must authorize all medical services (e.g. hospitalizations, diagnostic work-ups and specialty referrals) for a member[4].
governance	The manner in which something is regulated, often in medical administration, separated from management, e.g. boards govern ... administrators manage[2].
group model	A type of health maintenance organization (HMO) which contracts with physician groups at a negotiated fixed or capitated rate for a defined group of enrolees; in exchange, the HMO usually provides the facility, staff and administrative support for the physician group[1].
group practice	The application of healthcare service by a number of practitioners working in systematic association with the joint use of equipment and technical personnel and with centralized administration and financial organization[3].
health maintenance organization (HMO)	An entity that provides, offers or arranges for coverage of designated health services needed by plan members for a fixed, prepaid premium. There are four basic models of HMOs: group model, individual practice association, network model and staff model[6]. Under the Federal HMO Act, an entity must have three characteristics to call itself an HMO: (1) An organized system for providing healthcare or otherwise assuring healthcare delivery in a geographic area; (2) An agreed upon set of basic and supplemental health maintenance and treatment services; (3) A voluntarily enrolled group of people.

hold harmless clause	A section of a contract in which a party agrees not to hold another liable for a specific risk. For managed-care organizations, a controversial section of a contract with a physician that has the effect of decreasing liability to the insurer for non-covered services.
incentivization for optimal utilization	A theoretical concept whereby the above benefits, monetary or otherwise, would be paid for best practices, assuming that those could be determined and quantified. This is in contrast to fee for service (incentivizes over-utilization) or traditional capitation (promotes under-utilization).
indemnification	Protection or insurance against penalties incurred by one's actions.
indemnity insurance	Insurance coverage which reimburses medical expenses traditionally in a non-managed environment based on procedures and encounters after they have occurred. Payments are made either directly to the provider or to the insured[1].
indirect costs	Costs that cannot be directly linked to the provision of a specific good or service, for example rent and receptionist salaries. Often these are linked back to specific service by the use of a formula based on labor hours or direct costs. Also called overhead[2].
individual practice association (IPA)	A type of HMO in which a partnership, corporation or association of providers has entered into an arrangement for provision of their service. Practitioners provide care in their own offices and serve HMO members as part of their regular practice[1].
information technology	A popular generality that covers many innovations in the abilities of computers, microelectronics and telecommunications to produce, store and transmit a wide spectrum of clinical information in ways that will revolutionize medicine, e.g. electronic medical record.
integrated delivery system (IDS)	A regional healthcare system or network which provides a 'continuum of care from acute care and outpatient ambulatory care to skilled nursing and long-term care'. From a managed-care perspective, an IDS may contract to provide this wide range of services to a defined population within a geographic area[1].
Kaiser Health Plans	One of the first and one of the largest health maintenance organizations in the USA, based in California. Kaiser is a group model HMO.

managed care	An organized system of managing and financing the delivery of healthcare services which integrates the financing and delivery of appropriate healthcare services to covered individuals by arrangements with selected providers to furnish a comprehensive set of healthcare services, explicit standards for selection of the care providers, formal programs for ongoing quality assurance and utilization review, and significant financial incentives for members to use providers and procedures associated with the plan[2].
managed-care organization (MCO)	See HMO.
management services organization (MSO)	A management entity owned by a hospital, physician organization or third party. The MSO contracts with payers and hospitals/physicians to provide services such as negotiating fee schedules, handling administrative functions, and billing and collections[4].
market segmentation	Dividing a market into distinct groups of customers who differ in their buying behavior. Segments are typically based on demographics, or preferences (usually determined by surveys or analysis of purchasing behavior).
mature marketplace	A market in which sales growth is slow because the product or service has achieved acceptance and is reasonably well understood by most potential buyers. For providers, profits typically stabilize or decline because of increased marketing outlays to defend the product or service against competition[7].
medical necessity	The supplies and services provided to diagnose and treat a medical condition in accordance with the standards of good medical practice and the medical community[6].
member satisfaction	A measure of the satisfaction of insureds with their health plan. Usually determined by surveys.
NCQA	The National Committee for Quality Assurance (NCQA) is a private, not-for-profit organization dedicated to assessing and reporting on the quality of managed care plans.
network	A group of providers and facilities able to contract for a defined set of healthcare services[1].
opportunity cost	The cost of losing an opportunity, i.e. the value given up by using a resource in one way instead of in an alternative, better way[1].

outcomes	The art and science of measuring effectiveness of patient care in terms often related to quality and efficiency, e.g. cost, mortality, health status, quality of life or patient function and satisfaction[1].
outcomes measures	Quantitative indicators that offer some assessment of the results for a patient after care; for example, how long it took to restore the patient's ability to walk or to work[4].
over-utilization	Promotion of more services than might be necessary for a given patient or population, e.g. fee-for-service insurance.
patient-centered care	Healthcare that is closely congruent with and responsive to patient's needs, wants and preferences, e.g. physicians and other care-givers shedding their paternalistic image and undertaking the more laborious process of exploring optimal outcomes with the patient[2].
peer-review organization (PRO)	A physician-sponsored organization charged with reviewing the services provided for patients. The purpose of the review is to determine if the services rendered are medically necessary, provided in accordance with professional criteria, norms and standards, and provided in the appropriate setting[6].
per member per month (pmpm)	A method of payment whereby a network or provider receives a set amount of money per person every month under capitated payment arrangements[1].
performance improvement	An area that takes into account the sum total of providing more efficient clinical care, e.g. quality, cost, work flow, materials requirements, inventory control and labor.
physician hospital organization (PHO)	A contractual organization involving a hospital and its medical staff developed for the purpose of contracting directly with employers and managed-care organizations. This allows for the better opportunity to market hospital–physician services and achieve administrative efficiencies[1].
physician profiling	The practice of examining patterns or averages in a physician's practice, such as the average cost for an individual with a specific disease state.
point of service plan (POS)	A health plan allowing the covered person to choose to receive a service from a participating or non-participating provider, with different benefit levels associated with the use of participating providers. Point of service can be provided in several ways:

(1)   An HMO may allow members to obtain limited services from non-participating providers;

(2)   An HMO may provide non-participating benefits through a supplemental major medical policy;

(3)   A PPO may be used to provide both participating and non-participating levels of coverage and access;

or various combinations of the above may be used[6].

population-based medicine	Medical care which takes as its target a population, rather than individuals. This involves a shift from the classic paradigm of an individual physician providing comprehensive, continuous and affordable healthcare to patients as they present in the clinical setting to a population-based systematic approach that identifies persons at risk, intervenes, measures the outcomes and provides continuous quality improvement.
practice guidelines	See protocol.
practice style	The favoring of certain treatment options based on a physician's preference, which may reflect peculiarities among some groups of physicians (specialist–generalist, geographic location, etc.) Treatment based on practice style may lead to care that varies with respect to appropriateness, utility and cost, and the quality and quantity of resources utilized.
preferred provider organization (PPO)	A program in which contracts are established with providers of medical care. Providers under such contracts are referred to as preferred providers. Usually, the benefit contract provides significantly better benefits (fewer co-payments) for services received from preferred providers, thus encouraging covered persons to use these providers. Covered persons are generally allowed benefits for non-participating providers' services, usually on an indemnity basis with significant co-payments. A PPO arrangement can be insured or self-funded. Providers may be, but are not necessarily, paid on a discounted fee-for-service basis[6].
premium	A predetermined monthly membership fee that a subscriber or employer pays for the HMO coverage[4].
primary-care provider	A provider the majority of whose practice is devoted to internal medicine, family/general practice or pediatrics and serves as the primary access into the medical system for the patient. An obstetrician/gynecologist may be considered a primary-care provider[6].

protocol	Statements by authoritative bodies as to the procedures appropriate for the physician to employ in making a diagnosis and treating it. The goal of guidelines is to change practice styles, reduce inappropriate and unnecessary care and cut costs. You may hear these referred to as practice parameters, clinical practice guidelines or protocols[4].
quality of service	The quality of medical and nursing care. Third-party payers and agencies frequently initiate, encourage or mandate to establish quality assurance programs. Medical practices can be measured or compared to assess the level of excellence in the medical or nursing care provided.
relative value scale (RVS)	The compiled table of relative value units (RVUs), which is a value given to each procedure or unit of service. As payment systems, the RVS is used to determine a formula which multiplies the RVU by a dollar amount, called a converter or conversion factor[6].
resource based relative value scale (RBRVS)	A method of determining physicians' fees based on the time, training, skill and other factors required to deliver various services, developed by the Health Care Financing Administration (HCFA) to provide a more equitable physician reimbursement system for use by Medicare recipients[4].
risk	Possibility that revenues of the insurer will not be sufficient to cover expenditures incurred in the delivery of contractual services. Often considered a four letter word (in a negative sense) by physicians, e.g. 'There's no risk in this for me, is there?'[3]
risk management	A program of activities to identify, evaluate and take corrective action against risks that may lead to patient or employee injury and/or property loss or damage with resulting financial loss or legal liability.
risk pool allocation	The process by which any profits or losses in an at-risk capitated contract will be dispersed among the hospital and physicians. Often the trickiest part of determining a risk pool allocation is among the different physician groups and specialties[2].
risk-sharing agreements	A contract through which an HMO and contracted provider each accept partial responsibility for the financial risk and rewards involved in cost-effectively caring for the members enrolled in the plan and assigned to a specific provider[4].
single specialty networks	A group of physicians in the same medical specialty who have joined together to share the risk of providing care to their patients who are covered by a given health plan.

staff model HMO	A type of HMO, similar to the group model, in which physicians are salaried employees who provide their services exclusively to HMO enrolees[3].
stewardship	The act of choosing service over self-interest, e.g. to replace the traditional management tools of control and consistency, stewardship organizations will offer partnerships and choice at all levels to their employees as well as to their customers and hold themselves accountable to those over whom they exercise power[8].
stop loss insurance	Insurance purchased by an HMO or health insurance company to protect itself or its contracted medical groups against losses above a specified amount as a result of caring for a policy holder. Also referred to as reinsurance.
systems approach	A way of thinking about events, processes and organizations in which the economic, organizational and social context (systems) in which they occur are seen as essential to shaping, defining and motivating them.
third-party payment	Payment for healthcare by a party other than the enrolee (for example, by an insurance company)[3].
total quality management (TQM)	A system for integrating quality-related efforts throughout an organization so that all the functions can focus together on the efficient satisfaction of the customer's needs. Total quality management often involves participation across functions and up and down the hierarchy in an organization (see CQI)[9].
under-utilization	Promotion of the use of fewer services than might be optimal for a patient or a given population, often incentivized through traditional capitated contracts.
utilization	The frequency with which a benefit is used – for example 3200 doctor's office visits per 1000 HMO members per year. Utilization experience multiplied by the average cost per unit of service delivered equals capitated costs[4].
utilization review	Evaluation of the necessity, appropriateness and efficiency of the use of medical services and facilities. Helps ensure proper use of healthcare resources by providing for the regular review of such areas as admission of patients, length of stay, services performed and referrals[4].

withholds   The portion of the monthly capitation payment to physicians withheld by the HMO until the end of the year or other time period to create an incentive for efficient care. The withhold is at risk, i.e. if the physician exceeds utilization norms, he/she does not receive it. It serves as a financial incentive for lower utilization[4].

References

1.   The Governance Institute. *Healthcare Terms and Abbreviations for Boards and Medical Leaders*, 1997
2.   Klasko S, Shea G. *The Phantom Stethoscope: A Field Manual for Creating an Optimistic Future in Medicine*. Franklin, TN: Hillsboro Press, 1999
3.   Huntington, JA. *Glossary for Managed Care*, 1998
4.   American Medical Specialty Organization. *Definition of Terms*. AMSO
5.   Stahl D. Anatomy of a management system. *Nurs Manage* 1997;28(12):20–1
6.   United Health Care. *The Language of Managed Care and Organized Health Care Systems*, 1997
7.   Kotler P. *Marketing Management*. Englewood Cliffs, NY: Prentice Hall, 1991:350
8.   Block P. *Stewardship*. San Francisco: Berrett–Koehler Publishers, 1994
9.   Berwick D., *et al. Curing Health Care*. San Francisco: Jossey Bass, 1990:31

Appendices

Appendix 1: elements of employee handbook

(1)   Mission statement;

(2)   Basic philosophy;

(3)   Employment policies:

    (a)   Equal employment opportunities;
    (b)   Work hours;
    (c)   Regular and overtime pay;
    (d)   Performance reviews;
    (e)   Vacations;
    (f)   Holidays;
    (g)   Personal and sick days;
    (h)   Leaves of absence;
    (i)   Jury duty, etc.;

(4)   Benefits:

    (a)   Health;
    (b)   Dental;
    (c)   Life insurance;
    (d)   Short-term/long-term disability;
    (e)   Worker's compensation;
    (f)   Retirement programs;
    (g)   Tuition reimbursement;
    (h)   Employee assistance programs;

(5)   Employee hygiene/dress code;

(6)   Organization chart;

(7)   Individuals in the practice;

(8)   Legal information;

(9)   Pertinent information;

(10)   Family and medical leave act policy;

(11)   Interviewing techniques:

       (a)   Recruitment is an ongoing process designed to identify the best individuals for the job;

       (b)   Write a job description;

       (c)   Prescreen applications;

       (d)   As appropriate, consider personality tests;

       (e)   Score the candidates immediately after seeing them;

       (f)   Consider 'how would you handle' questions;

       (g)   Check references;

       (h)   Monitor turnover for the position.

Appendix 2: managed care[*]

[*]Adapted with permission from the Ortho–McNeil Institute, *Practice Planning Tools*, Optimistic Future Program 2000. Golden, CO: Medical Education Collaborative, 2000

Definition of managed care terms

(1)   At risk: capitation has an intrinsic inherent risk that the capitation payment represents complete reimbursement, regardless of level of services performed.

(2)   Adverse selective: the problem with attracting patients who will require a higher level of services than the population in general and exceed the medical budget.

Covered lives

These are potential patients who are eligible to use services and for which the physician is reimbursed on a per-member, per-month basis, regardless of whether or not services are utilized (see Glossary).

Stop-loss insurance

This is a form of reinsurance that provides protection for medical expenses above a certain limit, generally on a year-by-year basis (see Glossary).

Utilization data

This is historical information on how insured individuals used a healthcare plan's resources in prior years.

Withhold

A percentage of the capitation is withheld every month and used to pay for cost overruns. Managed-care plans use 'fee for service', also without a certain percentage of the fee to cover medical cost overruns (see Glossary).

CPT coding recommendations

Run a computer report of all current procedural terminology (CPT) services provided within your practice over the past 12 months by CPT code.

Be cognizant of CPT changes with respect to your speciality. These occur on an annual basis.

Be advised of ICD-9-CM changes that occur on an annual basis.

Relevant value units (RVUs)

One should be aware of the RVU use for each CPT code provided within your office setting over the past year. Multiply the RVU by the number of encounters for each given CPT. This calculation provides the total RVUs provided by your practice during the year for each specific CPT code (see Glossary). For instance:

CPT code	CPT encounters	×	RVU	=	Total RVUs
99213	213	×	$1.13	=	$240.69
59400	110	×	$41.52	=	$4567.20

'Total RVUs' represents all the work performed by the physicians within the office on an annual basis. You can then calculate cost per RVU, by taking your total overhead cost for the year and dividing by the total RVUs. This is one method of co-ordinating cost with respect to level of reimbursement.

Cost per CPT code can also be calculated as follows. Identify the CPT code and multiply the RVU by the cost per RVU. This will establish the cost for each CPT service. For example:

CPT code	RVU	x	Cost per RVU	=	Cost per CPT
99213	1.13	x	$33.63	=	$38.00
59400	41.52	x	$33.63	=	$1396.32

Cost savings within the practice

(1) Encourage communication among staff members with respect to ideas for cost containment;

(2) Put the due date on the back of the envelope and mail accordingly;+

(3) Purchase supplies in bulk as often as possible;

(4) Monitor overtime costs for staff;

(5) Billing and collection: efficiency within this system, i.e. the ability to track delinquent accounts is obviously important. A mechanism for the tracking of submitted bills that have fallen out, for whatever reason, must be identified and followed up. Monitoring of this process is of extreme importance.

Suggested reading

The Ortho–McNeil Institute of Physician Practice Development. *Practice Development Workshop – Career Planning Tools*

World-Wide Chamber of Commerce Directory. PO Box 1029, Loveland, CO 80539 (telephone (970) 663 3231)

Index